THE LIFE A

EL

THE CONTROVERSIAL CAREER OF TERRY VENABLES

HARRY HARRIS

EMPIRE
PUBLICATIONS

First published in 1994
This edition published 2021

EMPIRE PUBLICATIONS

1 Newton Street, Manchester M1 1HW

ISBN: 978-1-909360-90-7

CONTENTS

STEVE CURRY

MY CO-AUTHOR, Steve Curry, former *Daily Express* chief football writer, died aged 76 in August 2019. Steve and I were the founder members, along with Colin Gibson, then of the *Daily Telegraph*, and Stuart Jones of *The Times*, of the "Morris Men". It is hard to know whether we were given that title as a compliment... but there was no doubting the power of the unit as we enjoyed enormous influence within the football industry, to the extent that we were, as a unit, consulted by then FA Chairman Graham Kelly about the suitability of Terry Venables to become England manager.

I asked Steve to help me in writing a definitive biography of Terry Venables way back in 1994. I wanted Steve to concentrate on his life and times, while I put together the hugely complex investigation into his business dealings.

This new updated book on El Tel is a tribute to the work of Steve. The last edition of the book stopped short of Euro '96 which was arguably Venables greatest hour, and the new book reflects that in a new assessment of his career, which coincides with a new documentary film, to which I have contributed.

Steve began his career at the *Blackburn Times* and went to the *Lancashire Evening Post* before moving to their London office and beginning a stellar career on Fleet Street.

He joined the *Express* in time to report on England's World Cup win in 1966 and became chief football writer in 1982. In 1998, while working for the *Sunday Telegraph*, he was named Sports News Reporter Of The Year.

David Emery, who worked alongside him longer than most before himself becoming sports editor, said: "There were a few young lads who went on to have significant roles in the paper and there was a great feeling of camaraderie. Steve pulled some big stories and had some great contacts."

Of his passing the Football Writers' Association tweeted:

"Steve was a great larger-than-life character, a top reporter, former FWA Chairman and Life Member. Our heartfelt condolences go out to his wife Carol and family."

On the FWA website friend and colleague James Massop wrote an emotional tribute: "Superlative journalist, whimsical companion, friend of football: Steve Curry was all that and more.

"His endless qualities glowed throughout the many years so many of us knew and admired him. Players and administrators entrusted him with their thoughts, hopes and apprehensions. His years at the Daily Express were dappled with exclusives.

"He was a marvellous fellow traveller too, especially in those days when we Fleet Street men travelled on the same charter aircraft as the England team. He had a fine singing voice and standing in the aisle, would give his finest, with a song about "Old Shep" being one particular party piece."

Harry Harris

FOREWORD
By David Seaman MBE

TERRY VENABLES' relationship with his players can be best summed up as - "his greatest asset" - a remarkable, one of a kind, game-changing gift. Terry had the perfect relationship with his players and displayed some of the best man-management skills I've ever come across.

I have first hand experience of his dealings with me when he took over as the England manager from Graham Taylor. I had been left at home for the previous Euros where Nigel Martyn and Chris Woods had been preferred, which left me as the No 3 choice under the previous manager. But as soon as Terry arrived he took me to one side at the training session at Bisham Abbey and told me that I was his No 1. You cannot imagine the confidence that inspired in me and how positively it affected my game as usually you are always left guessing, but Terry came right up to me and wanted to make the point that there was no doubt in his mind who he wanted as his No 1. That transformed my outlook in training, my standing in the team and my mindset heading into the competition.

Euro '96 was a magical time for the players and of course for Terry Venables. Terry wasn't the only manager to have had Gazza under his feet occasionally, so he asked me to take him fishing to calm him down as he was starting to get nervous and nerves were already starting to affect the rest of the team. Of course that fishing trip turned into one of the maddest moments in our build up to the Euros as the *Daily Mirror* photographer Arnie Slater was hiding in the bushes to get a picture as he had heard that Gazza, Ian Walker and I were going fishing before the Spain game. We actually reenacted the scene for a new film about Terry's life and that was the first time I discovered the lengths that the photographer, Arnie, would go to to conceal his undercover shots.

When we spotted his long lens that day, we started to row back in from the lake and Gazza went ballistic demanding that Arnie hand over the pictures! Arnie refused and tried to make a quick getaway in his car so I phoned the fishery owner to lock the gates to make sure he couldn't escape! But when Gazza demanded the film from the camera the photographer had already hidden it in his underpants! Gazza was furiously shouting, "Give it to me', and Arnie was shouting "no chance, no way." In the end Gazza just reached in to the passenger seat of the car and grabbed the phone saying you can have this back when you give me the film.

The photographer wouldn't talk to us so Gazza started letting his tyre down!! Arnie panicked and rammed his car through the wooden gates, speeding off. I told Gazza to press redial on the phone and it went straight through to Piers Morgan! Next day there was a classic *Daily Mirror* headline "Gazza's Armada, Able Seaman and Walker the Plank"!

This was the kind of constant scrutiny the team was under and this was what Terry was dealing with day in and day out, but he was so adept at keeping a calm head, blocking out all the noise and keeping the whole team focused and on track.

Of course Euro '96 was a special tournament, played on home soil with huge expectations and even the build up was something out of the ordinary, including the much talked about trip to Hong Kong, where we played a Pub XI, beat them 8-0 and were allowed a night out afterwards. I sat on the hotel bed watching a rerun of the Arsenal/Sheffield Wednesday Cup Final and fell asleep, no word of a lie! Of Course the lads went out on the lash and the rest is history but I only found out about the infamous "Dentists Chair" the next morning. And by then it was in all the papers and I was devastated as it sounded like a cracking night out!

As for the tournament, it highlighted all of Terry Venables man management skills. He was an English manager of England, so he completely understood the levels of expectation weighing on the players, alongside the fan-frenzy that was at fever-pitch. He had the total respect of the players because he had already achieved so much with Barcelona and at other clubs, but the way he handled all the different personalities and characters, the pressure from the press and the expectation of the fans was a true testament to his strength of character as a man and his ability as a great manager.

Terry Venables was the greatest England Manager of my career; he is a gentleman, a fierce competitor, a brilliant tactician and an England footballing legend.

David Seaman MBE
75 caps for England - 1988-2002

INTRODUCTION

A Great Manager and Coach...Euro 96 Remembered

TWENTY-FIVE YEARS on from Terry Venables' finest hour, when he almost led England to their second major trophy, 2021 will see Wembley host the final of the European Championships. Should Gareth Southgate somehow lead England into that game then he will have gone one better than the man many regard as the finest England manager since Sir Alf Ramsey.

Euro '96 was the focus of a new film about the life and times of Terry Venables to which I contributed with their TV crew spending four hours in my office. The film, authorised by the Venables family, wanted it to be a fair and balanced account and, despite my prolonged scrutiny of El Tel's business life and his resulting ban by the DTI, I never doubted Venables' abilities as a football coach.

In fact when it came to the appointment of Venables as England manager, despite all the allegations hanging over his head, I endorsed his appointment when asked by the then FA chief executive Graham Kelly who sounded out a select group of chief football writers.

Venables' conviction throughout his entire career was that it was, indeed, his destiny to become the manager of England's football team. When that objective was achieved, just a matter of days after his 51st birthday, it had been a passage negotiated by the most circuitous of routes and not without its casualties. It was a story of single-minded purpose, of sometimes tortuous ambition and of a thousand mistakes.

Perhaps only Venables could have been handed the most prestigious position in English football after having been sacked acrimoniously from his previous post. For the appointment itself was a paradox; since the time the Football Association abandoned its amateur, and quite ludicrous, practice of selecting

England sides by committee and appointed managers from within the professional orbit there had been strict guidelines as to suitability of candidature.

Alf Ramsey was lured from Ipswich Town in February 1963 in the wake of England's failure to meet with success in the 1962 World Cup staged in Chile. He was not the first choice, the job having been turned down by Burnley manager Jimmy Adamson. But he had proved a highly successful manager of Ipswich Town, who in 1962 had won the League Championship under his painstaking tutelage. It was a momentous choice for he was, of course, the architect of the highest point in English football history, the memorable victory in the 1966 World Cup finals.

His reign lasted 11 years and 113 games before the post was passed, after a brief and hugely entertaining period of caretakership under the jolly Joe Mercer, to Don Revie, by the mid-Seventies quite the outstanding candidate following his success in building the Leeds United side. It seemed a logical and sensible choice. But Revie was to last just three seasons, his relationship with the then Football Association chairman Professor Sir Harold Thompson increasingly estranged, the two men quite incompatible. Revie walked out on England in the summer of 1977, lured by the lucrative money being offered by the United Arab Emirates. In his place came Ron Greenwood, the retired manager of West Ham United and an acknowledged coaching authority. Among the talented men he introduced to his England 'team' was the young and thrusting Terry Venables as coach to the England Under-21 side, where he worked alongside David Sexton, who had himself been interviewed for the manager's job along with Bobby Robson, Jack Charlton and Lawrie McMenemy. Also involved in the England set-up were Robson and Don Howe, and it seemed the FA had settled on a policy of succession, with Greenwood likely to hand over to one of his team of coaches at the end of his own tenure.

Venables' work as both a coach and a tactician was already being universally recognised. It was an aptitude for organisation that he had enjoyed since he was a boy playing football in Dagenham, ironically also Ramsey's birthplace. He had ended an illustrious playing career which had included selection for his country at every possible level, amateur included, in 1976.

Malcolm Allison, who had bought Venables as a player at Crystal Palace, was the man who insisted he turned to coaching and Venables had become the club's manager by the time Greenwood seconded him for part-time England duty. Nothing clouded Venables' own vision of his future. He had persistently and unwaveringly expressed his ambition to one day be in charge of his country's football team. But perhaps it was the very nature of his ambitions in life that seemed to retard him in fulfilling the one task to which he was best suited. The men who run the Football Association have, to a very large extent, allowed the game to rule their lives. The FA Council, who set the standards and approve all appointments, were for the most part sitting in their ten headquarters in Lancaster Gate, central London, because they had dedicated their entire lives to the game. They are largely county representatives whose devotion to duty to the game at grass roots is rewarded with a seat in the chamber of power. Often, they are almost anonymous men whose thinking has not been tainted by some of the sharper manoeuvres of the professional game. Oddly little has changed down the generations to such an extent one of the potentially best FA Chairman, Greg Dyke, opted out of a final year in office because he could see no route to proper reform. He described the FA as being run by white middle aged men in blazers.

★

At the height of Terry Venables' popularity there were always two sides to his complex character.

For years, Venables was perceived as a man to whom football was a means to an end, the base around which to build a business empire and, competent though he was within the parameters of the touchlines of a football field, he proved less than successful when he has diversified into a variety of innovations, expanding his creative and ingenious mind, that wondered from the training ground. From co-writing a novel, to trying to re-invent the wheel, then onto business and trying to buy Spurs.

In some FA circles, in short, East End Tel was seen as a bit too streetwise for the staid FA. What did he want with all his business connections, they argued? And was he really involved in any sharp practice in securing the money to buy his own football club? Why couldn't he be content with simply managing a club and running a team? And what of his friends and business associates? Has one of them not been involved in some 40 failed companies? Some were valid reservations.

For there is no doubt Venables had what his former chairman Irving Scholar described as 'a grasshopper mentality'.

His father Fred, to whom Venables was devoted, wrote in his own book about Terry, *Son of Fred*, the following appraisal: 'Terry's problem is that he has always been a workaholic. Everything is performed at 100mph. He lives at that speed, works at that speed and drives at that speed. I don't know how he sleeps, probably with his brain racing at the same speed. There have been many times when I have worried that he has taken on too much but he has always assured me he is in full control - I don't think Terry could ever be happy just having one thing on his mind. He would get bored.' This paternal insight gives the essence of the man. He had a fertile mind and it allowed him to lead a very full and innovative life.

At the age of 17 he made himself a limited company, one of 12 he had through his working life and a number of which finished in the hands of receivers. But on the field, his teams rarely lacked in ideas, for Venables sought always to make the game better by improvement. Whatever else might be said of him as a businessman, as a football coach he had few peers.

It is rare, indeed, for a man to have managed four football clubs, as Venables did at Crystal Palace, Queen's Park Rangers, Barcelona and Tottenham Hotspur, and not to have made enemies within the dressing room. Yet, he has always been a players' man. Therefore those 'enemies' within dressing room were not that many, certainly not to the deluge of enemies, and questionable aquaintences he brought upon himself his his relationships with directors.

Ray Bloye, the former chairman of Crystal Palace, was bitter that Venables raided his old club for players when he became manager of Queen's Park Rangers, effectively dismantling what had been described as the 'Team of the Eighties'. He finished up at loggerheads with Scholar at Tottenham. The former Spurs chairman, in his autobiography *Behind Closed Doors*, described him as a man born with a silver tongue. Their relationship soured badly as Venables announced his intentions of staging a management buy-out of the club. He ultimately achieved this objective courtesy of a partnership with Alan Sugar, who, like himself, had begun life in a deprived East London and who built himself an empire that began by selling car aerials from the back of a van. Only, Sugar's empire now constituted a skyscraper to Venables' council house! This partnership, formed in June 1991, was to prove the most acrimonious of all, and tracing its development constitutes a major part of this story of Venables' rise, fall and rise again at Euro '96.

Indeed, the one English chairman with whom he enjoyed a concordant relationship was Jim Gregory, the former chairman of Queen s Park Rangers, an ex-second-hand car-dealer who built up a successful property business. The two powerful and ambitious characters hit it off instantly, sharing an eye for the main opportunity and an ability to think on their feet. It had been Gregory's intention to sell the QPR team and club to Venables while retaining ownership of the Rangers stadium, but this deal was not to be completed before Venables was somewhat surprisingly lured away to Barcelona to enjoy what was to become a crucial part of his football education. Venables was reluctant to leave his blossoming Team of the Eighties but here was the main chance, where he felt that by broadening his experience in Spain, he might further his chances of becoming the England manager once Bobby Robson's sojourn in the chair was completed.

When the post became vacant in 1990, however, his name was not even in the frame. In short, football's hierarchy had decided that Venables' diverse interests and his desire to own his own football club were not compatible with holding the England post and when the shortlist was drawn up, it included just the names of Graham Taylor, Joe Royle and Howard Kendall. It was a shattering blow to Venables' pride and, in a postscript to his father's book, he wrote: 'After what happened in the summer [of 1990], I now regard the prospect of managing my country as a thing of the past. But that does not mean I might not turn up at a World Cup in a few years' time as manager of another country. On the Continent they have a different approach to international management. It's a good job, but not the best job. I discovered that big clubs like Barcelona and Real Madrid often prefer their managers to have had international experience before they are appointed and not the other way round as in this country. International management is a normal job and this has set me thinking. There is no reason why I could not manage a country that is not my own and if the same people are involved at FA level in a few years' time, I am not sure I would even want to manage England if the opportunity arose. I haven't been terribly impressed by some of the people I have met on behalf of the Football Association and I found their actions this summer [i.e. in appointing Taylor] both strange and amusing.

'I would have thought a successful career managing Barcelona in Spain would have counted for something when they were going through the suitable candidates for the England job. I am not being presumptuous when I say I would have expected to be included in any batch of three. Amusing because the more I look at the sort of people who made the final decision, the less aggrieved I feel that I wasn't asked for an interview. These are people most football fans - and many managers and players, too - would not recognise if they tripped over them in the street. We all talk about the FA but few know who they really are. I can't take the FA seriously if they put Joe Royle on the shortlist having never managed higher than Division Two, when I'm out of the running. I regarded the national job as the best in football but the events of the last few months have diminished my feelings for it. I'm no longer interested in managing England - sod 'em, forget it. I'll do something else.'

Venables wasn't the first 'People's Choice' and darling of the media to be overlooked. The same thing had happened to Brian Clough in 1977 when Ron Greenwood had been appointed. The public believed that the FA wanted someone to fit into the blazer mould and toe the line, they didn't want a maverick, a troublemaker. Yet they picked Don Revie and look how that panned out! Even in recent times, the FA have blundered their way through the selection process of an England manager, most notably picking Sam Allardyce. I was asked on radio by an excitable host looking for an upbeat pronouncement on the new England appointment, for my opinion the day Big Sam was announced at the new England manager. My response shocked the genial presenter. I told him it would all end in tears, sooner rather than later, and wondered whether anyone at the FA ever did their due diligence on potential England managers. When I said sooner or later, even I didn't imagine it would last just one match!

Yet when Graham Taylor went after the debacle of failing to qualify for the World Cup in the United States, the timing found Venables out of work and looking for a job. Jimmy Armfield's part in the appointment of Terry Venables was a crucial one for, without him, it is unlikely the Football Association would have taken the risk with him because of their concerns about his business dealings. Armfield had played 42 matches for his country, but he had become an influential 'father figure' within the game with his role with the BBC as a radio pundit and co-commentator, and the FA trusted his judgement and the role he fulfilled in engineering Venables' entry through the doors of Lancaster Gate was without doubt his most distinguished.

From the moment Graham Taylor did the honourable thing

and resigned his post, the selection of England's next manager was never going to be easy. There was a deep division within Lancaster Gate as to which direction they should turn, since there was not one really outstanding club manager born the right side of Hadrian's Wall. Dare they follow the example of Germany and France and select a former international player without club management experience? After all, Franz Beckenbauer had won a World Cup for West Germany in Italy in 1990. This was the route favoured by the key man at Lancaster Gate, Sir Bert Millichip, and he very much liked the look of Queen's Park Rangers' Ray Wilkins; he had the right pedigree, was the right age and the right type with an unblemished character. But then the FA chairman would have settled for Bryan Robson, Kevin Keegan or Gerry Francis. He did not want, at any price, Ron Atkinson or Terry Venables. There was more to managing England, he believed, than an ability to coach. There was an image to be maintained, one that did not accommodate brashness, flashiness or the lure of the fast buck.

However, elsewhere in the austere steel and glass HQ in central London, chief executive Graham Kelly was not exactly pulling in the same direction, and not for the first time. Here was a power struggle into which the choice of a new manager now slotted. Kelly, portrayed as somewhat of a Dickensian figure of fun in many quarters, was largely misunderstood. He had grown into the position for which, ironically, he was headhunted by Millichip, and developed into an able administrator.

Sir Bert, a distinguished member of the UEFA executive who has weathered the years of hooliganism in English football with a heavy heart and a stout resolve to eliminate it, needed to delegate. He was no buffoon, but had a full diary and he was almost 80. Taylor's resignation, accepted on 23 November, turned the ignition, and Kelly, with an astute masterstroke, decided on an inspired course of action. He knew the public had little faith in the FA international committee to make the right choice. After all, this was the body of men who had for years turned their back on the clamour of the crowd for Brian

Clough and had amazingly not even included Venables on their 1990 shortlist when his claims were at their strongest.

It would be a masterstroke of diplomacy, he decided, to bring in a professional whose own credentials were immaculately beyond reproach. He had grown up in Blackpool knowing Jimmy Armfield to be an avuncular figure without an enemy, a man who had stuck by Blackpool, his one club, captained his country, managed Leeds to a European final and been a respected commentator on the game. On 30 November, Kelly asked Armfield to help find the pulse of the professional game and he was flattered. He had kept his contacts by working as a respected soccer reporter for the *Daily Express*. He accepted a job with the FA to be a consultant on a five-man sub-committee set up to appoint the new man and would seek a manager the experts felt was right for the job.

Kelly said it was time that the FA came down form its Ivory Tower and consulted all the constitute parts of the footballing family, the media included, and hence it came to pass that Kelly sought the advice of the senior chief football writers, myself, on the *Mirror*, plus Steve Curry of *The Express*, Colin Gibson of the *Telegraph* and Stuart Jones of the *Times*, calling this group into his hotel room during an England trip to ask our opinions.

Jimmy Armfield set about his task with some relish, driving the Peugeot that came with the job the length and breadth of Britain. Nobody with a meaningful voice would be overlooked and to that purpose he bought his own little black book into which the results of all thoughts and meetings were jotted. He knew the candidates and gradually and diligently saw them all, mixing his meetings by addressing managers who could not be in the frame but whose counsel might be valuable.

Alex Ferguson, the most successful club manager in the country, was one of the first, George Graham another. He saw much of Howard Wilkinson, a man for whom he had deep respect and who he wanted to see in a senior role within the FA. He dined with Gordon Taylor of the PFA, chatted to Johnny Giles and consulted Dave Sexton and Bobby Robson. He even talked to the men who had relinquished the post, Graham Taylor and Lawrie McMenemy.

And then there were the candidates: Kevin Keegan, Gerry Francis, Trevor Francis, Glenn Hoddle, Ray Wilkins and Bryan Robson. And that provided the shock. Nobody, he had thought, would turn this most prestigious of jobs down but Keegan did, his task at Newcastle unfulfilled. Gerry Francis hedged, favouring retirement rather than a possible rope around his neck. Wilkins still wanted to carry on playing. They were millionaires, men of means who didn't really need the money and who, in any case, might be taking a cut in salary with the prospect of being labelled vegetables as compensation recalling how the *The Sun* painful and personally branded Taylor 'The Turnip' across its back page - the start of the personal attacks that undermined the position of England manager, and heralded the title "The Impossible Job".

Far from being the one job that no Englishman would ever turn down, the press had turned it into a poisoned chalice.

Armfield's was a painstaking search and while he turned every stone, the FA were inevitably accused of dragging their feet as names were flung into the ring on a daily basis. One newspaper, which had already handed the job first to Don Howe and then to Keegan, claimed they had a world exclusive that Venables had the job before his name had gone before the committee. But they were right about one thing. The more Armfield asked, the greater the crescendo for Venables, by common consent the country's outstanding coach. It was time he was spoken to… Before the break for Christmas, the two talked. Venables desperately wanted the job and, yes, he was immediately available. Armfield made up his mind. He summoned the committee to their third meeting and told them plainly that Venables was their man. Worries about his business interests might be investigated, but if they wanted a winning team this was the coach to provide it. He had the overwhelming backing of the players, the Premier League managers, the media, and the country and should be seen forthwith.

If 1993 had been an *annus horribilis* for Venables, then 1994 looked full of promise as Venables left his club in Kensington on 5 January to take the short ride for interview with the FA sub-committee set up to make the new appointment. To keep their meeting secret, they had hired the Football League's commercial offices in the heart of London's West End and well clear of the 'spies' at Lancaster Gate.

The meeting was chaired by the FA chairman, Sir Bert Millichip, and chief executive Graham Kelly, the self-same men who appointed Graham Taylor and whom Venables had suggested might debar him from interest this time around. They were joined on the committee by Liverpool director Noel White and Oldham Athletic chairman Ian Stott, with Armfield there as a consultant. And now Venables was telling them how much he wanted the job, how he saw it as his ultimate challenge as a football coach. But there was no real need to sell himself as a strictly football man. Armfield had already done that for him, with a little help from the then Premier League chief executive Rick Parry, now heading up the Football League. He did, however, need to persuade them that he had dropped his business interests.

Parry, along with former Crystal Palace manager Steve Coppell and QC Robert Reid, had been enquiring since the autumn of 1993 into irregularities in the transfer dealings at Tottenham Hotspur. Amazingly, and despite undisputed evidence of irregular payments to agents, Parry now told the sub-committee that Venables was in the clear and would not be liable for charges under the FA's regulations on transfers!

That was certainly a major obstacle cleared for Venables, on 5 January, and just the news he had wanted to hear on the eve of his 51st birthday. But there were other aspects of his business life the committee wanted to discuss. It was spelled out to the potential new man that the FA did not want a manager who was still operating as an entrepreneur and that he should keep a distance between the post he would fulfil and some of his friends and business associates who spend a good deal of time at his Scribes

West club. They were his business adviser Eddie Ashby, whose presence at Tottenham Alan Sugar had found so abhorrent, not least because of his assault on the *Guinness Book of Records* for the number of insolvencies he has been involved in. Then there was Eric Hall, Venables' friend since he was in his late teens, known to Fleet Street as a football agent, to Venables as an adviser, or, as he affectionately calls him, my 'agent extraordinaire' and who was rarely seen without a bright jacket, fat cigar and using the expression 'monster, monster' about any deal he made.

Perhaps Venables should be admired for his loyalty to these people, for, by shedding them, he would certainly still have been chief executive and co-owner at Tottenham. England certainly didn't need them and didn't want them and Venables was told in plain language by Armfield that their involvement in any connection with the Football Association would lead to a swift termination of Venables' employment. The vital question now was: could he distance himself from them? Or did he want to?

There was also Venables' own outstanding claim for wrongful dismissal. Could the FA have their new manager involved in protracted High Court litigation? Daily, issues clouded an impending announcement. Venables talked of a 'smear campaign' and suggested he was being forced to defend himself when he had done nothing wrong. The FA had been given two other names by Armfield, Gerry Francis and Howard Wilkinson, so they were not totally committed to the one option. They stalled nervously pending an appearance by Alan Sugar, the owner of Spurs, before the Premier League to give evidence of alleged Tottenham irregularities while Venables was chief executive. Still nothing to implicate him emerged. Meanwhile, Armfield spoke again to Gerry Francis on Monday, 17 January, to establish his position on the management issue. He stated that Venables was the best man for the job. Armfield saw Glenn Hoddle the next day. He said the same.

Wembley was booked for a Thursday press conference on 20 January to announce Venables' appointment, when a major article in the *Financial Times* regarding the way Venables raised the money to buy Spurs made them stall again. This was no lurid tabloid headlines, Kelly decided. It was an accusation in an establishment newspaper and had to be investigated, as it had been in this book and by myself in the *Mirror* at great length. The press conference was called off.

Meanwhile, Millichip had told the world's press that Venables was their man, a premature statement which forced the FA into a corner, for it gave them no escape route. The drama was suspended while the European Championship draw was held, but on Monday, 24 January, the committee reconvened in the Midlands and decided they could wait no longer. During the two days that followed, Venables discussed his contract details with Kelly and Armfield and the announcement was ready to be made on Thursday, 27 January. But this was the same date as the funeral of Sir Matt Busby and, out of respect for his memory, one last delay was made in announcing the appointment.

So, at 2pm on Friday, 28 January, Venables became England's eighth post-war manager at a Wembley press conference, though his appointment was public knowledge two days earlier, despite the fact that the FA refused to confirm Venables was their man. Even the day before, Graham Kelly was still talking of the 'new incumbent'. Venables, dismissed out of hand by Kelly and Millichip in 1990 as too much of a risk, was now their Prodigal Son, the FA's most controversial appointment to the post. It was a triumph not so much for reason as for common sense. But above all, it was testimony to Jimmy Armfield's powers of persuasion.

Venables was happy to leave Scribes in the capable hands of his second wife Yvette, who Venables married in December 1991 and who was known to all the Venables clan as Toots. She had cared for the fine detail of Venables' life since he was in Barcelona and she knew that if her man can't wire a plug then he can find the current in a football team with electrifying perception. His memory for the detail of a football game was unrivalled. Only when he moved away from the pitch and into the executive offices at Tottenham, it was a bridge too far. There are many of his admirers who believe Terry's big mistake in football was not to test the elasticity of the rule-book, but to take his eye off the ball and direct it onto the balance sheet. By the time he moved to Tottenham he had undergone enough setbacks in his business ventures to make him realise that he should stick to what he was good at.

But he still insisted that outsiders had the wrong view of his entrepreneurial activities, and in his newspaper column he stated: 'I do not run a business empire. I have just one business that I consider to be a very exclusive restaurant club in the West End of London. Like a lot of managers in football, I became involved as a failsafe, a method of looking after my family should anything go wrong with my football career. Nobody could possibly argue with the correctness or wisdom of that when you remember what happened to me at Spurs. It has been an important part of my life in the eight months I have been out of football. Although it has been run by my wife, I have become more and more involved recently, though, of course, it would not cut across anything I do in football.

'What I find astonishing is that so many people seem to consider it strange for someone in my position to have interests outside football. I would think there are other prominent names far more involved in business than myself. It is a form of insurance against things going wrong in a professional sport not noted for its security. From the moment I turned professional, my parents advised me to prepare for the future and it is the sort of advice I have passed on to my players. When I became a manager I only ever looked a year ahead. I have done that for 20 years now. I knew how easily it could all collapse around me - and wasn't I right?' His determination to be the chairman of his own football club was noble enough in principle, but he was stepping from the world of penalty kicks into pinstripes and, sharp though his mind can be, this was uncharted territory for him. Alan Sugar wanted him to stick to team sheets, not balance sheets.

The two Venables personae were almost enemies. Had he stuck to football, Venables would have been leading an England side to the World Cup in the United States. The fact he didn't get the post in 1990 was not so much the fault of the FA as the fault of Terry Venables. But the financial spoils from the game alone could never satisfy his appetite for money. He loved football, but did he love money more?

He got his hands on enough of it to be able to go with Alan Sugar into a joint purchase of Tottenham in June 1991, both men providing £3 million - almost spending money to Sugar but a veritable fortune to Venables. He borrowed to meet the initial payment, but then had to find more again to maintain his equality with Sugar as the two men were obliged to take up more shares in a mandatory offer for the company. How he obtained those loans and the dubious nature of his allies and their involvement spawned more lurid headlines, increased my own surveillance into those activities, and eventually I was at the centre of a *Dispatches* TV investigations with Martin Bashir, who is now himself under investigation for using questionable methods to get the Princess Diana interview which made his name. It was during this time that I got to know Bashir very well, and found him ambitious, aspiring, and willing to do whatever he takes to be first to the punch. Unfortunately, where the football world was concerned, he was not in the same league when it came to my contacts and circle of influence at that time.

It was always going to end in tears between the ambitious Venables and the wealthy Sugar. The equality disappeared when there was a rights issue and Venables had to borrow a further sum, while Sugar bought many more shares. How Venables acquired this money is detailed here, as is exactly whose hand was on the tiller. It was his own uncertainty in the world of finance which led to the appearance of Eddie Ashby, who was to describe himself as Venables' 'personal assistant' and who took over Venables' old manager's office at White Hart Lane.

Venables was burdened with huge interest payments, but he always insisted the investments were not a concern to him, though in one unguarded moment he told a newspaper: 'If the chance came again I might not do it. But I'm in it and so be it. I have borrowed a lot of money. It cost me £3 million and the interest is colossal. But I had no option. It was either pay it or don't do it and I got caught up in the emotion of it all with everybody saying "You have to save us." But I didn't intend to go in so deep. I was thinking of putting up a smaller amount, £500,000, to buy a smaller club like Barnet but everybody got so carried away with the Tottenham thing so that in the end I felt I was going to be a rotter if I didn't do it. Certain people said they would put up the money and didn't so I was left with the bill.'

Just five months before Venables was ousted from Tottenham in a blaze of injunctions and legal paper-waving, he was extolling the virtues of his partner Sugar, the man who would unseat him. 'We are on the phone to one another every day,' Venables revealed. Clearly, what was said down the telephone lines was not always what Sugar wanted to hear and there were storm clouds gathering. Venables wanted to do things his way and claimed: 'I put my money in, my whole life is on the line so I am going to do it my way. It is everyone's right to criticise, and I'm not bothered by it. It is like everything else in life. If people are with you, they will give you the benefit of the doubt. If they are not with you, they will look for the wonky side, find fault. I can live with that.'

But he lived with Sugar with increasing difficulty and the rift was already apparent when a book by the former chairman Irving Scholar, *Behind Closed Doors*, revealed that Sugar was not overly impressed by Venables' business acumen. Sugar and his family owned 48 percent of the club. Later, when Tony Berry sold his shares, Sugar would have control of 50.1 percent of the company. He was really making the major decisions. Sugar was concerned, too, about the skeletons in the cupboard and he told the *Sunday Times*: 'All sorts of cretins are turning up saying we owe them money.'

The rift grew steadily more serious through the spring of 1993, with behind-the-scenes rows as Sugar turned all his attention to the fine detail of how the club was being run by

Venables, while at the same time having to continue to operate his electronics empire. It was clearly now a fight to the death and it seemed there could only be one winner. Sugar had the scent of Venables' blood and he called a special board meeting at the ground on 14 May to do a Julius Caesar on Venables, with the other club directors as his co-conspirators. Venables knew before the meeting that the swords were out: 'I have been summoned to a board meeting and it will be my future that is under discussion,' he said. 'It is unexpected, though there have been differences of opinion with Alan Sugar. I am going to fight it. I have not done what I have over the last few years to take this lying down. I feel the club has done extremely well in profits, gates and on the playing side. All the signs of success are there. I don't know why this situation has arisen, but my life is in here. We had the beginnings of something special and it is being threatened.'

What was being threatened was Venables' authority. Sugar was suggesting that the club's computer system could be linked to the main computer at Amstrad's headquarters to save on costs, which the chief executive opposed. When the matter was discussed at board level, Sugar lost his temper with Jonathan Crystal, the barrister and director who was a Venables ally. Before storming out of the meeting on 6 May, Sugar 'threw' Venables a letter telling him he was sacked. And on 14 May he was formally fired, with Crystal registering a vote in favour of Venables and Tony Berry abstaining.

Venables came to the ground for a ten o'clock board meeting. By 11.50am it was all over and Venables was out. He went to Chingford to tell his father Fred and from there he travelled to see his lawyers for a 1pm briefing at which he asked them to seek an injunction to reverse the board decision until a full hearing later in the month. The court case was heard in mid-afternoon, with Venables now having moved to the Royal Lancaster Hotel. He poured champagne there for his long-standing friend, Denis Signy, and his wife Pat, who had for many years been the stalwarts in the running of the Football Writers'

Association. He stayed there until 4.30pm, viewed the headline in the *Evening Standard* which read: 'Tel Out In Tears' and grinned: 'That's a bit over the top.' Some of his closest friends had now gathered at Scribes and, as the evening progressed and while the lawyers talked in court, he was drinking more champagne at £6 a glass and watching Ceefax for news of the hearing. At 9.20pm the news filtered through that the injunction had been given and that Venables was back as the club's chief executive, at least until the next hearing on 25 May. The fans who had gathered that day, both at White Hart Lane and outside the High Court, were Venables' supporters who had labelled Sugar a 'Judas'. But, essentially, there had been a clash between the two men as to who should run the club. Sugar had on numerous occasions asked Venables to get rid of one of his associates, Ashby. He felt that Venables should be concentrating his efforts on football and allowing him to run the business side. But, after the bloodletting, Sugar did say: 'If Terry was not surrounded by certain people he would still have a job.' He was referring to Crystal and Ashby.

Although nothing of substance was ever proved against Crystal, it was Ashby who caused Sugar the greatest concern. He was an undischarged bankrupt who at that time had been involved in 43 companies, 16 of which are in receivership, eight in liquidation and 15 struck off by the Register of Companies. Under insolvency laws he would be debarred from involvement in the management of any limited company. Yet he seemed to have been playing an active role in helping Venables run the football club and an insider would reveal: 'He was Terry's eyes and ears on the commercial side.' If they would not be parted, then Sugar was certainly going to be parted from Venables. He made an offer to buy his shares at the original purchase price plus nearly £500,000 in severance pay. It was turned down and both men went to war, Venables hoping to challenge Sugar's public credibility and Sugar in turn knowing Venables would be stretched financially to haul their quarrel all through the courts of law. Sugar knew Venables would enjoy press and public support and was prepared to play it as dirty as Venables wanted.

There were allegations of 'bungs' on transfer deals, of selling Gary Lineker on the cheap and of Venables' involvement in various businesses that financed his stake in the club. These were to be the focus of a BBC television documentary for *Panorama*, which Venables has said will be the subject of a libel case and at that time he claimed to have issued a writ, though one has not been received. The *Dispatches* documentary I had been involved with also aired a few days after *Panorama*, much to Bashir's delight, only because Channel 4's scheduling meant that it was screened a week later than envisaged.

Venables' fight for financial compensation for his Tottenham contract was the centre of another outstanding lawsuit, which Venables was determined to pursue even in his new role as the coach of England.

Venables' story is of one man's fight to rise above the historical image of the professional footballer; of a determination to break the established mould of management, to prove it was possible to own your own football club. In these grandiose ambitions, there was no doubt Venables overreached himself on the financial front, and it was to cost him a personal fortune as well as damage his reputation. It was, indeed, a harsh lesson in the world of big business, for perhaps this book will show that Venables never quite had enough to make his dreams come true. But all his life Venables has been a fighter and, in landing the post of England coach, he wrote another chapter about his remarkable life of a man who always wanted to be liked and it wasn't difficult to like him.

Will he be best remembered for his the glories of Euro '96 when he almost brought football home, with a brand of football that was the hallmark of his genius as a football coach, or for his failed businesses and his battles with the new Lord Sugar, who once told him 'You're Fired!'?

CHAPTER ONE
From Humble Beginnings

It was 14 May 1993, but it might just as well have been March, for there was a hint of Julius Caesar and the Ides about the overthrow of Terry Venables. The plotting, manoeuvring and conspiring to topple Venables from his seat of power at Tottenham Hotspur had been under way for some months. A partnership that had never been built on much more than business necessity was about to end in a welter of accusation, counter-accusation, acrimony and messy, endless and very expensive lawsuits that would cripple Venables financially. It was not the way that he would have chosen to go in a career in football that was based on achieving goals that did not necessarily have a net behind them.

The irony of it all was that the man wielding the dagger of Brutus, the man who would deliver the unkindest cut of all, was, like Venables, a person who had climbed from the humble origins of East London to achieve a status and wealth that lifted him above the humdrum existence of that sprawling area east of St Paul's Cathedral. And Alan Sugar, the multi-millionaire head of the electronics and computer empire Amstrad, had the muscle to end the dream that had taken root in the streets of Dagenham in the early Fifties.

Venables' ambitions never wavered almost from the time he could walk. His family came from the town famous for Ford motor cars and a girl pipers' band. He was no different from any other kid in those austere post-war years where sweets were still rationed and the family unit was a strong bond. Certainly, there was no deprivation in the Venables household, but every penny had to be worked for and perhaps some of the grandiose ideas he would nurse through his adult life stemmed from the very austerity of those early days.

Fred Venables was in Nova Scotia, Canada, when his wife

Myrtle gave birth to their only child at 313 Valence Avenue, Dagenham, on 6 January 1943 and it was some time before his ship returned home for him to get the first glimpse of a son he little believed then would develop into one of the most outstanding talents the game of football has produced in its modern history. Indeed, in that small council house, life had none of the extravagances with which Venables would surround himself in later life. His mother had to go to work in a local café to supplement the family income to a degree where Fred could afford a return bus fare from his ship's base at Chatham, Kent.

It remains a matter of deep pride for Venables that his father, to whom he has been so devoted, saw that the family were fed and clothed, and the bond between them was cemented by Fred taking his son with him when he found himself a job as a lorry driver for £6 a week at the end of the war. With his parents at work, it was Venables' maternal grandfather Ossie who was the first to encourage his grandson with a ball at his feet. Like a million children before and since, he would play in the park with little awareness that what he was doing would lift him to the pinnacle of a game that so many children would aspire to play professionally.

It was from this ordinary start that the Venables family fostered their son's interest in sport, though the father would recall that when Terry was first taken to watch football in Barking he did anything but take notice of events on the pitch, a natural urge for involvement rather than detachment that was to stay with him throughout his life. If Barking bored him, football boots beguiled him and his feel for a ball began to take shape. Fred would dispatch him to the comer shop to buy cigarettes, but young Terry would not make the journey without a tennis ball at his feet. Such concentration cost him a fat lip when he collided with a post box, but it was this fascination with a ball that very often helped make young players in those years before the distractions became too varied.

Certainly, when school started, Venables was already familiar with a football and it was around the age of 11 that he started to play for Lymington School, with his father and grandfather invariably offering their encouragement from the touchline. But the man on whose word young Venables depended was his schoolmaster, George Jackson, whose enthusiasm for the game was limitless and whose desire to see his kids do well surfaced in his touchline behaviour. He was in his early twenties but had lost his leg and would stomp along the touchline offering his walking stick as the likely source of retribution should his players not deliver the results he was looking for. It was the kind of conduct that Venables would, in later life, deplore from schoolmasters, believing they should put the emphasis on learning how to play the game and not on making sure the school won their matches. Yet the two men remained firm friends as Venables' career developed. So, although Venables would no doubt have graduated anyway, he felt he owed his promotion to the Dagenham schools side to the teacher who once snapped his walking stick in two in his temper with his young charges.

Like so many talented youngsters, Venables' sporting dexterity extended beyond the soccer pitch and his cricket and distance running skills made him something of a *Victor Ludorum* at Lymington, though academically he suffered for his affection towards the sports field. His appearances in the district side inevitably brought him to the attention of the scouts who scoured the playing fields for potential stars and it was West Ham, the local club, who were quick to invite him to their academy to develop the skills that were already in evidence when he collected his first trophy as a teenager, one so enormous the kids could barely lift it. You didn't have to be the most talented of observers to realise that Fred and Myrtle Venables had bred a future sporting star. But they were not alone in that respect in their very productive sports district.

By now, the family had moved to Bonham Road in Dagenham and five doors away lived the Browns, whose son Ken would become an FA Cup-winner with West Ham, playing alongside Bobby Moore against Preston North End in 1964.

Then, just across the road, was Bill Allen whose two sons Les and Dennis went into the professional game, with Les playing on the winning Tottenham side at Wembley against Leicester in the 1961 final. They were slightly older than Terry, but would pick him up en route for yet another game and it was all his mother could do to keep pace with the dirty washing.

Those games in Valence Park, Dagenham, would go on till darkness fell and served only to intensify the feeling of his parents that there could be just one career for their son whose enterprise, even in those formative years, knew few limits. Though a young trainee at Upton Park, Venables was not regarded by his father as old enough to watch the senior side and he would instead travel to the main London railway terminals when he knew a side from the midlands or north was due to arrive at one of the capital's stations. Little did he know then that some of the players whose scribbled names he cherished so dearly would confront him sooner than he thought as he was ushered into professional football at the earliest possible age. But he still regarded that autograph book as one of his prized possessions.

Venables knew his destiny even then. When his class was asked to write, as all young children in their early teens invariably are, what he wanted to be in adult life he satisfied himself with the one-liner at which he would become so adept. 'When I grow up, I'm going to be a footballer,' he wrote simply. His master admonished him, saying he had witnessed millions of essays saying exactly that and that only one in a million ever made it. 'I'm that one in a million' was the straightforward reply. And he meant it. It was only a matter of time before the knocks on the front door of the Venables home would reveal another scout. For, although it was West Ham who were training young Venables, it would be another of their London rivals who would eventually persuade him to cross the city and sign for Chelsea, the team from the fashionable Fulham Road. Somehow it seemed to be the most appropriate environment for his developing flamboyant personality.

Jimmy Thompson, the Chelsea chief scout, was not so much

a scout as a phenomenon in the Fifties, a man whose name was synonymous with some of the great names of the era. A former Chelsea forward himself, he had brought Les Allen, a Venables neighbour, into the game in 1954, even though it was subsequently to be Tottenham and QPR who enjoyed the best years of his career. His great coup, three years later, was to entice a scrawny East Ham kid called Jimmy Greaves to Stamford Bridge and now he was knocking at the Dagenham door of Fred Venables to give his sales pitch on behalf of Chelsea and their manager Ted Drake.

It was a difficult decision for the Venables family, since Terry had become used to the atmosphere at West Ham and his parents were regular guests of the chairman Reg Pratt. But Jim Thompson was different, a larger-than-life character who dispensed with the trilby, then part of a football scout's uniform, in favour of a bowler hat, pinstripe suit and rolled umbrella. He was something of a sporting entrepreneur, a horseracing man as well as a soccer scout, but his reading of the form as far as young Venables was concerned was accurate.

Fred Venables recalls with some humour that Thompson would hide in the bathroom of his house rather than be caught under the Venables roof by other visitors interested in the future of his son. He also remembers how Thompson's stealth as a scout, hiding behind walls and seeing an opponent round every corner, caused much mirth among the Venables family. But he was determined not to allow Venables to go anywhere but Chelsea. As Terry graduated to the London Schoolboys so the interest in him intensified.

It doesn't take long in the closeted world of football for notice of a rising star to spread and now the scouts descended on Dagenham from much further afield than the environs of London, with Manchester United among the interested parties. This was all taking place in advance of young Venables' 15th birthday, so it was little surprise that the young man had some confidence about the direction of his working life.

For Fred and Ossie, the days of taking buses and trains to

see matches were over. If they wanted to see Terry playing for England Schoolboys in Northern Ireland then Manchester United would be only too delighted to foot the bill. They did, too, sending Fred and Myrtle by train to Manchester and plane to Belfast, where Harry Gregg, United's Northern Ireland goalkeeper, was charged with looking after them while Terry played against Northern Ireland at Windsor Park. Other inducements were there for the taking as the interested clubs fought for the services of the rising young star. Fred could have swapped his battered old van for a brand new car if he could talk his son into signing for this club or that, but when the time came to make a decision this single-minded youngster took it entirely on his own.

Like the businessman he was to become, Terry kept his options open and, in addition to his sessions with West Ham, he trained with other London clubs. His summons for an England Schoolboy trial in Doncaster coincided with his having to make a decision about leaving or staying on at school. The trip north was really no more than a formality and Terry moved straight into the England side where his authority and robust presence marked him down as outstanding.

The time had arrived for the young Venables to make his choice of club and he must have felt as if he had been standing in front of a jeweller's shop window with a free choice of what to select. Would it be West Ham, the side that first gave him the feel of a professional club? They had an excellent man coaching the kids called Malcolm Allison, who was to figure so largely in Venables' later life at Crystal Palace and who was to become a trusted friend and adviser. Or would it be Tottenham, the side he supported as a boy and who had on their books his hero Dave Mackay? Matt Busby had been a charming man to deal with, so United was a possibility. But secretly young Venables had already made up his mind.

Jimmy Thompson's fatherly advice had always made an impression on young Terry and, for all that the other clubs could offer, they were not able to give him the companionship of his pals. He wanted to have familiar faces around him and told his father so. The next day it was Ted Drake who was the lucky man to get the Venables signature on the piece of paper. The chase was over and so, effectively, was any chance of Terry Venables staying as the kid next door. The beguiling world of professional football was beckoning and young Venables, already an England Schoolboy star, was waiting for the challenge.

CHAPTER TWO

Blue is the Colour

THE FORMS VENABLES signed after strolling down the Fulham Road were amateur, for he had set his heart on playing for England in the Olympic Games of 1960. He earned less than he might have done as a result of having to work outside of football for his money. He travelled from his East London home to the city with the rest of the commuters before changing trains and making his way to his new place of employment. These were the carefree days of Venables' life when nothing on the horizon seemed clouded. The game came easily to him, even though he was prepared to work diligently and unstintingly to improve upon the natural ability with which he was blessed.

The progression from international schoolboy football to youth football was a natural one and made effortlessly. Venables once said: 'Football is an extension of being at school, doing what you enjoy and not really thinking about the future. You finish training, have a bite of lunch, play snooker, talk football. And a lot of players go on doing that until they are 32 and it is all over. It is only then that they panic. When there was a maximum wage before 1960 then the change from being a £30 footballer to a steady £20-a-week job wasn't too difficult to adjust to. But in these days when players earn big money the change is a dramatic one.' For Venables the game of football was his true meaning in life and while he was still on amateur forms he played a match that was to be significant for the football history record books. He played a game for the England amateur side at Dulwich Hamlet. And that appearance was to make him the only player ever to have represented his country at every possible level: schoolboy, youth, amateur, Under-23 and full. Moreover, with amateurism now a dead expression in football, it can never be repeated.

Venables, indeed, was still an amateur when, at the tender age of 16½, he was pushed into first-team action by Chelsea manager Ted Drake in the 1959-60 season - and the opponents that day were the team from nearest his home, West Ham United. He played alongside Jimmy Greaves and his Chelsea hero Johnny Brooks. Older and wiser than the young Venables, he had enjoyed a successful career at Tottenham before moving to West London. Terry would relate the tale later of how Brooks sauntered over to him at half time and, instead of getting the words of encouragement for which a debut boy might be hoping, was asked how he thought Brooks was playing!

Those early right-half appearances for Chelsea told us much about the quality of the product honed on the playing fields of Dagenham, for here was a natural leader, precocious and exerting an influence far beyond his years. There were, of course, some naive faults to be ironed out by Drake and if he did not immediately win a regular place in the side, then on the training ground he was being taught the nuances of the professional game by a man whose own goalscoring exploits at Arsenal, 136 goals in 182 games, became legendary.

When the 1960 Olympic squad was selected and the expectant Venables was not chosen, he wasted no time in committing himself to the club with a professional contract in August 1960, with a salary of £1,000 a year in the winter and £930 in the summer - hardly the kind of money to send you rushing for the share pages of the *Financial Times*. And yet Venables was ready, at the age of 17, to make himself a limited company and so begin the long and fateful delving into money-making enterprises that was to bring him to the brink of ruin more than 30 years later.

It was an innocent enough move, some might say innovative, but it had the backing and encouragement of his parents. There were, it is true, too few genuine advisers and a surfeit of hangers-on around footballers in those days when players had just earned their emancipation from the restraints of the iniquitous maximum wage, thanks largely to the campaigning of Jimmy

Hill, the bearded one of Fulham whom Venables takes great delight in mimicking when he is in one of his showbusiness moods. The services that the Professional Footballers' Association have since put in place to advise their members of pensions and investments were still some years away and a young, streetwise lad like Venables decided this was the moment to go it alone. He told his father that no camel-coated shark was going to take 20 percent of his earnings.

It is ironical, then, that it should be in these impressionable teenage years that Venables first came to make friends with Eric Hall, who now acts in his interest and is known throughout football as a man who likes a reasonable percentage from his clients. His relationship with Hall has been one of the more mystifying of Venables' loyalties to those he befriended in his youth.

Perhaps he needed advice of some sort with his initial business experiments, for, almost without exception, they were unmitigated disasters. Though football was his career, making money was his game and he embarked on a number of what can only be described as get-rich-quick schemes. The most notable of these sounds today as if, in those early days of the Swinging Sixties, it might have been quite imaginative and certainly would have had a novelty value. It had the ingenious name of a Thingamywig. The idea was to make a hat with a wig inside it so that a lady wearing curlers might venture into the street without the offending appendages being noticed. You could buy them blonde or brunette and friends and family were delegated to do the marketing and selling. It failed to make him rich. Undaunted, he then hauled in a few mates, including current *Independent* sportswriter Ken Jones, to start a tailoring business. That, too, folded without making money and Jones commented wryly: 'We had good suits and bad debts.'

But, just as the business ventures were proving that perhaps Terry was over-stretching himself, there came from across London the harsh Glaswegian tones of Tommy Docherty to take over the coaching of the West London club. The Doc's abrasive playing career was reaching its finale, and when the call came from Chelsea it was one he felt he could not refuse.

The chemistry between the Doc and Venables was wrong from the start, possibly because they were alike in so many ways. Both of them had been brought up in areas where you lived on your wits and survival was the nature of life. Both had very strong personalities and a ready wit, so it was not difficult to see that there would be a serious clash of personalities at some stage along the way. Docherty saw there was a rich vein of talent running through the club: Peter Bonetti, Ron and Allan Harris, Bobby Tambling, Barry Bridges and, of course, the irrepressible Venables. Whatever differences might eventually surface, Docherty was shrewd enough to assess that the potential at the Bridge was quite outstanding. But what he hadn't bargained for was the departure of Jimmy Greaves to AC Milan.

As Jimmy Hill and his fellow players were locked in the discussions that would lead to the new freedom whereby players were able to negotiate their own pay, the Italians were already offering players the kind of money that was impossible to refuse - and Greaves didn't. The start of the following season, 1961-62, was a traumatic one for Chelsea without him, and it didn't exactly foster the relationship between Venables and his new coach when Docherty came out of playing retirement to take his place. For the 18-year-old Venables it was a serious blow to his pride.

Docherty still insists that had Greaves not made his move to Italy, there was at Chelsea the basis of a side that would have lifted the Championship half a dozen times. The irony is that, had Greaves stayed in West London for just a few more months, Chelsea would have been in the position to offer him the kind of salary that had lured him to Italy and to an unhappy phase of his exceptional playing career. 'Trying to replace Jimmy in the side was virtually impossible,' the Doc reflects now. 'We only won two of our first six games and it was at that point I decided to play myself and it was Terry Venables who made way for me.' Though it was a move that didn't help foster the relationship between Venables and Docherty, it worked for the team that day because they defeated Sheffield United 6-1.

Docherty played just four matches in that comeback spell before being called in by chairman Joe Mears to be told he was to be the club's new caretaker manager at the age of 33, the youngest manager of the time in the First Division. But the team was on a downward spiral and Venables one of seven teenagers in the side. They were short of the experience that can be so invaluable in a backs-to-the-wall survival situation. The Chelsea directors kept their nerve, however, and it was something of a surprise when Docherty was given the manager's job on a permanent basis. When he was called in to see them, he expected the sack.

But not even the ebullient Venables could save Chelsea from relegation that season and they plunged into the Second Division. But Docherty knew that with the young players he had, and with experienced players like Frank Blunstone, John Mortimore and Frank Upton to guide them, there was no reason for that to be more than a passing hiccup. So it was to prove, as Chelsea came surging back to the First Division, though it needed a nail-biting victory over Sunderland in the penultimate match of that 1962-63 season and a home win in the final game against Portsmouth to get them back there.

There were 55,000 inside Stamford Bridge for that last game against Portsmouth and, having squeezed through at Sunderland, they were not in the mood to allow the position to slip. The Doc now had a tough full-back from East Stirling, Eddie McCreadie, in his side and had also bought Derek Kevan to counter the heavy mid-winter pitches. They were in that promotion side along with three of the club's outstanding youngsters, Ron Harris, Bobby Tambling and, of course, Terry Venables.

Venables was already emerging as not only a fine player in his own right, but a master reader of the play, a manager on the pitch in a sense, which didn't always captivate the man who had the title. Chelsea were back among the fashionable clubs and the next three seasons were to be ones of consolidation where the fruits of the club's exceptional youth policy were gathered. In the first season back the club finished a very acceptable fifth position, just seven points behind champions Liverpool.

At the start of the 1964-65 season, 30 players, 90 percent of the club's professional playing staff, were under 25. Venables was still some months short of his 22nd birthday, but there were even younger men beneath him in 17-year-old John Boyle, John Hollins (18) and Ron Harris (19). Peter Bonetti and Bobby Tambling were 22, Barry Bridges 23 and full-backs Ken Shellito and Eddie McCreadie were positively ancient at 24! However, there was one further piece in the puzzle to be supplied by the Doc and he brought in George Graham from Aston Villa. Docherty was uniting two men whose friendship was to endure through some of the darker days in Venables' life.

But throughout this Chelsea period, Venables' forthright views on the game began to emerge increasingly and not always in the way that Docherty appreciated. He was a strict disciplinarian who liked to be in sole charge, but there were times when the young Venables would question his motives, examine his game-plan and, on the occasions he felt it was necessary, change it during the course of a match.

But the team were doing very well in 1964-65, topping the First Division for a while, and Venables' part in the renaissance was recognised by Alf Ramsey, another Dagenham boy who had made it to the summit. When Venables was selected for the games against Belgium at Wembley and Holland in Amsterdam in the autumn of 1964, it completed the set for the young Chelsea skipper of having represented his country at every level.

Venables may have made a faux pas that didn't endear him to the England manager. Alf had worked hard to distance himself from his Essex upbringing and had even taken elocution lessons to straighten out his accent, so Venables got the famous stonewall look from Alf when he sidled up to him and told him he knew his old next-door neighbour! Whether it was this, or his performances in the matches that meant Venables played only twice for his country at senior level, we shall never know.

Perhaps Venables' England career suffered because he was introduced at a period when Ramsey was experimenting with various formations. In the run-up to the 1966 World Cup, England had no competitive matches, because they qualified as of right as hosts of the 1966 finals. In his first match against Belgium, he formed a new left-sided partnership with Alan Hinton against a side which featured eight players from the Belgian champions Anderlecht. Similarly, in his second match, he was alongside debutant Alan Mullery. Though Venables let no one down, Ramsey decided that what he really needed was a ball-winner in midfield - a role that was to go to Nobby Stiles. Venables' England career was over before his 22nd birthday.

It was also the period when England's most explosive player, Bobby Charlton, was effectively operating from a forward midfield position, and the competition for the other places in the midfield was at its keenest. In the end, perhaps Venables' flamboyant personality was not quite in keeping with the image of the archetypal Ramsey player.

However, his career at Stamford Bridge was reaching a climax. Chelsea had won the League Cup 3-2 over two legs against Leicester City, with Venables very much a part of the side, scoring one of the goals, and they had already knocked West Ham and Tottenham out of the FA Cup on their way to the semi-final. They had even accounted for AC Milan in the Fairs Cup, the predecessor of the UEFA Cup, in a play-off match of memorable excitement. Then, suddenly, the wheels seemed to come off as the side dipped out of the FA Cup to Liverpool and slipped to third place in the First Division.

One of the club's outstanding matches, postponed from earlier in the year because of the weather, was against Burnley at Turf Moor. Docherty took the side to Blackpool to prepare for the match and, though he was a strict taskmaster when it came to training and playing, he also believed in the theory that players needed time to relax off the field. However, they were under trust not to abuse the rules and regulations he imposed. 'I had let them go out many times on previous occasions and they never let me down,' he would recall after the event. 'I had no objections to them having a drink so long as they were back in the hotel at a reasonable time. All I asked of them was that they behaved like professionals and in accordance with the wages they were being paid. But, that night in Blackpool, they let themselves down, they let me down, they let the club down and, above all else, they let the fans down.'

The Doc had asked the players to be back in their hotel by midnight. But some of them returned within the curfew time and then decided to make another sortie out again via a fire escape. In not closing it after their departure, they had alerted a hotel porter who had also received complaints from other guests about persistent noise. The Doc, his suspicions raised, asked the porter for a master key to the bedrooms to check all his team were safely in their beds. As each room he searched revealed emptiness, it dawned on him that his players had abused his trust and he returned to the lounge asking the porter to alert him immediately the players returned. It was a long wait.

It was at four o'clock that the tip-off came, by which time Docherty had brooded for almost four hours and was furious. He went to each bedroom in turn and was even more incensed when he found the errant players tucked up but still fully clothed. He knew that Venables was by now something of a leader for the players. 'I might have known I would have most trouble with Venables,' the Doc recalled. 'He was always the ringleader, they all looked up to him. He wasn't even in his room, so I went back later and asked him where he had been.

'He claimed he had been in Eddie McCreadie's room but I knew that was a lie because I had checked his room earlier and it had been empty. But he still denied that he had been out of the hotel, which made me very angry.' That anger was still evident the next morning when Venables, George Graham, John Hollins, Barry Bridges, Eddie McCreadie, Bert Murray, Marvin Hinton and Joe Fascione were handed rail tickets and told to go home. The hotel porter's last act was to inform the press and when the eight arrived in London they had a huge audience of cameramen to greet them. Inevitably, the team lost to Burnley by a 6-2 scoreline and the chances of lifting the league title were gone.

There was no coming back for Venables and Docherty after that incident, for it was almost as if a partnership that had always bordered on a form of mutual tolerance at best had now exploded. Yet the respect for Venables' football brain must have always existed in Docherty, for when there was a scouting mission to be done on Roma, the club opposition in the first round of the Fairs Cup in 1965-66, it was Venables who sat next to Docherty on the flight over.

The first leg of the match at Stamford Bridge on 23 September 1965 was memorable for many reasons, not least the fact that Chelsea overcame the provocation of their Italian opponents to triumph 4-1 after McCreadie had been sent off. Venables was in his glory, scoring twice from cleverly taken free-kicks. Though he was carried off just before half time Venables returned to start the second half with a hat-trick goal. It had been one of his most effective performances, not only for the way he had marshalled the team but for the glorious goals that went with it.

Nobody connected with Chelsea could have envisaged what was to happen to the team and its supporters in Rome in the return leg. The Italians couldn't even wait until the start of the match before showering the team and its officials with rubbish when they went out to inspect the pitch. Stones the size of golf balls were hurled at Tommy Docherty and chairman Joe Mears. But that was as nothing when compared to the deluge that was thrown down at them once the teams were on the pitch: eggs, coins, concrete, fruit, lighted cigarettes and even broken glass. A parcel full of warm liquid was flung at the club's medical officer, Paul Boyne, who remarked: 'I shall always try to believe that it was tea.'

But it was after the game that the real bombardment came. For, despite having armoured vehicles and riot squad police at the front and back of the team coach, windows in it were still shattered by a barrage of stones and bottles. One beside Eddie McCreadie was smashed, who had just put a sports bag by his head for protection. It was remarkable that no one was seriously injured. Roma were banned from European competition for three years because of this.

The phone rang on a Friday at Venables' home in Bonham Road and his father picked it up. 'It's Tommy Docherty,' the voice said. 'Tell Terry he's not playing tomorrow and that he is no longer captain.' Venables had been made captain of the club while still in his teens, though he shared the role with other players. It was curt to the point of being rude and it was the signal that the battle for a voice on how the team should be playing was over, with the manager, as might be expected, the victor. It was a devastating time for Venables for his personality suited the environment he was in at Chelsea. They were the Kings Road club and this was the Swinging Sixties. Venables somehow symbolised the vigour and the verve of the time. It was a good time to be young in London, especially if you were an icon of the generation, a boy with talent and good looks. It was, perhaps, the first time things had gone wrong for the lad who had broken out from the deprivation of the area in which he had been brought up.

Docherty saw it as a straight sell-him-or-succumb-to-him situation. Venables was the voice of the players in the dressing room and Docherty would recall later: 'He started to challenge my authority in training. He would make sarcastic remarks about what I was trying to put across. He wanted to be Mr Big in front of the lads. But there can only be one boss in a football club and this was developing into a major clash of personalities. He was a thorn in my side and too cheeky for my own well-being.' Docherty was to reflect that he considered Venables' position within the club for a good 12 months before deciding that he must go to Joe Mears and make a declaration that there wasn't room for the two of them within the club.

The chairman backed his manager while realising that Venables was a favourite among the fans and a true leader on the field of play. His days had been filled with his burgeoning desire to talk and educate himself on the game of football and there were long and heated afternoons with his Chelsea pals in the café bars of the Fulham Road talking football. Venables had proved at Chelsea that he was a bom leader. There is little doubt that the re-emergence of the club as a football force was as much down to Venables as it was to Docherty.

Venables was innovative in training, constantly suggesting new ideas, particularly for set-pieces. Even then, he was emerging as a masterful tactician with an easy grasp of what was required. When he wasn't actually directing operations at the heart of the side then Chelsea were never quite the same force. Through the spring of 1966, Venables' form began to suffer with the constant dressing-room friction and when Charlie Cooke was bought by Docherty from Dundee, Venables accused him of having brought in a replacement for him before he was out of the door. And that was exactly how it appeared.

It is ironic in the extreme that Venables' final game for the club should have come in the Fairs Cup at Barcelona, the club where he was to enjoy perhaps his headiest success as a manager in years to follow. He was in a losing side that night and was told by the Doc that he had played his final game for the club. It didn't really matter since he returned home to make a quick move across London.

Venables had been placed on the Chelsea transfer list in April 1966, just weeks after his wedding to Christine McCann, and now he was on the move to Tottenham. His father took the call from Bill Nicholson at the Barkingside home in which Terry and Chris had set up and the young Venables said he would be delighted to go to White Hart Lane. No sooner had he put down the phone than it rang again, with Ron Greenwood of West Ham United on the other end asking the same question on behalf of the club Venables first trained with as a boy. But it was Tottenham, the team of Mackay, Mullery, Greaves and Gilzean that appealed to Venables. It was the wrong choice.

On the face of it, they seemed ideal for each other since

Venables was the cavalier playmaker, an extravagantly gifted player with brimming confidence. In that month of May, just before the World Cup in which he might have been participating, it seemed an ideal marriage. Tottenham paid £80,000 for him, and at the start of the 1966-67 season, in the heady aftermath of English World Cup success, Spurs looked ready to take on all comers. So what was it that went wrong? From the start there was no rapport between the slick Venables and the demanding Spurs fans. They sorely missed John White, cruelly struck by a flash of lightning on a golf course at the peak of his career, and they compared the 23-year-old Venables to their fallen hero.

In fact, the Venables way did not really suit the Tottenham style of one-touch football where the movement was constant and sharp. He was never the quickest of movers and he was more like the American quarterback, holding possession until he saw the right forward detaching himself for reception of the ball. By doing this in the Spurs team, he was restricting the flow and it frustrated the fans. In his first season, however, there was one glorious satisfaction. Spurs reached the FA Cup final and their opponents were Tommy Docherty's Chelsea. It was a sweet revenge for Venables who felt he had left Chelsea prematurely and over a clash of personalities.

For that day at least, Venables was able to set aside the criticism from the Spurs fans. That would not spoil his day and in any event he was determined that Tommy Docherty would sit on the bench and squirm while he helped his new club lift the FA Cup. And that they did, by a 2-1 margin.

But it was an oasis in Venables' time at Spurs, for he continued to be the target of a campaign from the terraces and in trying to appease them he was trying to play the way they wanted rather than the way he knew best. On reflection, Venables must have wished he had chosen West Ham.

On his very first day in training he had been kicked up the backside in a five-a-side by Dave Mackay and from there it went downwards. And, come the summer of 1969, it was time to move on.

Les Allen, a former Tottenham hero himself and a Dagenham lad, came to the rescue and Venables joined his third London club, Queen's Park Rangers for a £70,000 fee in June 1969, and it was to be possibly the happiest phase of his playing career, even though he was initially dropping in to the Second Division as the club had just been relegated. But the rapport with Allen was immediate, the chemistry of two boys who had risen above their background yet who had never forgotten their roots. They were to be good for each other in those days, because Venables was in need of rehabilitation after having had his confidence eroded at White Hart Lane.

Indeed, it is surprising that with the problems he had there as a player he should choose to make the North London club his target for ownership all those years later. Was there, perhaps in his subconscious, an inner desire to compensate for what were probably his unhappiest years as a player?

However, it was at Rangers that his instincts for leadership, never deeply buried beneath the surface, really blossomed. Perhaps when Les Allen was replaced by Gordon Jago it was even more of a signal for Venables to flourish as a leader, for Jago did not see his ebullient nature as a threat, as Docherty had done, but more of an asset to be encouraged and fostered. But it was not an environment where motivation, humour and spirit were much of a problem. With players like Venables, Rodney Marsh, Stan Bowles and Frank McLintock around, it was never going to be dull. Rangers elevated themselves to the First Division as runners-up in 1973, playing football that was captivating even if they did have trouble filling their small ground in Shepherd's Bush.

Jago, a natural extrovert himself, loved the dazzling image his team were giving the club and they were stepping out of the shadow of being an incidental club tucked behind BBC Television headquarters into the spotlight where they were capturing as much attention as the big clubs in North London and, more especially, bigger than Chelsea who were just a couple of miles away. The style of play exemplified by Bowles and Marsh was an ingredient perhaps only now being fully appreciated, for such characters are now missing from football. They bred wonderfully witty remarks like the one about Bowles. It went: 'If he could pass a betting shop like he could pass a football he'd be a rich man.' The riches, though, were for those who witnessed that period of the club's history and somehow they reflected the personality of Venables. But once again fate was to take over a situation that seemed settled and successful.

It was almost as if the pages had been turned back to Venables' days at Chelsea, only this time it was Jago making the decision to move this most talented of men on to Crystal Palace, his fourth London club. It came as a shock to the players and the fans.

'I am very rarely lost for words,' Venables said at the time. 'But this is one of those occasions. I really find it very hard to talk about it.' Jago also refused to shed light on the subject though, perhaps, like Docherty, he had seen in Venables a threat to his own strength within the club. But it left the Rangers manager with a desperately unhappy dressing room, with McLintock, a senior professional, registering his protest and Gerry Francis, who felt he was learning so much under the influence of such a good teacher, accepting taking over the captaincy only with the greatest reluctance. Yet the move to Selhurst Park did have its compensations for Venables, for it meant he was going to play under Malcolm Allison, the man he had so admired when, as a boy in his early teens, he had trained with him at West Ham United.

Here were two personalities that developed exactly the right chemistry. This was an era when managers were perceived to be much more dour than Big Mal with his fat cigar, his bunnyclub girlfriend and his palate for the finest champagne. There had been 15 years since Venables first listened to Allison's futuristic views on the game, but now as a mature player he was even more ready to lend an ear to those inventive ideas that sprang from one of the most fertile coaching brains this country has ever produced.

In 1974-75 Crystal Palace began their first season

experiencing Third Division football. It was a change for Venables and he could not have imagined how his life was about to undergo a dramatic shift of emphasis. Allison had seen more in Venables than just buying a player and he knew that here was a man he could perhaps groom in his own image. The way things panned out, that objective was easily met. Ironically, QPR tried to buy him back just two months after selling him to Palace, Jago perhaps realising just how much Venables was missed. But the bid was refused and it was perhaps as well for football that it was. For, after just 14 games in the Palace side, Allison called Venables into the office and told him it was all over. His playing days had ended and it was time all those bright ideas that crowded his mind should now surface in the capacity of coach. The invitation coincided with Venables suffering increasing problems with a heel that was diagnosed as arthritic. It was the close of a playing career conducted round the London clubs which had been colourful, controversial and committed but which had been the ideal apprenticeship for what was to come.

CHAPTER THREE
The Playwright

Terry Venables had never been happy with the stereotype lifestyle of a football player where training was followed by an afternoon in the billiard hall or the betting shop. His nature was much more restless than that and there were always new goals to be reached, whether it was behind a microphone at the Hammersmith Palais, making suits for Norman Wisdom or, the most successful of his many diversions, writing books and television series.

Venables had always maintained that he had a need that extended beyond the smell of linament, if he was ever to achieve total fulfilment. He was to reason: 'Football is really only an extension of being at school, doing what you enjoy, what you might do for fun anyway. A lot of players don't really give too much thought to their future, though in the modern era they are encouraged much more to take heed of what might happen when their careers end in their thirties. They train, play, talk football and maybe play snooker and suddenly, when it is all over, they panic because they are faced with a dramatic drop in their wages.

'Years ago we had a maximum wage, £20-a-week players, and when they finished playing they would get an £18-a-week job and it wasn't too drastic a change. Now they are earning thousands of pounds a week it is a different story. Football also tends to make you lazy and maybe unreliable. They are 20 years old and they are at the top of their profession. In a more ordinary walk of life you might aim to reach the top around the age of 40. They tend to shy away from what other people would consider hard work. It is a matter of saving money, buying a business and then getting someone else to run it for them. Life is about knowledge as well as money.'

So Venables reached out, tentatively at first with his wig

business and then a £200 investment in the tailor's shop that went wrong. But all the time Venables was learning the pitfalls. In between times there was also the music business, for Terry had crooned with Joe Loss at the Palais when he was just 17. He had dressed in flannels and his England Youth blazer, with the three lions boldly displayed on the breast pocket. It earned him harsh words from Tommy Docherty, but was only an extension of his stage days in Dagenham when he joined a song and dance troupe called the Happy Tappers. The showbusiness bug has stayed with him through the years, even to this day. He is to be seen, without much persuasion, singing Sinatra numbers on the Karaoke nights in his Kensington club, Scribes West.

The man who often comperes those evenings is Eric Hall, the cigar-smoking agent who began his working life in Tin Pan Alley in the Soho offices of Mills Music where his pal in the packing office was Elton John. In the afternoons, Venables, George Graham and the Chelsea clique would spend their spare time there. Tony Hiller, who was later to write the Eurovision hit 'Save Your Kisses For Me' for Brotherhood of Man, was at Mills Music too, and Venables wondered if he could become a songwriter. But he was no Bernie Taupin and the idea of becoming a music writer went the same way as most of his other early business ventures, down a cul-de-sac. But he was a great believer in the principle nothing ventured, nothing gained and he saw yet another avenue, not writing lyrics this time, but books.

He was still only 19 and developing apace as a soccer player when he had his first meeting with the man who was to give him the drive and the incentive to pursue a writing career. He had not, after all, had the benefit of an exceptional education, but what he did have was a strong and vivid imagination. Just as he was to be innovative as a football coach, so he brought that fertility of mind to the typewriter. Gordon Williams was a Scottish journalist in his early forties who Venables met almost casually at Chelsea's training ground in Mitcham. He had just been made captain of the side and the relationship between the skipper and the Doc was, for the time being at least, a harmonious one.

Williams was living in West London and had worked on a number of local newspapers and magazines. He was already a novelist with an escalating reputation. But that first meeting came while the budding footballer was just as fascinated by the budding author. Williams at the time was ghosting newspaper articles for Docherty and so was a regular visitor to the training ground.

The journalist was quick to see the drift. 'They were becoming stars and were being offered articles for anything between £100 and £2,000 if it was a big piece for a Sunday newspaper. They would then get someone to ghostwrite the article and an agent to handle the contract and finish up with maybe 40 percent of the money,' Williams would recall. 'As I discovered, a few of them were more intelligent than the press men being sent to write the articles. So I suggested they write their own articles and then they would keep 100 percent of the money. Some of them weren't interested but Terry had already started going into other areas, taking coaching courses, and I knew that he had been involved in other business pursuits like the tailor's shop in Old Compton Street.

'He turned up with this short story, typed, and asked me what I thought of it. He was a bit shy about showing it to me. It was incredible and I enquired as to how he had done it. He told me he had watched me tapping away and it had seemed easy enough and he went and bought a typewriter and wrote this short story about ticket touts. It was amazing because it was one of the best pastiche versions of Damon Runyon, that colourful, raffish, sporting chap and spiv, I had seen. But he told me he had never heard of Damon Runyon. Then I discovered he had never even read a book the whole way through, which had been a point of honour bearing in mind the essay he had turned in at school which had simply said he was going to be a footballer.'

Venables remembered that first sortie into the literary world. 'It was about a footballer and it was called *The World of*

Sammy Small. I would write bits of it while Chelsea were away on European trips.' Williams, who had written the book from which the film *Straw Dogs* was produced, had made a firm friend and he admired a footballer who would take the trouble to go out and buy his own typewriter so he could try his hand at becoming an author even though he had never actually read a book through himself. From accurate long passes to fascinating short stories, here was a footballer who had brains at both ends of his body.

The friendship flourished, but it was while Williams was compiling the brochure for the FA Cup final between Spurs and Chelsea in 1967 that Terry's talents again alerted his mind. Part of that publication was to profile each player in turn, with the players providing their own thoughts. While Williams interviewed the rest, Venables wrote his own, the only player among the 22 to do so. He had already got the message that in using an agent and ghostwriter he was halving his own share of the proceeds. He wrote a missive called *Jokes The Fans Don't Hear* which was published almost unaltered in a magazine and the thirst for further publications was fostered.

What Williams had spotted in Venables was a quick, inventive brain and a wonderful ear for his native Cockney dialogue. It seemed he had an ear like blotting paper and it was then that his co-author suggested: 'Come on, let's write a book. Give it one day a week.' But Venables was in Williams' West End office daily; the two men from opposite ends of the country sitting over their typewriters as the ideas poured forth. Williams, the more accomplished typist, set them down on paper.

They came up with a futuristic book and the title, *They Used To Play On Grass*, was perhaps more prophetic than Venables and his co-author could possibly have envisaged. Venables was so excited at what was happening in that tiny office that he would recall later: 'It was the most exciting thing. I was describing an imaginary match and I found that I couldn't get the words down fast enough to keep pace with the mental images. It was almost as if I was turning on a tap because the words just kept flowing.

Looking back it was probably the first time that the football and the words had fused together. I was describing something that was really exciting me and the adrenalin was flowing. It was funny because Gordon would be hovering behind me, wondering what the score was.' Venables had really caught the creative bug, and he was consumed by it.

But when the book was published there was scepticism all round, largely because no one quite believed that a footballer, even one of Venables' wide-ranging talent, could have produced a novel of quite such fascinating content. The book was reviewed not on the literary pages but on the sports pages and was treated there almost flippantly. There was the snobbish belief that a footballer was incapable of producing the thought and creativity that went into the book, whereas the truth was that much of it was written by Venables himself.

Williams said: 'Unfortunately, as a result of Terry's position, the book got gimmicky publicity and was never really taken seriously enough. That was the reason we decided in any future literary ventures we would use a pseudonym. Venables was always aggrieved that the effort he put into those books should have produced such a wary reaction about his input into them. So many business ventures then and since have carried a sportsman's name as a selling point without the individual concerned having contributed even the germ of an idea.'

With Venables it was certainly very different. 'People always asked if I really did have anything to do with the writing. They seemed to think: "Ah, yes, a thick footballer. He can't put two sentences together." Those people don't know just how many afternoons went into the production of those books.'

The significance of *They Used To Play On Grass* should never be obscured, for in it were the concepts of artificial pitches which Venables was to introduce at Queen's Park Rangers in the years that followed. Another visionary concept was the idea of the British Cup which, even now, remains a constant talking point within football.

Because of the reaction to their first collaboration, it was under the name of P.B. Yuill that the books about private detective James Hazell were first published. Ernie Yuill had been a close friend of Fred Venables and his family in earlier years, when they worked together in the London docks. He would go with Fred to watch Venables play in his school matches and would occasionally baby-sit when the young Terry was just a short-trousered boy. Williams, by coincidence, had an uncle of the same name so they decided that their next venture into the literary field would carry this pseudonym. That left no room for Venables to be subjected to any raised eyebrows and ensured that any work would be judged solely on merit.

'What we needed was an idea,' Williams recalls. 'Then came the day Terry rushed up to me. He had been involved in an important match [for Chelsea] against Nottingham Forest in the season the club went on to clinch promotion [1963], He babbled something to me about babies and maternity wards.' What had struck Venables during that fateful football match was what might happen if babies in a maternity ward were accidentally switched. Venables then explained: 'I really began thinking about this when I went to see my first baby in hospital. The tiny identity tag had slipped from her wrist and dropped onto the floor. There were ten babies in the ward and it made me wonder about two mothers leaving the hospital with the wrong babies.' But the more they tried to re-create the drama of such an eventuality, the more they felt it needed another dimension. They had reached a stage where one of the mothers had been involved in a car crash and needed a blood transfusion to save her baby's life.

'We tried to trace the story through the minds of the mothers, one from Bethnal Green, and poor, the other one rich,' Williams explained. 'But as neither of us was particularly keen on babies or mums - in that sense - we found the only way we could tackle it was through a cynical so-and-so like ourselves.' That is how Hazell, the Cockney private detective who was to become the subject of three hardback books and a smash-hit television series was born. His job was anywhere in London and through him Williams and Venables were able to capture the atmosphere of the city. It was Macmillan who published those books, *Hazell Plays Solomons*, *Hazell and The Three Card Trick*, and *Hazell and The Menacing Jester*.

It was widely believed at the time that the name Hazell was inspired by one of the Rangers players, Tony Hazell, a defender and midfield player who dourly graced the London football scene of the early Seventies. In fact, it was the name of a lad from Venables' past, a centre-half from his younger days. Venables always insisted: 'He is not any one person. People said he was a mix of Bobby Moore the footballer and Billy Walker the boxer but he was really nobody in sport. Hazell was a combination of the characters I have met in the East End of London.

'He was really a typical Londoner but we searched for a name with a female ring to it because we wanted the character to have a little bit of femininity. You know how they talk in the East End - "ducky" and all that. Some of his mates called him Shirley because he had fair, curly hair. But we wanted him to be typical of the area I was brought up in, a bit of a "jack the lad". We didn't realise just what we were creating at the time.'

But this lovable Cockney character, stumbling his way through life, was really far removed from the man who had created him, since Venables' own conception of his career direction was much more clinically mapped out. He was determined his own life should not be lived solely within the parameters of professional football and he abhorred the thought that he might ever feel so involved in it that he would conform to the Bill Shankly belief that the game was more important than life and death.

It was not until four years after Hazell had been created that it eventually came to the small screen as a television series, starting in 1978, a period in which much happened to Venables' own life as it focused between Crystal Palace and Queen's Park Rangers. He had diversified and it had helped him relax from the pressures of managing Palace.

There was no question of the world of writing taking over from football, which was the mainstay of his life. But it was football that helped give him the basis for his character. 'What happens in life is what happens in football,' he would reflect. 'One minute you are a hero and 90 minutes later you are a villain. But what writing had in common with football was that it was hard work. When I would sit down with Gordon we would create something in the typewriter and feel it was good. Then you read it again and know it can be improved. There were times when I thought Gordon was an absolute bastard, but it is only when I would relate it to the football job that I could accept the search to get it right. On the training pitch that is what you do with players. You make them work to hone their skills and to make sure that the end product on a Saturday is the fruit of patience and the desire to get it right.'

Venables had found an outlet that was more satisfying than the miming in the clubs, the amateur attempts at singing Sinatra songs with the Joe Loss Orchestra, the Jimmy Durante impersonations. This was professionalism of the highest order and it was, perhaps, the first time that Venables had gone into business and produced something that was successful and lasting.

When the books were turned into a TV series, the auditions were conducted in his father's public house in Chingford and the lead role went to Nicholas Ball. The irony was that Venables, who loved to have a stage on which to work, was now the man in the background supplying the words. His own sharp wit, his facility with the one-liner were all emerging from the mouth of an actor. In some ways this would gall the frustrated vaudeville star lurking in Venables. The natural showman in him was part of the appeal and, having cut his teeth so early in his top hat and bow tie as a member of the Happy Tappers, it was no great surprise that he should continue to crave an audience and seek the company of those who worked in the Soho music industry.

As Venables grew up, so the heroes were as much Sinatra as Blanchflower and those infant and adolescent turns in the clubs and pubs of Dagenham gave him his love and feeling for the world of showbusiness. The showmanship wasn't always appreciated, not least where Tommy Docherty was concerned, and progress in a talent show run by Butlin's was curtailed by Docherty, as was his attempt to earn money as a dance-hall singer after his aforementioned debut on the stage of the Hammersmith Palais. There was an offer on the table for £100 a show. But Docherty, in short, gave his young, emerging talent a final ultimatum: be a singer and you can forget about football. It wasn't really a difficult choice for although Venables might well have been able to negotiate a professional singing contract of sorts, there was no question that his real aptitude was for football.

But this was a restless mind at work and though he would be the heart and soul of training and the unofficial chairman of the endless football discussions that followed it in the cafés on the Fulham Road, Venables still needed something different to occupy his mind. His brush with the showbusiness world would take him to the offices of Mills Music in Denmark Street where he found in the packing department young contemporaries in Elton John, still Reg Dwight in those days, and Hall.

The friendships formed during those long afternoons of daydreaming have endured, notably the one he cemented with Hall, who was to move on from brewing the tea to become a record plugger and an agent for various young actors and singers. But it was probably due to Venables, and their friendship, that Hall moved into the world of football, never straying far from Venables' side in recent years as well as being the representative of a number of his Tottenham players. Hall's Havana cigars have become a part of the Venables entourage and he can still be spotted as the man who often greets the guests at Venables' West London club and eaterie, Scribes West in Kensington High Street. The showbusiness urge never left Venables, even at the height of his power as the man who owned and ran his own football club. The bond between Hall and Venables remains stronger than some people who see Venables as a guru of the game might like.

Hall was not in the wings when his mate did make his one major contribution to the world of crooning while he was manager of Barcelona. Venables' profile as manager of the club was much higher than it had been in England at Queen's Park Rangers and Crystal Palace for there are daily TV bulletins about the club in the football-crazy Catalan city.

One of the Spanish channels learned of his singing talent and invited him onto one of their highly rated entertainment shows belting out his favourite number 'I've Got You Under My Skin'. He was backed by a big band and if the rendition was not exactly going to make Ol' Blue Eyes shake in his highly polished crocodile shoes, then it was passably good and the video of his performance remains one of his family's most treasured possessions.

This act was in the way of a TV comeback for Venables since he first captivated the cameras as an entertainer while he had his boots on. The occasion was a First Division game at Derby County and as the camera panned on the Rangers, Venables wiggled his eyebrows up and down. It became a well-used piece of film and when the *Big Match* programme used it as part of their opening sequence for their excellent show, Venables became even more of a popular figure with a reputation as a cross between an athlete, comedian and entertainer. Little did we know then of the number of eyebrows Venables would make other people raise as his restlessness and eternal search for his own Utopia drove him on beyond his limitations. But first he had to prove that he could now accommodate all the innovative talent and leadership he had shown in the playing arena and utilise it in the field of coaching and management.

CHAPTER FOUR
Crowning at the Palace

MALCOLM ALLISON HAD SEEN much more than a player when he lured Venables to Selhurst Park, for his extraordinary perception had told him that here he was buying a mind that had already taken over from the feet. Allison was perhaps the best teacher any young coach could have had. Back in his West Ham United days, when tuberculosis had robbed Big Mal of a lung, he was a visionary, perhaps conscious as a player that he was merely serving an apprenticeship for the management route that would bring together one of the finest sides of post-war years, the Manchester City Championship squad of 1967-68, a team ahead of its time which played exceptional football and had players of great individual merit and collective brilliance.

Allison had then been the thrusting young coach, almost running ahead of his own ideas and needing the steadying influence of Joe Mercer to curb his excesses, both on and off the field. Those who remember Mal in those barnstorming years could see a parallel with the emerging Venables. Both had minds that were bursting with ideas, an ability to communicate that would have made them masters in any classroom while always permitting the freedom of expression that was to produce wonderfully gifted players.

When Big Mal called in Venables to signal the end of his career as a player, he commented: 'You are the only man in football I would take this advice from. By the way, happy New Year!' So it was that on New Year's Eve 1974, a chapter closed in the life of Venables and a new horizon suddenly appeared.

Allison had no fears of what the new partnership might bring, even though he sensed he was unleashing a vibrant new talent into the coaching sphere. He had witnessed the gathering influence Venables had on the side he captained at

Queen's Park Rangers and sensed that here was a personality who could supplement his own extensive experience in the field of educating players and producing football teams of excitement and promise. What they were able to do was bounce ideas off each other and they would plot and plan the next day's training for hours on end. It was as if the two men had a telepathy and there is little doubt that this period in Venables' career was the one that was to carry him forward to the pinnacle of club management in Spain some years later. In Venables' first full season as coach at Palace in 1975-76 there was work to be done for the side were in the Third Division. The ambition to climb out of that territory which so ill-befitted the fertile minds of the two men in charge burned within Allison and Venables, but as the season wore on they found their loyalties confused by an exceptional FA Cup run that had lowly beginnings in knocking Walton and Hersham out in the first round. But as Millwall (in a replay) and Scarborough followed, Allison and Venables were suddenly pitting their coaching skills against those of Leeds United, then managed by Jimmy Armfield but still with some of the great players of the Revie era: Peter Lorimer, Billy Bremner, Norman Hunter, Paul Madeley and Allan Clarke. Palace went to Elland Road and won 1-0 and now they were on a roll. As the publicity machine ground into action, so did Allison.

The cigars became bigger and he adopted a huge fedora hat to add to the image. The team posed for photographs in James Cagney suits while carrying violin cases under their arms. There were lunches for the press in the smarter restaurants of the West End. For Venables, there was particular satisfaction in having brought about the demise of Chelsea in the fifth round at Stamford Bridge with a 3-2 victory. Suddenly, the names of Jim Cannon, Nick Chatterton, Martin Hinshelwood and Peter Taylor were becoming recognised. Sunderland succumbed in the next round and so came a semi-final against Second Division Southampton at neutral Stamford Bridge, with most people quite convinced Big Mal and his sidekick would make it to Wembley, the Butch Cassidy and Sundance Kid of the footballing world.

It was a colourful and potentially historic moment, for Palace were set to become the first Third Division side to reach a Wembley final. Unfortunately, nobody had read that script to Lawrie McMenemy, the Saints manager, whose own profile at the time was hardly that of a shrinking violet. The big ex-Guardsman had some nifty lads of his own, Peter Rodrigues, Nick Holmes, Mick Channon and Venables' old Chelsea chum Peter Osgood. Big Lawrie's team swept to Wembley at Palace's expense, there to defeat mighty Manchester United in a memorable final. Sadly for Palace, this disappointment was not cushioned by finishing fifth in the Third Division and missing out on promotion by three points. Chairman Ray Bloye decided that summer it was time to split the partnership and Allison was sacrificed, allowing Venables to take full control in the summer of 1976.

It was a sad parting for the two men had like minds and when Allison had described Venables as 'the most impressive young man I have ever met in professional football' he didn't realise that chairman Bloye was taking it all on board and quietly thinking that he didn't need Big Mal. The challenge for Venables was an immense one at the age of 33 and it meant another turning point in his life.

For some years he had been a significant member of the Professional Footballers' Association committee, a kind of roving football barrister, often engaged in the defence of his fellow members of the professional game. He was an early advocate of freedom of contract for footballers which was to give them a significant control of their own destiny. From his Welsh mother he had inherited a natural talent for advocacy and persuasive language. He was certainly applying that effectively on the training pitch where Allison increasingly left him to get on with it.

His captain at the time, Ian Evans, was also Welsh and he suggested: 'Terry transformed the side. He seemed able to isolate the weaknesses in players and would work on them so there was no way you could not improve under him. He always made certain that training was going to be interesting and his imagination at dreaming up unusual free-kicks was remarkable. We would spend at least two hours a week working on them.' Those sessions not only captivated the Palace players, they fascinated Allison, too. 'Terry emerged as a deep thinker about the game,' he says. 'He has an urge to absorb knowledge.' It is, indeed, interesting to reflect on some of the early philosophies Venables expounded and which are as appropriate today as they were in the late Seventies.

'The game's possibilities are endless but before they can be fulfilled there has to be a lot of thinking, and a lot of changes. First of all, we have to strip the game of fear because there are too many managers living day to day. Before we can give the country its super stadiums we need to ensure the basic security of the manager's post. How often do you see managers who have poured their energies into setting up a youth policy not being allowed the time to exploit that work. If you give him a cast-iron contract then he has a chance. At the end of that time his work can then be reviewed. That is the time it becomes fair to make judgements. Then, as you give the new manager a base for his work, you widen his horizons. You encourage him to be bold.

'The game has become corrupted by caution. We need to reward aggression and boldness with extra points. If you do that you change the emphasis of the game in one stroke without introducing any artificial element.

'It is also absurd to see highly skilled footballers ploughing through thick mud in mid-winter. The skill dwindles and the game loses its magic. I believe that ultimately soccer will become a summer game. Imagine the incentive to skill of playing on thickly grassed, true pitches. We are too rooted in tradition. We play on a Saturday afternoon because we have always done that. Evidence suggests Sunday would be more popular so we should put it to the test.

'We have to sweep away the absurdities like allowing teams

to come out of a 0-0 draw with a point each. How can you give a team a reward when it has failed to score? By one simple device the authorities could bring in a new era of attacking football. Wipe out the points for a goalless draw and the effect would be dramatic.

'It is also crazy we have so many stadiums in a city like London. We have to prune to make ourselves strong. And we have to be strongest at the top, with a Super League of 16 clubs.'

These were prophetic thoughts Venables offered when he first became a coach at Palace in 1975 and how true they still ring today. Some of them have been implemented in the meantime and others remain as vibrantly relevant today as they were 19 years ago when the then very youthful Venables first uttered them. This was the same man who was one of the first to sense the growing threat of the hooligans and who suggested: 'It might help to have grounds with seating only so we can get rid of the obscene fences that look like something from Auschwitz.' That remark, too, came ten years before the Taylor Report on all-seater stadiums that followed the horrors of Hillsborough caused by exactly those kind of fences.

It was evident from the outset that here was a light for the game, a torch that young players could follow. There was wisdom in his words and guidance for the young players who would heed his advice. He sensed that young men reaching the pinnacle of their profession early in their twenties would have problems handling what went with such swift elevation, so he was conscious of the value of leadership. It was with these ideals in his mind that Venables parted company with deposed Allison having learned a great deal from their brief and very kaleidoscopic partnership. 'I couldn't have done what I did without Malcolm,' he would reflect. 'He would remember the things that used to upset him at City when he was coach and Joe Mercer was above him and then make sure they didn't happen to me.'

It was at this time Venables first indicated his belief in a two-tier structure of management where the coach ran the team and the manager sorted out the contracts and dealt with transfer business. 'You need two men for one basic reason and that is: no man can coach the same players he is having arguments with over money.' Though one of the youngest managers in the league, Venables had prepared himself well for his new role in life and even those at the very top of the game were ready to acclaim him.

Don Revie, by now manager of England after his huge success at Leeds, had carefully monitored his rise towards football management. 'Nobody in the previous ten years and connected with English football had made a bigger impression on me than Terry Venables. I predicted he would reach the top as a manager when he first moved to Queen's Park Rangers as a player from Spurs. I delivered a lecture to a management course in St Helens and Terry was there. He fired more questions at me than anyone else on the course. There is an astute football brain there. He reminded me of myself when I was his age, because when I was 34 and looking to go into the job I went and quizzed Sir Matt Busby in just the same way Terry did with me.'

Venables was determined that he would run Palace democratically. He remembered only too vividly his days at Chelsea when Tommy Docherty would rubbish his opinions and at Spurs when it was Dave Mackay who did the talking. Even at QPR he urged Jago to allow free expression without challenging the manager's position and he insisted: 'A democratic system may be the most difficult to organise, but it is the easiest to make work. People have their say but if they can't make up their mind then you make the decision.' There was a reluctance among the young players at Palace to express their views, but by patient and painstaking insistence he eventually persuaded players to be frank and open in their thoughts.

Coaching, he would say, is largely a matter of organisation, telling which players to go where and teaching them the short cuts. But he would harness individual ability claiming it was self-defeating to stamp his personality on something that doesn't require changing. 'With the talented players, you put them in an area of the field where they are going to be most effective and just try to add refinements to their game.' By persuasion and some cajoling, Venables soon had the players responding to his own infectious personality. He was essentially charming them and in that first full season of 1976-77 the place was alive with fun and laughter. He would add his humour getting on all fours and saying: 'Give it a Sylvester the Cat' as he tried to teach one of his wingers how to creep up for a blind-side run.

He would never clutter his players' minds with too much dogma and if there was something new to be explained, he would devote an entire session to it rather than skip and jump from one tactic to another. The keyword for a Venables training session is simplicity, getting across one idea at a time. As Allison had said: 'There are certain things you can learn about coaching, but personality and leadership are essentials you are born with and Terry is blessed with both.' They were prophetic words and nobody around at the time was arguing.

Venables himself had taken on a new lease of life, refusing to dwell on the fact that he could no longer sit in the centre of midfield knowing that he was the driver and his feet were the gear-stick for the side. The Hazell series was making him financially independent so that he could be his own man. He was desperate to be a successful coach but at the same time he didn't want the game to consume him, to own him. 'There are a lot of genuine and dedicated people making a living out of the game, but there are conmen, too, and they are guys who don't have real ambition. They drift within the game. I want to be the best, at anything I do. If I ran a pub it would have to be the best pub in the district. If you have the belief then you have a chance. When I packed up playing and moved into coaching that's what I felt. I'd heard all the stuff about the mystique of coaching. But when you looked at some of the people who were doing it, then you had a sneaking fancy you would be OK.'

The fact that Arsenal had made an effort to lure Venables from Palace after Allison's departure could only have added to his belief that he was capable of lifting Palace away from the

Third and up towards the First. But he knew, too, that the club would offer him an opportunity of finishing his apprenticeship in the job away from the glare that would have focused on him at a place like Highbury. 'The foundations for a good club were there. They had the players with the right potential and I knew that the directors at the time felt strongly about progression. And, in any event, Malcolm had insisted I stay even though I told him I would go with him.'

One of his first problems was that he would be unable to keep Peter Taylor, his outstanding winger, at the club. He had been picked for England from the Third Division, but mixing with England players made him realise that to sustain an international career he would have to move on.

It was soon evident that Venables' decision to stay at Selhurst Park had been a good one as Palace, by degrees, started playing football in the Venables mould. And there was no restriction on his vision of what he could create. It was a time when Liverpool were at their pomp, but in January 1977 as Palace prepared to meet them in the FA Cup - they drew at Anfield and lost the home replay 3-2 -Venables was able to remark: 'In some ways I'd like to think Palace are becoming the Liverpool of the Third Division. But, in the long term, I am looking for more than they have to offer. Eventually, I want my team to be more complete. I believe we are one of no more than six clubs who improve players and help them understand the game they are playing. When I see some of the West German teams playing and consider how much nearer they are to perfection than anything we have in England I want not only to win games like Liverpool but also to play football that is visually exciting, which can stimulate the senses. If that sounds a bit much from someone in the Third Division then I can only say that our team is developing quickly.'

In that side was George Graham, who Venables had picked up on a free transfer. It was a reunion from the Chelsea days, though now, of course, Venables was the boss. Graham would admit in later years that their time together at Palace helped Graham considerably in his own ambition to reach out as a successful manager.

It was to be the best possible climax to Venables' first season in charge as the side scored 12 goals in their last four winning games to make it to the Second Division clinging onto the third promotion place on goal average. There was euphoria in South-East London, but the pragmatist in Venables knew that there was still much work to be done and he was not about to join in the general hysteria.

'I knew there was a lot to do before we could claim to have anything lasting. Malcolm and John Cartwright had set up a fine youth section at the club, but I was concerned about the way people kept going on about the potential of the place. Some of it was drivel because I have seen too many players with potential who are still waiting to fulfil it when they reach 30. I didn't want the players having their heads filled with this seventh-heaven crap. When we reached the top was when I wanted to hear about potential, not before.'

Helping him towards that objective was another of his former Chelsea team-mates, Allan Harris, who was to be a loyal lieutenant for the next ten years as Venables' own reputation soared. He knew now that the going would get tougher. 'Success can be worse than failure,' he said. 'If you fail you cry for a couple of weeks and then get back to work again. If you succeed you can only afford a week to enjoy it and think about it because the demands for greater success are enormous.'

Because of his success, Chelsea tried to entice Venables away from Palace that summer, but they had little joy for, with promotion assured and a youth side that had just won the FA Youth Cup, Venables felt he was sitting on a club capable of really going places. But it didn't quite happen in his second season of 1977-78, which was one of consolidation. Young players like Kenny Sansom, Vince Hilaire and Jerry Murphy were learning their trade from Venables. They in fact finished a respectable ninth place while Tottenham, having been relegated the previous season, leapt straight back into the First Division.

The season did have its compensations for Venables, however.

In January 1978, Ron Greenwood, confirmed as England's new manager after the defection of Don Revie to the United Arab Emirates, named an impressive list of managers and coaches to look after the interests of the England sides under his jurisdiction. Bobby Robson, whose Ipswich were a side Venables much admired, and Don Howe would run the England 'B' side, Dave Sexton managed the Under-21s with Venables as his coach, while Brian Clough and Peter Taylor were given responsibility for the youth side. 'Ron had twice tried to sign me as a player for West Ham and had been instrumental in fostering my interest in coaching. Working with him now is a great honour for me,' was Venables' reaction at the time.

Even during that season of consolidation there were further attempts to lure Venables away from his young side, with Birmingham City announcing their interest after the former England boss Sir Alf Ramsey quit the club when they failed to back his sale of Trevor Francis. But if there were some disappointments on the field at Palace, Venables had the satisfaction of seeing his Cockney character Hazell make his TV debut, played by Nicholas Ball. Still, it seemed Venables was in great demand and as the summer of 1978 came and went, so did further job offers, one to link up with Jimmy Armfield at Leeds United and another to manage the Australian national soccer side.

At the start of the 1978-79 season, which was to be a momentous one in his life, Venables was content to have his Palace side compared to that at Chelsea when he had bubbled along with Tambling, Bridges and the rest. They even had Allan Harris and George Graham, two of the old Blues Brigade, on the staff, though the team now featured more of their young stars: Peter Nicholas, Steve Kember, Ian Walsh and Terry Fenwick. They were even using Chelsea's former training ground at Mitcham. Venables was in tune with them because, he said, he could understand and accept the pressures young players were under. 'The key word was patience,' he reflected. 'You mustn't expect too much from young players. Those lads at that time had achieved results beyond their years and experience and it was necessary to keep everything in perspective.' The average age of the side was then just 20, so Venables sensed there need be no ceiling on achievement. He had them playing football that was attractive and uninhibited and he expressed a desire to create a side in the mould of the then great national teams of Holland, with their 'total' football, and Brazil.

The recognition for the side was matched by that for their manager and still the offers came in. Jim Gregory, the chairman of Queen's Park Rangers had ambitions for his own club in West London for whom he was providing a neat stadium in Shepherd's Bush. He was determined to entice Venables there and there was also a £200,000 tax-free job offer from the Middle East. But Ray Bloye and his Palace board resisted all-comers and insisted that Venables had a four-year contract at Selhurst which he would honour. One offer Venables was able to accept at the time came from Thames TV who wanted him to do a short spot for them on their Friday preview programme, a television 'in' where he didn't need to sing into a microphone, but offer analysis on the game he really did understand.

Venables was flattered by the interest but certainly not fazed. He said: 'I had worked bloody hard over the three years I had been at Palace, first as a coach and then as a manager. There were only two players in the side who had been with the club when I first started there and I had been told that if I could make it at Palace, I could make it anywhere. I know what he meant because financial resources were very limited and I really felt I needed to spend some money. But it was the challenge of reaching the First Division that was stimulating me more than the offers that might have been coming in for me.'

There were eight members of his Youth Cup-winning side now in the team and it is interesting in 1994 to reflect on the view expressed in 1978 by Venables about the education of young players. He said at the time: 'We undertook a three-year development plan for boys. We told John Cartwright, our youth coach, to take the pressure of winning off those lads for an entire year. Too many boys have been flung into matches instead of being taught the game, and schoolmasters are as much to blame for that as coaches. The best player might be fortunate to get one touch on the ball or one header in the game. In the first year at Palace, we concentrated on breaking down the individual skills like control, passing, heading to the exclusion of everything else. We have always over-stressed the competitive side of English football at too young an age.

'In the second year, we tightened up on the physical side, the competitiveness, the endurance but only after they had been given the confidence to express their skills. And in the third year, they trained harder than they had done in their lives. That way, when they reach the coach of the first team there is not a lot of work to be done on them.' They were actions very much in line with the Football Association's own thought process when they announced new plans for the preparation of young players at the end of 1993.

Indeed, the general sloth and lack of interest in improvement became a constant hobbyhorse with Venables which he would air on any occasion he was given the opportunity. There was something of a crusade about it. He told a meeting of the Football Writers' Association in 1978: 'Mainly through laziness we are not working at the things we should be working at and our football is nowhere near the quality we should be seeking. Too many players are content to play in the little plots of land their coaches tell them they should occupy. There isn't enough artistry and invention in our game. It's exciting enough with the ball flying from end to end, but when you look for the extra, special quality, it isn't there.' We have players of ability, but what is in question is their ability to grasp what they are being told.

'I also wonder about what they are being told. It seems to me clubs are happy to get the games over rather than learn something from it. Possibly this is because we don't have enough time to spend with our players. You play Saturday, patch up the injured, play Wednesday, patch the injured and play again Saturday. It is obvious we play too many games. If we cut them back then coaches might have enough time to teach the good things and players might have more time to understand them.' It was once again prophetic talking from Venables, for are these not the same problems that still sterilise the English game a generation on?

At least as Palace plundered towards increasing recognition, Venables was able to give vent to his high ideals as he coached the England Under-21s. It was the perfect break from the promotion race, a chance for him and his players to have a break from living in each other's pockets.

Back at Selhurst, Venables' young side continued to challenge for their First Division status. There was a slight hiccup at the start of 1979 as they drew six league games in succession. However, when it came to the final furlong they produced a fine gallop, winning five and drawing one of their last six matches to clinch their room at the top as champions of the Second Division after a home victory over Burnley. The gates all season had been gradually increasing and on the day they went up there were 51,801 crammed inside the ground to salute their precocious young side. For Venables this was a special moment as he had hurried his young side through two divisions in the space of three seasons and most of the players were his, including Ian Walsh and David Swindlehurst who scored the goals in that memorable game. It had been a tense night, for defeat would have kept Palace in the Second Division, a draw won them promotion but the victory ensured the Championship.

Venables, who had acquired a taste for cigars and champagne from his predecessor Allison, was able to enjoy both as his Palace side were christened the 'Team of the Eighties'. But it was to be a label they found it impossible to live up to.

The big red Jaguar that was Venables' gesture to status purred round London with its proud owner at the wheel. He had arrived in the First Division, where he felt his talents always belonged, two years ahead of his own schedule. His side had looked the most arresting since the Busby Babes and he would proudly tell anyone who wanted to listen: 'They have deserved to win the title. They have shown character under fire and done better than anyone could have hoped for. The tremendous thing about Palace's progress this season, from my own point of view, is I can still work within the time limits I have set myself - and I can still see this Palace team reach fulfilment. I was fortunate that when I took over, the club had been set up properly by Malcolm Allison, that a lot of undergrowth had been cut away. But I still reckoned it would take five years to establish the side in the First Division. It could be I will get four full years in the First Division with them. I am fascinated to see how far this team can go. I have had offers to move and I have been frustrated by the restrictions imposed on me in the transfer market when I needed to use it. But all the time I have been held back by the thought I could be walking out on one of the strongest foundations in English football.'

Nothing could re-create the bond that Venables had with his Championship side for he was more like an elder brother to the players than a boss. On the coach back from away matches his habit was to take off his jacket, light a cigar and sit at the back of the bus cracking jokes and joining in the fun. Nobody took advantage for they all realised that without the verve and vigour of their young manager they would not have made it to the top. He had always hated to be beaten as a player and, although he had instilled in his side a respect for the fineries of the game, an ability to scrap for the ball when it proved necessary was another part of his teaching. That side could certainly scrap, with Steve Kember the fulcrum for the players around him like Vince Hilaire and Jerry Murphy who added the sophistication.

Venables was now in an even stronger position to campaign for change in the game. The advocacy he employed as a very powerful PFA committeeman he now turned into a lucrative daily newspaper column where he tub-thumped for improvement by reducing the size of the First Division and making up for the lost revenue by introducing sponsorship, now accepted as a fact of life but at that time quite a new development in the game. Another of his longstanding beliefs, three points for a win, was aired again and this, too, was to be taken up eventually by the Football League.

Meanwhile, there was now the challenge of his debut season in the First Division and Venables used the break to bring in a bit of experience in Gerry Francis in midfield and Mike Flanagan in attack. The season started well enough as the side negotiated the first couple of months with a bunch of draws, a few wins and the odd defeat, good enough to maintain a place up near the Liverpools and Manchester Uniteds of the division. He resented any talk, either on the terraces or on the training pitch, that this might be a season for consolidation. He would explode: 'Consolidation is an excuse. It means you expect to lose a few games and you don't really mind. I think it is rubbish to suggest you use your first season at the top to find your feet.'

There were times that season when it did look as if the Palace team were having trouble with their footing as their results fluctuated. Chairman Bloye, meanwhile, was talking of making Venables his managing director as soon as the regulations permitted and yet contract negotiations dragged on and on until, in December 1979 there was another sensational and very tempting offer on the table for the talented Palace manager.

This one came from the New York Cosmos, owned by the giant Warner Communications company. They had players on their staff whose names were symbolic of some of the finest football in the world: Franz Beckenbauer, Giorgio Chinaglia, Carlos Alberto and Johan Neeskens and the appeal was great. Venables had always insisted he would not manage players who were being paid more than he was, so the carrot was a four-year contract worth £1,000,000. This was around six times more than Palace were offering, but Venables had to weigh against that the talent of his young side and his income from his Hazell series and from the public houses in which he was now involved, his father running one in Essex, his mother one in Wales, while a third one was under construction to be called the Laurel and Hardy. He also felt at the time that another three years in English football might bring him right in line to take over the England job after the World Cup of 1982.

But there were question marks in his mind. He said: 'The challenge of working with players like that was very appealing. But what was their attitude to it all? They couldn't possibly have the same commitment they had in their great days and there wasn't the level of competition to keep them at a high pitch. So what would it do for me? Would I begin to lose my edge as thc novelty wore off? It was a good question to ask myself because I thrive on the involvement I had at Palace.

'Money was important but only to the point where it makes you independent. I was offered the Arsenal job before I went to Palace and turned it down. People, some of them my friends, said I was mad then, but I felt at a club like that there would be too many comparisons with the past. What we achieved at Palace was ours. When we won the Second Division, I watched middle-aged men waving scarves and singing. They had had years of being second best and taking stick from their pals and now they were on top. That is something a lot of people don't realise about football, just how much it means to so many.'

So Venables stayed, but the first lever to dislodge him from Selhurst had been applied and when results over the Christmas period wobbled there were the first signs of unease and Venables found himself having to dismiss rumours of a mutiny within the ranks. Venables had also to rap the fans across the knuckles for their restlessness and remind them that the side had come a long way in the space of three seasons. But it was a fairly undistinguished season as the side finished just below halfway. Venables may not have liked talk of consolidation but it appeared that was just what the season was for his young side.

Before the 1980-81 season even started, Venables found himself embroiled in a delicate situation over a young player who, like himself, had been brought up in Corn Beef City, the name some of Venables' relatives used to describe Dagenham. Queen's Park Rangers' young striker Clive Allen had been bought in the close season by Arsenal manager Terry Neill for £1 million. Yet before he could kick a ball in the Arsenal first team, he was involved in an exchange deal with Venables which took him to Selhurst Park and sent Kenny Sansom to Highbury.

There were those who cried foul, implying that Neill and Venables had got their heads together on an 'arrangement' because Rangers had been unwilling to sell Allen to Palace. It was hotly denied by both managers as the controversy exploded and Venables shrugged his broad shoulders and suggested that such swap deals might be a way forward with so little money to spare in the game.

The loss of Sansom, a firm Palace favourite, didn't help the mood at the start of the 1980-81 season and Venables' 'Team of the Eighties' lost nine of their first ten matches to be rooted firmly at the foot of the First Division. This was not part of the projected planning. The express had been derailed and suddenly there was no longer the happy, buoyant spirit that Venables had introduced into the dressing room.

Once again, Venables found himself at a personal crossroads for things were moving on another side of London. Jim Gregory, who had appointed Tommy Docherty and sacked him 28 days later in 1969, had re-appointed him in May 1979 as manager of Queen's Park Rangers. It was a stormy relationship, with the Doc being told to leave in the summer of 1980 only to be reinstated after the players had staged a protest meeting. But they, like Palace, had made a dreadful start to the season and Gregory swung the axe again, claiming the sacking this time was not over results but over remarks the Doc made about Chelsea and for which Gregory had felt the need to apologise to chairman Viscount Chelsea. In any event, those stormy days down at the 'Bush' were to open another door for Venables.

CHAPTER FIVE
No Bull at the Bush

THERE WERE BOUND TO BE some blaring horns and dented bodywork as Venables negotiated his way from SE25 to W12. Venables had resisted the first moves by his old club Queen's Park Rangers and said he would honour his Palace contract. But he had sat through a difficult board meeting at which there had been criticism of his purchases of Francis and Flanagan. There was also disappointment that he had put goalkeeper John Burridge, a popular figure at the club who Venables believed was trying to hold him to ransom over a new contract, on the transfer list.

'After disagreeing with the board I sensed I would have to leave before the end of the season. I only stayed on the extra time out of deference to the players and the fact that they were bottom of the First Division. When I had spoken to the chairman he said the board didn't want me to go but they weren't going to stand in my way either. That was not convincing enough for me, so I spoke to Jim Gregory who made it clear [Queen's Park Rangers] wanted me very much. I put it in Palace's court by saying that if they agreed compensation I would go and if not I would stay. I put it that way deliberately to give them an out.

'But the crunch came when I asked Ray Bloye outright if he had approached any other mangers. He hummed and hawed and then told me that two managers had been approached and I decided if that was the way they were going to do things that was it. I had been loyal to them even when I had four or five job offers. I turned them all down. They couldn't have it both ways. I was very bitterly disappointed because it almost looked as if I had leapt into the life raft when the ship was sinking. But that was not the case.'

With him to Rangers went his assistant Allan Harris, his chief scout Arnie Warren and his youth team manager George

Graham. Their task was to lift Rangers from the Second Division and bring some belief back into the place. Venables missed the First Division, but it intensified his determination to get back there with as much haste as could be achieved within the restrictions of finance. Gregory and he hit it off almost from the first day, for the chairman respected his manager's capacity for hard work, while Venables appreciated Gregory's philosophy of letting him get on with it. Venables was forced to admit: 'There is not so much of a buzz when you are not in the First Division. The phone doesn't ring quite so often, but then at least that gives you more time to think and to plan. You become determined to build up the gates by having good teams playing good football.'

However, Venables set about the rebuilding of Rangers in a way that was to cause resentment, suspicion and investigation, for, with the money Gregory supplied to provide new players, he went back to his old club Crystal Palace. No harm in that since it was a habit of managers to raid their old clubs for favourite players, then as now. Suspicions were aroused when he took Mike Flanagan and Terry Fenwick to Loftus Road for £250,000. Of that fee, £160,000 was for Flanagan who, just ten months earlier, had cost Venables £650,000 from Charlton. He said at the time: 'The days of the big spenders are over. This may look a bargain deal, but that is the trend now. The bottom has fallen out of the market. It is a buyer's market now. The players were surplus to requirements at Selhurst Park and Palace could do with the money. There is just none around in the game at the moment and that is what makes prices tumble.'

The question a lot of Palace fans wanted answered was whether or not Venables would have sold those players at that fee had he stayed at Selhurst Park. And what of the man who did the deal on Palace's behalf? He was the new manager and old friend of Venables, Malcolm Allison. They were to be followed to Loftus Road in the same month, December 1980, by a third Palace player, John Burridge. The moves took place just one month before there was a boardroom change at Palace, with former chairman Ray Bloye giving way to a consortium headed by Ron Noades, a former Wimbledon chairman.

Very shortly after that takeover, Noades was to criticise bitterly those transfers, describing the entire package as 'a half-price deal'. He claimed the three players were worth double the collective £325,000 Rangers had paid. 'They were a gift. John Burridge went for £75,000 when he was really worth £150,000. Mike Flanagan went for £150,000 when he was certainly worth £300,000 and Terry Fenwick cost them £100,000 when he was probably worth £150,000.'

What had not emerged at that time was the existence of a company called Chris McCann Management Ltd which had among its clients both Allison and Venables as well as a number of the Palace players, notably Vince Hilaire, Clive Allen and Peter Nicholas. Also signed up was Kenny Sansom, transferred to Arsenal shortly before Venables parted company with Palace. Investigations showed that the company had been formed in 1979 as Aidstar Ltd, a name changed to Chris McCann on 22 November 1979. The directors were listed as Christine McCann and Richard Andrew Coomber. Christine McCann was the maiden name of Venables' wife and the documents stated that the firm was a subsidiary of Terry Venables Ltd, founded back in 1962 to 'exploit the talents of Terence Venables'. The directors of that company were Terry and his wife Christine.

When news of the existence of the McCann company surfaced in 1981, Venables sold his share to his partner Coomber, a former publicity manager at Thames TV who had an office in a small studio off London's Oxford Street. When he was approached about Venables' interests in the agency he was quick to point out: 'I have bought out Terry's shares in the company. He is no longer involved, though he remains on my books as a client.' Coomber admitted, however, that he also represented Flanagan and Gerry Francis on a non-contract basis.

The agency had started, Coomber said, after he had met Terry while he was publishing manager at Penguin Books, where he had handled the paperback edition of the Hazell novels. 'I then joined Thames and Terry Venables had become a friend. I wanted to start an agency but couldn't realise the finance and Terry agreed to fund me for a period of two years. The idea was to find a whole new generation of young footballers and to promote them. Because Terry was manager of Crystal Palace, I went there and signed the good young players on his books.'

Coomber was quick to contact the Football League secretary Graham Kelly to explain the nature of the operation, stressing that Venables was no longer part of the company. In that letter, he was anxious to absolve Venables of any tarnish and suspicion. 'I find it sad that something that started out as an act of friendship by Terry has been made to look sinister. None of these people is able to point to one action by Terry or myself that is improper,' he wrote.

Allison had left Palace after the Noades takeover and a month later Gerry Francis also switched to Rangers for a fee of £150,000. Three further players, Hilaire, Allen and Nicholas, all contracted to Chris McCann Ltd, asked for transfers.

Venables was quite open about his involvement when he was confronted in the first week of March 1981. 'I sold my interest in Chris McCann last week to Richard Coomber,' he said. 'When I went to Palace I told the chairman that we should have a commercial set-up to look after the players' interests. He wasn't keen to do it, so I did it myself, with his permission freely given. Richard Coomber was a man I had met in television and he didn't have the cash to get started, so I funded him. There is nothing sinister about the use of my wife's maiden name for the agency. It was a family joke. If I had really wanted to be devious I would have put it in a nominee. Richard signed up the people in demand, Malcolm Allison, Clive Allen, Vince Hilaire, Peter Nicholas and Kenny Sansom. He went for the younger players.' Venables agreed that he had kept his own connection in the company very quiet but added: 'I didn't make a secret of it either.'

Venables also admitted that once he had left Palace the problems began to mount. 'It was then that Ray Bloye drew the attention of the Football League to the situation. But I insist

I did nothing dishonest. When Allison returned to Palace the three players up for sale were offered to me as a package deal. I had to take all three and I did get a bargain.'

Yet there were players within the old Palace staff who would claim that it was once Venables introduced a commercial aspect into the club that there was a division among the players that became disruptive. The players who were given commercial work claimed there was jealousy from other members of the first-team squad. That might have led to rebellion had those outside the chosen few realised the connections between the Chris McCann agency, the players who were signed up as clients and their own manager.

When David Swindlehurst, a member of the promotion-winning side was informed of the connection after he had left the club and joined Derby County he would say: 'I knew nothing of any players being signed by an agency connected to Venables. But it certainly explains a few things.' Swindlehurst was able to guess the men belonging to the McCann agency and he said: 'Players like myself, who had played in the Third Division and helped the club to the First, would ask for a rise and Venners would fight it all the way. But young lads who hadn't been at the club five minutes were getting a better deal - interest-free loans and all that. I would often see Richard Coomber at the training ground and he seemed to have ready access to Terry's office but I had no idea what was going on.' Perhaps it was just that the agency signed the best players, who were always likely to attract the best money.

Hilaire readily admitted his own involvement with the agency. 'Richard Coomber approached me at the ground and asked if I wanted to be looked after commercially. In the first season I made around £5,000 from TV and commercial appearances. I didn't know at the time that Venners was involved in the Chris McCann set-up, but then there is a bit of Venables in all of us.'

No action followed the suspicions regarding the Chris McCann agency, which was put down to being another Venables business venture and so he sailed serenely on in his determination to create a team in his own image at QPR. He was the perfect foil for the chairman. Jim Gregory was a self-made man who had begun his business career with a second-hand car pitch and built up a property empire. He treated his football club as if it were a private club, fiercely proud of the way he had developed the neat little stadium and it almost seemed incidental whether the public attended just so long as he could take a seat in the directors' box and watch the side win football matches.

Venables' East London wit and extrovert nature appealed to Gregory, for it was possibly how he would have liked to be himself, though the image he presented to the world was that of being a very shy and introverted figure who could wheel and deal but who liked to stay very much in the background. Together they set about building their little empire behind the Television Centre and just along the road from the old White City. Gregory was ready to fund the deals that, in addition to Venables' old Palace players, brought in reliable defender Glenn Roeder and the highly talented Simon Stainrod. Rangers finished eighth in the Second Division at the end of the 1980-81 season, but the Gregory-Venables duo were already hatching something that was much more revolutionary than winning football matches.

Though they had built a fine stadium at Loftus Road, they had an awful pitch, with the enclosed stands making ventilation difficult. The forward-looking Venables had seen sport played on artificial surfaces in the United States and suggested that Rangers should pioneer it in Britain. Thus the summer of 1981 had the two men dashing to Canada to examine a new surface called Omniturf and they brought back their samples determined they would give it a try.

It was a poignant move for Venables. Almost ten years had passed since he had written, with Gordon Williams, the now famous book *They Used To Play On Grass*. It was a book looking into the future where football had freedom of contract, artificial surfaces, sponsorship, a super league, all-seater stadiums. At the time all these aspects were fictional, but all became fact.

Venables did much to implement some of those improvements, though it must be said that soccer has not proved to be a suitable vehicle for the all-weather pitches and the fact that the game's governing body FIFA bans international soccer on them has ensured that they have had restricted use. Yet Venables argued at the time that a consistent surface was what the English game needed. His theme was that the extremes of the English climate meant teams could play on lush grass in autumn, bone-hard surfaces in February and clinging mud in March. Artificial pitches would make the Pools Panel obsolete. Furthermore, the stadium could then also be used for other sports, hockey in particular, and for pop concerts, evangelical meetings or whatever any bright-minded entrepreneur could devise for the open air. There were sceptics everywhere and tampering with traditions was regarded as a smart-arse act by a weight of people within the game. But the Rangers pair were determined to push ahead with their scheme having secured the reluctant permission of the Football League, if not the Football Association.

Another significant event now took place in Venables' life, for in November 1981 Gregory appointed his manager onto the board of directors with the second largest shareholding in the company. It effectively made him one of the most powerful managers in the Football League and, more significantly in his own eyes, it was a step forward towards his ultimate ambition of owning his own club. 'His appointment, along with his shareholding, is proof of just how highly I regard Terry,' Gregory said when he made the move. 'He is actually the first manager I have allowed to buy players who I might not agree on, but that is because when it comes to judging players, I trust him completely. I have learned that if you want Terry to run your club then you have to take him as he is. If you put restrictions on him or try to influence his judgement then you are asking for trouble.'

Director or manager, he failed to get Rangers out of the Second Division that season. But what he did do to reward his demanding chairman was to carry Rangers on a romantic journey to Wembley and the FA Cup final. They had needed replays against Middlesbrough and Blackpool in rounds three and four and so were perhaps fortunate to reach the fifth round and a straightforward home tie against Grimsby Town. The sixth round success against Crystal Palace, with Clive Allen (another Palace old boy) scoring the only goal at Loftus Road was particularly satisfying for Rangers. So Venables was in the semis again, this time with West Bromwich Albion, then a First Division side, as opponents.

The last time Venables had been on the brink of Wembley, as coach at Palace, the build-up had been blessed with humour, champagne and cigar smoke. This one was approached much more professionally, for now he was a manager and director and there was a distance to be kept between himself and the players. He was able to reflect on the difference when he said: 'At Palace I was probably too close to the players and that made life harder when I became the manager there. That degree of closeness can be an encumbrance for a manager. One of the things I learned as I went on as a manager was to give the players a little bit of room.' It must have worked, for they won 1-0, Clive Allen scoring.

When he led his side out at Wembley, against his old club Tottenham, it was the fulfilment of another dream. He had played there as a schoolboy and a senior for England; he had collected an FA Cup winner's medal as a Spurs player, but now here he was in a smart suit at the head of his own team. It was not a classic final, a goal from Glenn Hoddle being equalised by Terry Fenwick to force a replay that Spurs won with a Hoddle penalty, though Rangers were handicapped by being without the suspended Roeder and the injured Allen. It had, even so, been an historic first full season, since Rangers had never before reached the FA Cup semi-final, let alone a final tie.

The wheels were certainly now in motion and at the end of 1982-83 Rangers positively sailed into the First Division finishing champions with ten points to spare over Wolverhampton and 15 over Leicester, the other two promoted clubs. The artificial pitch really had become a wall-to-wall magic carpet for the club, though there were still mutterings that it had given Venables' side an unfair advantage in that they had the facility to train on it daily.

In fact, what the club were doing was to train on grass during the weeks they were away from home and then on the carpet when they were at home. Rangers always allowed the visiting side to train on it 24 hours before the game, but many managers felt there was a technique involved in playing on it successfully. Certainly, Sheffield Wednesday and Chelsea were the only sides to win on it in the promotion season. But what was clear was that players with a good touch and feel for the ball could flourish on it and Rangers that season went up on a tidal wave of one-touch football that was a pleasure to watch.

Venables had surrounded himself again with a team of familiar faces, with Frank McLintock running his reserves and George Graham, tempted out of retirement, in charge of the youth side. Graham had been out of the game and was thinking of becoming a publican when the call came from Venables. It was to be a momentous move for the man who went on to manage Millwall successfully and then collect two First Division Championships with Arsenal.

Then, quite suddenly, there was consternation. Gregory, a man who always worried about his health, decided he wanted to sell Rangers. And the man he wanted to sell it to was Venables. Here was an opportunity, at last, to fulfil a dream that has sat increasingly with Venables since he first went into management. Venables told him: 'If you are selling it may as well be to me, as to someone I don't get along with.' The die was cast.

However, it is one thing wanting to own the club and quite another putting the financial package together and that was what kept Venables fully occupied amid the celebrations of promotion in that summer of 1983. Gregory knew his man and sensed the challenge would be too much for him to resist. 'If you start work in a fish shop your ambition is always to own it,' he would say.

In Venables' case, it was more a matter of the man from the shop floor moving to shop steward, union boss and then owning the factory.

Venables, at the time, had developed his own philosophy on the finances within football. As negotiations continued he would say: 'Fortunately, I have always respected money, all the time I have been a manager. I've seen blokes in my game thinking about buying a player and saying "Sod it, it's not my cash. I'll take a chance." I can honestly say I have always thought: "Hold on, Terry. If it was your money, would you spend it on this lad?" I have made a few bob and I have put a lot of it into this effort. It's my business. It's what I have been involved in since I was a kid. I am not going in for social or political reasons or because it's a bit of a chuckle. I'm in it because I love it and I know what it is all about.'

In the same interview, Venables gave the broadest hint about the extent of his ambitions which were ultimately to lead him into the whirlpool of Tottenham and the murky waters that brought his downfall at the club. 'You have to stretch yourself,' he said. 'I have seen players who were so good they could have played in their best Sunday suit and still been better than anyone else on the park. The trouble is they prefer to play in their best suits and the game comes too easily for them. Well, I'm going to put myself out. I'm following a great act in Jim Gregory, who built the ground, bought the players and turned the club into something that can go into the First Division next season and not be afraid of letting itself down.'

The idea was for Venables to buy the club, lease the ground from his chairman for 20 years and take over the players' contracts and try to make it work. The price was a modest £1 million. Some of the business fatcats who sat at the head of boardrooms felt there was something not quite right about a manager taking over the store from the owners. They feared that perhaps this man might gatecrash their cosy meetings where they could make sure there was a them-and-us situation. Venables could see the snags and the problems, but to Gregory it was a much more simple matter. 'If he owns the gaff, no other club can come and nick him off us.'

Once again, Venables appeared to be ahead of the game and the idea was that the club bring in an executive to develop the leisure side of the business, making the optimum use of the artificial surface. But, as the summer dragged on, far from owning the club, Venables was again the target of other London chairmen. Gregory told Arsenal he would fight them to keep his manager and Tottenham's Irving Scholar was told he couldn't afford him.

Little did Gregory know then that eventually Scholar would get his man some four years later. As it was, Venables had other things to address, like his club's first season in the First Division, and he started the 1983-84 season as the managing director of Queen's Park Rangers. He looked as though he would be there for life. It was a good start in the top flight for the club, too, as his side, with Clive Allen and Simon Stainrod leading the attack, finished fifth and earned themselves a place in the UEFA Cup. But for Venables there was a much more permanent European move brewing as Argentinian master coach Cesar Menotti walked out on Barcelona and they began to look towards England for his successor.

CHAPTER SIX
The Reign in Spain

TO GRASP THE ENORMITY of managing Barcelona Football Club, it is necessary to know the soul of Catalonia, the strip of Spain that runs from the north-east border with France down towards Valencia, embracing the beaches of the Costa Brava and the cities of Gerona and Barcelona. The awesome Nou Camp Stadium is home to what is not so much a football club as a parliament to the five million Catalan people, even though only 120,000 of them can squeeze into its vast bowl. Barca symbolise the Catalans' independence from the national forces of Madrid and give the games between the clubs of the two major Spanish cities an edge no other club matches could possibly equal. Real Madrid and Barcelona, two names from the world of football whose meetings transcend sport and embody the history and the politics of a nation.

Therefore, to manage Barcelona is to have custody of a heritage and it is a post that has tested the nerve and the will of some of the game's most evocative names, Helenio Herrera of Italy, Rinus Michels of Holland, Hennes Weisweiler of West Germany, Cesar Menotti of Argentina.

Michels, who managed his country to two World Cup finals and to a successful European Championship in 1988 has said that results for Barcelona are far too important: 'It is not a sane mentality. The task is not to change Barcelona but to live with it, succeed with it. There are great wells of disparate energies there, obscene wealth, constant seething destructive undercurrents. Enter with a sound heart, an instinct to know which current to swim with and watertight legal advice and the opportunities for high profit and quick success are abundant.' It was a seat that, in the spring of 1984, Menotti, architect of Argentina's 1978 World Cup victory decided he could take no longer. The move to find a replacement began, while back in England, Venables already had his nose in a Spanish language book.

The Barcelona post had been offered to Bobby Robson in the early Eighties while he was still taking Ipswich Town into Europe season after season. They had played at the Nou Camp, and Jose Luis Nunez, the vastly wealthy president of Barcelona, had been impressed with the way Robson's side played. Bobby had wanted the job badly, because he knew the kudos that went with it. But he was conscious, too, of the possibility that he might soon be in line to manage the England side. He was being tugged in all directions.

Barcelona were prepared to pay him wages of around £100,000 a year, then a very large sum, yet they were reluctant to pay the Ipswich directors compensation for stealing their highly regarded manager. The Cobbold brothers, who ran the East Anglian club, were happy to release him to England, but if the foreigners wanted him then there would be stiff resistance. Robson was concerned, too, about being able to communicate, as he had no knowledge of the language. The offer faltered on the uncertainty, and when Robson discussed the situation with Venables, he stressed his concern about the language. Football coaching is so much a matter of communication that Robson felt it was vital. So, too, did Venables, and he set about learning Spanish, not because he saw himself as the future manager of Barcelona but because he felt that another language might eventually be of value to him.

It typified his opportunism, though his reasons for choosing Spanish, as opposed to Italian, French or Japanese, were that he had been told it was the easiest language to learn and because he used to go there for his holidays! The continuing successes of English clubs in Europe and our domination of the European Cup was alerting the big clubs to the advantages of employing an English coach. And so it was that in May 1984 the rumours of an impending move for Venables to the lucrative pastures of Costa Brava began to circulate. On 21 May he went across for an interview.

He was not the only coach in the frame. Nunez also had in

mind the Swiss-German Helmut Benthaus, who some of the club's directors felt might be a more suitable choice to handle the brittle temperament of their German superstar Berndt Schuster. He was felt to be the player around who the new coach would build his side, since the departure of Menotti was almost certainly to be followed by that of his protégé Diego Maradona. Benthaus had just won the Bundesliga with Stuttgart. Also linked with the post was Michel Hidalgo, whose French national side was about to win the European Championships.

But Nunez had a known affection for the English game and had been frustrated since failing to entice Robson to Spain. He had, indeed, asked Robson's advice as to who the most suitable candidate might be. He had told him it was Venables. Meanwhile, the same choice was being suggested to Menotti by his friend, journalist Jeff Powell of the *Daily Mail*. So, at the age of 41, Venables had told his friends that he was going over to Barcelona to take a look at the surroundings and that he was one of several people the club wished to interview for the post.

After 48 hours of painstaking negotiation, the job was offered to him with a salary in excess of £150,000 a year, twice what he might have expected to earn with any club in the English First Division. Venables had never been a man to underestimate his earning potential in any of his dealings either in sport or outside it, but he would claim that on this occasion the challenge of Barcelona superseded the huge financial rewards that would go with it.

'I am looking for the challenge, the excitement and the experience,' he said on accepting the job. 'I am going to be running a great club in a foreign country where the game is a religion. You know, too, you are working with players of a different nature and temperament to the English player, with potential superstars. If I want to ultimately manage England, which I do, and hope to then win a World Cup, which I would, then I need to discover all I can about international football. I became fascinated by the Spaniards' passion for the game while I was in Spain for the 1982 World Cup, working for the

England manager Ron Greenwood, and since that time I had a gentleman's agreement with Jim Gregory at QPR that I could make my own decision about any offer from Spain as well as any chance to manage England.'

The story goes that, at the interview, Nunez offered Venables a cigar, but when he opened the lid the box was empty. Venables produced one of his own from his sock, telling the most powerful man in Barcelona: 'It's the only place to keep them and make sure they don't bend!'

Venables' very first task in charge of his new club was to sort out the position of Maradona, the remarkable but temperamental Argentinian superstar who had really created his own problem within the club.

Maradona was not in good physical shape and had deep financial problems. Venables, although he had not yet taken over at the Nou Camp, discussed Maradona's predicament with three of the Barcelona directors on a six-hour chauffeur-driven journey to San Sebastian. Juan Gaspar, one of the millionaire members of the board, translated since Venables' emerging Spanish was still short of conversing on players' contracts. Maradona, they decided, was psychologically not ready to continue playing for the club and with a £6 million bid for him on the table from Italian club Naples, the decision was made to sell.

Maradona, meanwhile, was agitating for the move, while stressing his motives had nothing to do with the imminent arrival of an English coach. Venables admitted that he would have preferred Maradona to stay because he relished the prospect of handling the man considered as the world's most talented player. But it was Maradona who said: 'Physically and psychologically I am destroyed. I have been unhappy in Barcelona for some time and my reasons for wanting to leave have nothing to do with the arrival of Mr Venables.' Venables said: 'His problems really started before I went there. He was a nice lad but I could see there might be some difficulties. I felt certain people might latch onto the England-Argentina connection so soon after the Falklands conflict, especially if there had been any problems between us. I just told the directors that I would welcome a quick decision so that if I had to make a fresh start I could do.'

So it was that Maradona departed, with he and Venables barely having the opportunity to get to know each other. But the new man had other things on his mind. There were battles to be won with the supporters of the club, because while Venables may have enjoyed a high profile in English football, few had heard of him in Spain. They had trouble knowing what to call him and, while the press at home had slipped easily into El Tel, the locals, wrestling with their 'V's' settled for Senor Ben-ah-Bless. The distinguished aforementioned Herrera did not help matters by announcing in print that there was no such thing as a good English coach and that the new man would be lucky if he lasted a week.

Venables decided that the first people to be won over were the Barcelona media. The city has three daily all-sports tabloid newspapers and they devoted to Barcelona and Venables the kind of space the English papers reserve for Princess Diana. Every sigh and syllable is recorded, every move analysed and examined. This was real goldfishbowl territory. 'There was the problem of acceptance,' Venables would record. 'But I worked hard at it. I gave them time which they appreciated. You do get a great deal of exaggeration in the Spanish papers, more so than in England, because they have more space to fill, especially among the sports-only papers. Five pages per day were devoted to the football club. At first I took terrible criticism from them, but by the time we were pre-season training for my first full season I had won them over. I came here knowing what the pressures would be and I wasn't disappointed at any time during my stay there.'

That first pre-season at the club's training camp in the Pyrenees haven of Andorra was an exciting one for the new coach who now seemed to be at the summit of his profession. It was as difficult for the players as it was for the new coach and his trusted assistant, Allan Harris, who had quickly followed Venables to Spain. The players had been used to conversing with Menotti in his native tongue. Venables employed a former language master and Oxbridge graduate, Graham Turner, then living in nearby Taragona, to be his mouthpiece, a partnership that stayed intact throughout his period in Spain.

Though Venables' mastery of the language was to improve almost daily, he liked to have Turner alongside, especially at official press conferences because, for one thing, it gave him thinking time. 'It is difficult to discuss things when you are not well-versed in the language,' he would say. 'But the main thing was I was able to get my message across. Personal relationships are a valuable extra, but there is no reason you can't make the team efficient just because you don't speak to them too much.'

The only player Venables could relate to, however, was Steve Archibald. He had bought the Scot as a replacement for Maradona, even though the club had been anxious for him to buy Mexican international striker Hugo Sanchez from Real Madrid. Venables explained: 'I knew Steve, and I felt comfortable with him. As it happened, Sanchez would also have been a good buy, but I felt it was important that I won that little argument, to establish that I wanted to choose my players because they were quite capable of bullying you into situations. I tried to sign Steve from Aberdeen when I was manager of Crystal Palace, but he chose Tottenham instead. But I remained a great admirer because when one of my teams played against him he was always a threat. He was the right age (29) and had the right temperament for Barcelona. Other players might have taken a year to get themselves integrated and you just don't have that amount of time to wait at this club.'

Venables had inherited a first-team squad of 27 players - far too many in his view to make things manageable and he immediately reduced that to 23. The problem with clubs in the Spanish League is that when any member of the first-team squad is not selected, he just doesn't get a match. The reserve side operates quite separately in the Second Division and has its own stadium and following. It meant that some players might wait for months to play a competitive game and the problems of match fitness are inevitable in that situation.

It was, indeed, a different concept to the one Venables had left at QPR. There, he was responsible for all aspects of the running of the club, with administrative matters occupying a great deal of his time. Here, his sole responsibility was to run the club's teams. Since there were 16 of them, beginning at the age of ten, it was not quite as straightforward as it seemed.

He slipped comfortably into the Spanish lifestyle, living initially at the Princess Sofia Hotel, one of the smartest in the city and owned by one of the club's 18 directors. It was just a five-minute walk from the stadium and, as he settled into his new job, Venables would hold court in the lounge bar of the hotel, often with an attendant posse of visiting English sports writers.

The size of the club suited the extent of Venables' ambition and, even in the earliest moments of his time there, he saw it as a possible stepping-stone towards managing the England team. He would tell his early visitors from Fleet Street: 'This is a great experience, a new experience and I am going to enjoy it. Bob Paisley said it took him 20 years to get his European experience with Liverpool. I am taking a short-cut. If ever the England job comes my way, I would be better prepared for it for the time I am spending at Barcelona. If the England job doesn't happen, well, I've learned a new language and had a new experience and I won't have lost by it.'

And it was with that attitude that he set about his work that first season of 1984-85, studying videotapes and written dossiers of his own and other Spanish players, earnestly working at polishing up his Spanish and accepting what he was taking on when 50,000 fans turned up for the traditional presentation of the players in the stadium for a photo-call. He addressed them that day in their native Catalan language, a sure-fire way of winning over their hearts.

But if they fell for Venables' personality, then the football his team produced that season would put him on the level of deity. All the signs had looked good in pre-season fixtures, not least one match the club played against Boca Juniors from Argentina. Menotti had been in the stand and made some unfortunate assertions about returning to the club. But he squirmed in his seat as Barcelona won 9-1. He was forced to say afterwards: 'This job is the most difficult in club management anywhere in the world. But, given time, I am sure Terry Venables will succeed because he has a football brain. But the fans and the politics of managing Barcelona make 12 months here as punishing as five years anywhere else.'

Though these warnings had no real meaning to Venables at the time, it was dawning on him the daunting task he had set himself. 'The trouble was that the scale of the club meant my biggest problem was that everything was out of proportion. There are so many opinions, and you have to live with everybody pushing and pulling in different directions. The only way to succeed, I believe, is to be single-minded. Let others get on with the debate and concentrate on doing what you know you are good at. Everything seemed to be accelerated. There were few shades of grey. If you won, the acclaim was at crescendo level and if you lost then the sack seemed round the corner.'

Into that climate Venables began his new job with the most awesome match possible, an away fixture against Real Madrid in the Bernabeu Stadium, itself almost as forbidding as the Nou Camp. 'It was like having your main course as a starter,' Venables recalled. 'If there was ever a case of being thrown in at the deep end then you have it. They get upset enough if you lose a pre-season friendly, let alone the showpiece game of the season.'

Venables had befriended a Spanish entrepreneur, whose pet name was Manolo and who owned a restaurant in Las Ramblas, the centre of Barcelona nightlife. They would, through the course of his stay in Spain, be the firmest of friends and became business associates in various land and property ventures. He introduced Venables to the Capri Beach resort where he would be able to relax, away from the attentions of the fans in the city, for his profile was to take-off after that first match in Madrid when Venables brought home a 3-0 victory for the Catalans and cemented his relationship with the club's millions of followers. It was, indeed, a heady start to his first season there, and it continued as the club went beyond their previous best start to a season of 12 matches without a defeat. From being simply a popular figure, Venables was now being hailed as a messiah.

He now needed privacy, as his presence in the Princess Sofia created traffic jams outside the hotel. He found it in his apartment, with its view over the stadium and out towards the Mediterranean. It was a haven from those who hung on his every word and, as December came, the animated talk of the side winning their first championship for ten years was becoming deafening, as all the repressed emotion of having lived in the shadow of Castillian Madrid came pouring out from the Catalans.

It was a fascinating scenario and a vivid indication of just what football success meant to these fiercely partisan people. Scenes of anticipation like these had not been witnessed in Barcelona for a decade when Johan Cruyff, the player, and Rinus Michels, the manager, won the title. But the Barcelona side now challenging for the ultimate prize had Venables' individualistic stamp on it. Under Menotti, they had been a side structured to accommodate the fickle Maradona's outrageous talent. But Venables had turned them very much into an 11-man unit with a collective unselfishness that was contrary to the flamboyant Spanish character. Venables went on record as saying: 'If you let this lot play instinctively they would need 11 footballs between them.'

What was equally important for Venables was the part Archibald was playing in this running success story. He had taken comfortably to life in Spain and to the blatant differences in how the game was played away from the demanding strictures of the English First Division. His selfless running and passing were essential to the success of the side, as was the level of fitness that Venables and Harris had been determined to build into their side.

There was, indeed, an English 'look' to the side, for Venables had dispensed with the sweeper system so favoured on the Continent. 'We attacked with three and aimed to get five or six going forward,' said Venables. If some of the outstanding defensive players, notably Alesanko and Alberto, were Menotti men, then they were being deployed differently by Venables. It was a pressing game, with similarities to the 'total' football Holland had devised. Best of all, it was directing Barcelona towards their ultimate ambition of wresting the title from Madrid.

As the momentum gathered that season, so did the acceptance that every side Venables had coached or managed seemed to be acquainted with success. Through his successful times at Palace and Rangers, there was always the lurking suspicion that achievement was related to some kind of East End instinct for survival, rather than to an ability to outsmart the opposition through straightforward tactical talent and awareness. Perhaps this was due to his fetish for punctuating his deliverances to the press with his sharp one-line wit. Those comic utterances, of course, had less significance to the Spanish press, besides which he was offended by any suggestion that he survived only through being one sharp thought ahead of his critics. As the New Year of 1985 was ushered in, it became increasingly apparent that Venables was leading his new club towards their goal. No other club could get near them.

The signing of Archibald had proved a master-stroke. The Spanish press had christened him 'Archi-goles' and he was co-ordinating their attacking football brilliantly, while the exceptional Berndt Schuster was organising things behind him. 'The great thing about Steve, as far as the rest of the side were concerned, was that if you gave him the ball you could expect to get it back. He won the respect of the other players here and they knew that his footballing priorities were the right ones. He was not concerned with trying to look that good himself by going past opponents. If he can pass, get into the box and then take the return pass when he is in a scoring position, that suits him fine. In addition to being able to compete with the hard men when the pressure is on, he has the capacity to stay cool and make a rational decision when he is in front of goal. If, for example, he can't get a proper striking header on the ball he'll knock it across goal and give somebody else a chance of putting it in,' Venables said.

He was equally lyrical about the capabilities of Schuster, who was the other significant player in that 1984-85 side as an instigator. 'At the time he was as good as any midfield player I had worked with or even seen. He was criticised before I arrived in Barcelona as being a player who stood around admiring what he had created, but I didn't find him that way. He operated on the basis there were two ways to get possession - from your own team-mates or to win it from the opposition. He works hard to win it off the other side. He is not only gifted, he is prepared to work hard at his game and you don't get too many like that. He attracts the ball and when he gets it he can deliver the killing pass.' What Schuster had helped Venables to do was make the changes he saw as essential to build a Barcelona side in his own image.

The team now challenging for the title played to Venables' own strategy, but it had not been easy for him to change their basic attitudes towards how they played the game. He would explain: 'They had the tendency to want to show off their individualism in an area of the pitch where it was going to do us the most harm. They were technically superior players to the ones we had been used to working with and there was the need to achieve the right balance. I had to drum it into them that there are times and places on the football field when passing is more productive than trying to beat people. I told them to keep their ball skills up their sleeves so they could suddenly hit the opposition with the unexpected in areas where it would do the most damage. I worked hard for them to press the ball, hustling the man in possession with three or four players at one time and trying to rob him in parts of the field where we could counter-attack quickly, efficiently and effectively instead of falling back and only winning it when their whole team is in front of you. If you can win it halfway through their team, you may only have five guys to get past to reach their goal. It sounds very simple, but when you get players to do that, life becomes an awful lot easier.'

Life, indeed, seemed easy for Barcelona as they captured the title on 24 March 1985 with a 2-1 win at Valladolid, with four matches in hand. The euphoria that night was beyond description, the celebrations lasting for days on end. Venables had achieved in one season what was to be a standard that would be difficult to live up to. Barcelona finished the season ten points clear of their nearest rivals and 19 points ahead of Real Madrid.

The reputation of the Dagenham boy knew no limits. 'A miracle has happened,' said the club's vice-president, Nicolau Casaus. 'This Englishman has brought us tranquillity. He has introduced brains into an institution that has always been ruled by the heart. We have been plagued by tension and nerves, but Terry is such a calm man and he has brought that quality into our football club. Not just into the players, but into the fans as well. You have your Iron Maiden in Margaret Thatcher and we have your Mister Wonderful and we want to keep him.'

It was heady stuff from an emotional people. Casaus knew all about heroism, for he had fought against the forces of Franco in the Spanish Civil War and had been sentenced to death by the dictator's regime. It was a sentence later commuted to life imprisonment and, after serving six years, he had become a trade unionist and then a leading industrialist. He knew better than anyone what the football club meant to the people of Catalonia. 'Our area was the centre of resistance to Franco and, for 40 years, all form of political expression was forbidden here. Our only means of self-expression was through football. Terry was intelligent enough to quickly grasp what the club meant to all Catalans. We have never been popular in other cities in Spain, but Terry has even helped to improve that image by holding a press conference in every place he visits. He seems to have people eating from his hand in all parts of the country.'

All of this was music to Venables. Whatever else he might have lacked, he loved the sense of occasion and he was now able to bask in the glory of what he had achieved, to sit back and read reports from around the world about the clubs who would like to entice him away from his new Spanish home. They were wasting their time. He had a wonderful lifestyle and the chance now to make a bid for the European Cup, one prize that had eluded Barcelona throughout their history and which their arch-rivals Real Madrid had at one time monopolised.

Yet his fame was not without its price. Rumours of a rift in his marriage with Christine continued to circulate, and he knew that some Sunday papers were camped outside his house in Loughton where Chris had stayed with their two daughters, Nancy and Tracy. But it was not until the following spring, and with a heavy heart, that he announced the breakdown of his marriage. It was concluded without acrimony, and Nancy even joined Venables in Barcelona. Amusingly, the paparazzi had taken photographs of him on his apartment balcony and sold them as being the boss with a mystery blonde, when it was, in fact, Nancy.

There were other things Venables missed about home, his Sunday lunches with his father, the pubs he owned and which his parents were running, and the lads in the West End, his old mates from years gone by who loved a natter. But he knew that the rewards were high and the challenge still inviting for a man reaching for the ultimate goals.

By now his Spanish was more than adequate, though Turner was still employed to do the interpreting. 'I didn't always like to risk speaking it,' Venables would tell his mates, and then recall the press conference when he interrupted Turner's answer and told him: 'Don't give them your version of what I said - just tell them exactly what I said.' But Venables actually found some benefits in the language problem. 'One advantage of not knowing the language is that you don't have to socialise with the team if you don't feel like it. When the mood takes you, you can cut out all the irritating small talk and get straight down to business. On the pitch I use body language. The eyes and hands can say it all. And you can let a team-mate know exactly where you are planning to go by setting your body to go there.'

One place Venables could use his own language was in front of the BBC television cameras and they snapped him up in the wake of Barcelona's championship success to be their summariser for England's 1985 tournament in Mexico City and for the World Cup in Mexico the following summer, a role he has continued for the BBC ever since.

Another contract he signed that summer was to improve his salary, even though winning the title had brought him over £200,000 with the built-in bonuses. Yet he knew that in 1985-86 he had an awful lot to live up to and it wasn't going to be easy. Nor was it, for Real Madrid were staging a spirited attempt to regain their title as the country's leading club. All this was almost bearable for the Barcelona fans, just as long as Venables delivered them the European Cup.

It was not a route without its moments of anxiety and good fortune. In the very first round, after winning 2-1 away to Sparta Prague, they seemed to be set for comfortable progress into the second round. But an indifferent home second leg, in which they lost 1-0, sent them through only on the away goals rule. Again, in the second round they appeared to be in trouble, for though they defeated FC Porto 2-0 at home, the Portuguese side fought back splendidly at home and it needed a Steve Archibald goal in a 3-1 defeat for them to progress, again on the away goals rule. It was not an easy passage they were negotiating and when the quarter-final draw pitched them against Juventus it appeared to be anybody's tie.

Barcelona won the home leg by a Julio Alberto goal and few supporters, even in Spain, believed that would be enough against the reigning champions. But Barcelona showed immense discipline in Turin and, again, it was Archibald with a goal in the 1-1 draw who saw them into the last four. It had been a troubled route to the semis, and when they went to IFK Gothenburg in the first leg of the semi-final and lost 3-0, you would hardly have invested 100 pesetas on them pulling the tie back at the Nou Camp. It was a torrid night in the huge stadium, but amazingly

Pichi Alonso scored a hat-trick to take the game to penalties, with Venables' side triumphing 5-4.

It was the fulfilment of a dream for the club's fans, for they had never been near reaching a European Cup final and it didn't seem to matter to them that they had finished second, 11 points behind Real in the championship, so long as they won the European Cup. The opposition were Steaua Bucharest, considered rank outsiders, and with the game being played in Seville, everything seemed set for Venables to add the European crown to his championship and thus establish himself as a real Catalan legend. There was drama even before the game was played. Archibald, so crucial in their advance on the final, had not played since the quarter-final against Juventus because of recurring hamstring problems. He had read of the results Bryan Robson had achieved through visiting Richard Smith, a Dutch physiotherapist, and requested, as a last resort, that he should visit him.

The Barcelona doctor, Carlos Bestit, refused permission but Venables overruled him. 'Terry told me I had nothing to lose,' Archibald said. 'I rang Bryan Robson who fixed it all up for me. It was as if a miracle had been performed on my leg. I was like a dead body when I arrived in Amsterdam with about five injuries on my right leg. But I was feeling an improvement within hours. I came away from there realising how ignorant I was about my body. As a result of that visit I changed my eating and sleeping habits and I feel physically fit and mentally content. He has enabled me to overhaul my entire outlook.'

Three hundred coaches, six trains and over a dozen charter planes carried the Barcelona fans down to Seville for what was being labelled as 'The Historic Dream'. It was a poignant final, too, for it came 12 months after the horror of Heysel and Venables knew the significance of that. He said before the game: 'It is not enough just to be here. We have to win and win attractively. We want to put on a bit of style.'

Unfortunately, style meant much less than victory to the Romanians and, with an extremely well-disciplined defence, they strangled the life out of a disappointing match. It was 120 minutes of sterile football and the misery was accentuated by four missed penalties in the shoot-out. The press turned on Venables and the 4-4-2 system he had employed against Bucharest. 'Deception', screamed one of the more hurtful headlines Venables woke up to in the 12th-century walled city of Carmona where the Barcelona side had made their Cup headquarters.

'I'm afraid my players thought it was going to be easy, though I had warned them it would not be,' said the crestfallen Venables. Yet he was dignified in defeat and it may well have been that match that persuaded him to prolong his stay in Spain. There had been suggestions throughout the spring of 1986 that he might be ready for a return home. Both Peter Hill-Wood, the Old Etonian Arsenal chairman, and Tottenham's dynamic Irving Scholar had been carefully monitoring Venables' position and Scholar, with a home in Monaco and a fervent interest in European football, had been an occasional visitor to Barcelona and had had lengthy dialogues with Venables. The man who was the centre of attraction had even hinted that he might take a year out of football to take stock of his future.

Nunez had been so anxious about losing his coach that he had contacted Bobby Robson again to ask for another recommendation and had been given the name of Howard Kendall. But the continuing run in the European Cup changed that and after the defeat Venables said: 'If I had won the trophy, what would I have had left to prove at the club? Now I have to get up off the floor and prove myself.' Venables and Harris had sensed the bitter disappointment of the club's directors for they had been virtually ignored at the lavish after-match banquet in Seville, attended by King Juan Carlos. 'We understand their feelings,' said Venables. 'When you win they shower you with gifts and when you lose they ignore you. The fans are the same. When we paraded the championship, there were over a million people on the streets of the city, but when we go home from Seville there won't be a soul at the airport to greet us.'

But Venables refused to be submerged by the defeat and was already working towards the future. He knew that, with Archibald approaching 30, there had to be a replacement. He had made up his mind that the player he most wanted was Gary Lineker, then 25 and unquestionably the rising star of the English game.

'There is no secret about why I went for Gary,' he explained. 'It is simply that he was a goalscorer and I needed to replace Archibald, who had been one of the best strikers I have ever worked with. He was a good signing for me because he helped me to win the League in my first season. I knew about Lineker, because we had met a few times and I was impressed with his intelligence, which for a player moving abroad can be quite important. You knew that he would be able to settle down in Barcelona and you knew that he would pick up things easily as Archibald had done. He would be interested. He had his own devices anyway and I'm not saying I added much to that. But if you wanted him to do something he would respond and his running and positioning became better. There were things he couldn't do and his heading ability was only adequate. What I liked about him is that he had everything worked out. He prefers it when he knows what he is supposed to be doing as a player.'

The deal was agreed before Lineker took part in the 1986 World Cup in Mexico, and it must have given Venables particular delight to see him emerge in that competition as the leading scorer, even though England were knocked out at the quarter-final stage by Maradona's two goals. With the fee of £2.2 million already agreed, Venables must have felt happy and secure with his new signing. He had also taken Mark Hughes to the club from Manchester United, and the difference in the fortunes of the two players was marked.

Lineker settled almost immediately and took to the lifestyle. He and his wife Michelle rented a luxurious, four-bedroomed house in a secluded small estate with close security for residents and they were quickly swept up in the laid-back lifestyle, dining at the finest fish restaurants. They both attacked the Spanish lessons vigorously and mastered the language in an amazingly short time. Hughes, on the other hand, found the language difficult. He was a single man in what can be a lonely city and, despite the efforts ofVenables and the Linekers to make him feel at home, he never came to terms with life in the sunshine.

Lineker's contentment, on the other hand, was reflected in his football. Though it was a different game, and he was now encountering the defensive sweeper in just about every game he played, he made the necessary adjustments to his technique and, as he maintained a goal ratio of one every two games, he became the darling of the Barcelona social set, cementing firm family friendships with Jose Carreras and Montserrat Caballe.Venables was delighted to have Lineker follow the example of Archibald, as he worked to put the European Cup disappointment behind him. Lineker scored three goals against the champions from Real Madrid and it is interesting to record that in 13 meetings with the club's arch-rivals, Venables was a loser only once. Lineker would score 21 goals in 41 games in his opening season, a fine haul in Spanish football, though not enough to prevent Real Madrid taking the title, with Barcelona once again runners-up.

Venables' delight at the way Lineker had responded was offset by his frustration over Hughes, for whom he had paid £1.7 million. Perhaps the problems of loneliness that beset him off the pitch were responsible for his poor performances on it. His frustrations with the language didn't help, but nor did the fact that he was not finding goals easy or the service to suit his strengths. There were problems, too, with the Spanish referees. Hughes' game has always been a physical one and by diminishing that, the Spanish match officials were helping minimise his effectiveness.

'One of the main problems was that the things he got away with in English football are frowned on in Spain,' Venables says. 'All of a sudden, that physical part of his game was taken away and it was frustrating for him. He would be constantly pulled up by referees. It wasn't basically his fault. He had just gone from one kind of game to another. Gary was perhaps fortunate that his game had never depended on physical confrontation. The insecurity in football tends to result in your entire world revolving around how you are performing on the pitch. If things are going badly, then everything else is affected and you find you can't even cough properly. Mark was really down at the start and, even though Gary and Michelle had him round to their home, he obviously felt that he was getting in the way. He and Gary were different types socially, but they were good for each other. On reflection, Mark, at 22, was perhaps a bit too young to try his luck abroad. Perhaps if he had waited another two years it might have been different. But once the fans turn against you at a club like Barcelona, it is very difficult to get them back again. I think he honestly would have preferred being with his mates at home sinking a few pints.'

Eventually his girlfriend came out to join him, but by then it was too late. The press were relentless and Venables knew he had to take some form of action. What he did was to frustrate Hughes even further. In Spain, the manager names a pool of players for a block of matches and anyone omitted is isolated without competitive matches to play in. After he was sent off in a UEFA Cup tie which the club lost, this was the action Venables reluctantly took with his Welsh international, restoring Archibald to his squad. That was certainly the beginning of the end of Hughes, for at the start of the 1987-88 season an alteration to the rules made by the Spanish Football Federation meant that Venables needed to make a choice between Hughes and Berndt Schuster. The German won and Hughes was soon to be on his way to Munich and thence on to his return to Old Trafford and to glory with Manchester United in the inaugural Premier League season.

A success ratio of two out of three British signings was acceptable to Venables, who insisted that he had bought British not to anglicise Barcelona's football, but simply to ensure that he had players he knew might score him goals. His objective, he insisted, was to blend the English and Spanish styles of play.

He wanted the flair of the native players aligned to the mental toughness of the British player. Lineker, in turn, had formed a partnership with Venables that was to serve them both well back at Tottenham in years to come. It was the way Lineker came to terms with playing against the sweeper system and his ability to adapt that made him such a favourite with Venables.

It is possible they learned from each other, for Venables was quick to recognise Gary's own grasp of the basics of goalscoring. 'You would rarely see him hit a shot over the bar. He will usually hit it low and make the goalkeeper work. You get so many strikers who want to give it a blast, but he concentrates on hitting the target. He knew that by keeping it low there was always some possibility for him. In the big moments, when it was important, he always kept his head. He might have gone ten matches without scoring but it wouldn't bother him. He wouldn't panic because he knew that eventually it would turn round. He got the most out of himself as a footballer with his runs and the way he deceived defenders. He would find positions on the field that would take the pressure from his suspect control.'

Their relationship was a fruitful one and they both enjoyed that first full season together, even though it did not bring them the second championship Venables had set his heart on. And, for that reason, the pressures on him began to build. Any lingering doubts about his future in Spain were dispelled when the 1987-88 season began with three defeats - two of them at home.

In a series of meetings at the club and in the Princess Sofia, terms were worked out for Venables' departure in what was later described by his interpreter Turner as 'half a sacking and half a resignation'. Terry's reign in Spain was over, but it had been a profitable one in so many ways, financially certainly, but also in terms of experience. It had been an exhilarating and exciting chapter in his life and one that had brought him one of the game's most coveted championships and a penalty shoot-out away from a European Cup. It was certainly an experience he emerged from with his dignity very much intact and his reputation enhanced.

CHAPTER SEVEN
Venables Wins his Spurs

IRVING SCHOLAR SACKED David Pleat with a particularly heavy heart. As a manager and coach, he had nothing but respect and admiration for Pleat, and it was a great disappointment that it should be influences from outside the game that were to bring about the situation where the Tottenham chairman had little alternative but to show him the door. The fact that Pleat's personal problems came to breaking point at the time Venables was being replaced by Barcelona was merely coincidental and Scholar, on reflection, would hardly describe it as a happy coincidence.

However, a new manager had to be found and Venables was just about as attractive a prospect as a club the size of Tottenham could contemplate. Scholar had carefully watched Venables' climb towards managerial respect and their paths had almost come together in 1984 after the resignation of Keith Burkinshaw as the Tottenham manager. It was at the time Venables was managing director of Queen's Park Rangers and there was a strong possibility of him buying the club from the owner Jim Gregory, a purchase that never materialised.

'I received numerous telephone calls from friends and associates of Terry Venables suggesting he would be very interested in the position if it were offered to him. But we never seriously considered him,' Scholar says. 'He had always given the impression of being easygoing and jocular and we were concerned about the discipline - a point Terry and I actually talked about when I got to know him much better while he was with Barcelona.'

The two men had to come together in Venables' first season in Spain when Venables turned to Tottenham for his one significant purchase of that season: Steve Archibald. Scholar began to warm to Venables in those talks and in subsequent social meetings in Spain, impressed by his natural charm and by his apparent ease at dealing with the media. That change of heart about Venables, and the knowledge that he had broadened his coaching experience in his three years at Barcelona, now persuaded Scholar that Venables might be the right man to take over the club.

A meeting with the agent Dennis Roach, who was involved in the negotiations for Tottenham to host the Frank Bruno v Joe Bugner fight, led to the two men discussing Venables' whereabouts in the wake of his departure from Barcelona. Roach contacted Scholar with a number for Venables in Florida and in the middle of the night, English time, Scholar made his first contact. Scholar recalls: 'I came straight to the point. If he was interested in the Tottenham job then I was prepared to fly out and meet him within 24 hours. I told him there was no point me flying thousands of miles if he was going to leave me in limbo and his answer was: "Irving, go and buy a ticket to Miami". I felt that here was a real chance to solve our search for a new manager.'

In a real cloak-and-dagger operation, which entailed Scholar travelling under the name of Arnold and being ushered to the aircraft door at Heathrow down a labyrinth of corridors, he was bound for Florida without having been noticed by the press agencies whose job it is to monitor the comings and goings of well-known people through the airport. Waiting at the gate at the other end was Venables, tanned, smiling and obviously happy to see Scholar.

Venables was staying at the West Palm Beach resort hotel, a sprawling complex with holiday homes dotted around the grounds and with its own golf courses, home to the American Professional Golfers' Association. Even in the vehicle the hotel had laid on to pick up Scholar, the chairman could see Venables was bulging with enthusiasm.

Scholar recalls: 'He pulled out a piece of paper and a pen and marked 11 blank positions representing the team. It was a thing Venables and I were to do many times over the years to come. He wanted to know how many of the current players did I believe were capable of being filled in on that piece of paper - players who might win the club the Championship. This, he said, was the ultimate test. He said: "If you are going to start, you must start looking at the very highest point in your quest for achievement." I told him I felt it would be better for him to discuss this with the coaching staff at the club, but he insisted I should do it.'

When Scholar undertook the exercise, there were only four names on his sheet and Venables said: 'What you have done there leaves seven blanks and that represents a big job ahead for whoever is appointed your manager.' One dinner and lunch later, the two men began to talk terms. Venables wanted only a two-year contract, but Scholar pushed him to make it three. Venables also insisted that he needed a six-week period to sort out his various business affairs before taking up his new position sometime in mid-November.

Venables' original plan had been to take a year out away from the pressures of the game and take stock of the state of football in various European countries before resuming the hunt for a new job at the start of the 1988-89 season. Scholar wanted to announce his new capture immediately and explained: 'Because we were on the other side of the Atlantic, where football means little and the big names are relatively unknown, I turned journalist and photographer myself. We had just introduced the Spursline at the club where the fans could ring in and hear the day-to-day news from within the club. The trouble was, I didn't have a tape recorder so we went to the local supermarket and bought one. We then sat in Terry's car in the car park and did a ten-minute interview, with a disbelieving Terry wisecracking his way through it. I had taken my own camera with me to America and Terry's then friend and now his second wife Yvette took pictures of us sealing his agreement to join Tottenham.'

That picture was to adorn the front of the Spurs programme the following Saturday and was then sold to a national paper for several thousand pounds, with the money going to a children's charity. And, back at home, his mother turned up one of Terry's old schoolbooks in which he had predicted: 'I want to play for and then to manage Tottenham.'

For the latter privilege, Scholar paid Venables around £150,000 a year, a signing-on fee of £50,000, with bonuses and other benefits; it was a package over three years that was worth around £600,000 and made him one of the highest paid football managers in Britain. From the Florida sunshine, Venables watched the results of the club he was about to manage and what he saw was not very encouraging. The day after his signing, the club went out of the Littlewoods Cup and the following Saturday went down 3-0 at home to Wimbledon. Scholar and Venables talked by phone, but it made depressing listening and the talk turned to who might be his assistant.

Scholar suggested Peter Shreeves, who had his heart in Tottenham and had been responsible for the grooming in the reserves of players like Glenn Hoddle. But Venables decided that Allan Harris, his old friend and assistant at his previous dubs, would work alongside him and he nominated Monday, 23 November 1987 as his date for starting the job.

His first match in charge was against Liverpool on 28 November. It came at the end of a spell in which the team had lost five and drawn two of its previous seven matches and, despite a crowd of nearly 47,500 and the highest of expectations, it was another disastrous afternoon: Steve Hodge was sent off and the side went down 2-0. Tottenham then had two weeks without a game, this being the season when the First Division was reduced to 21 clubs, giving each one two free Saturdays. Venables had time to take stock of his staff and get over his initial message as to how he wanted the game played.

It was not to bring him a change of fortune in the next game, again at home, with Spurs losing 1-0 to Lennie Lawrence's Charlton. It was now clear to Venables that what he had taken on was a serious reconstruction job. In his first season at Barcelona he had needed only to replace Maradona by Archibald. Here was a different set of circumstances.

But, as that process of rebuilding got under way, so there was to be the first disagreement on policy between Venables and his new chairman. Scholar the businessman favoured buying young players, because he felt they were an appreciating asset rather than players in their later twenties who, at the end of their contract, might have little re-sale value. However, Venables wanted players of maturity and experience to bring a stability to what was a side lacking in belief. He wanted Terry Fenwick, one of his former Crystal Palace and Queen's Park Rangers players who may have been 29, but was also one of England's defenders in the 1986 World Cup in Mexico. Scholar was not happy with the salary Venables wanted to pay the veteran defender, believing Fenwick's demands to be high in relation to the existing wage structure at the club - he was paid more than Chris Waddle.

The new manager got his way, despite the chairman's own reservations. The relationship, however, remained good. Scholar was press conscious and warmed to the way Venables could handle the media with his mixture of sharp humour and the facility to find a phrase the headlinewriters would like. If Venables had learned one thing from Docherty, it was the value of the right kind of publicity. Scholar suggests: 'We had a good, frank and open relationship, though I was surprised how often he would seek my opinion on players and team matters. I would tell him the job was his, not mine, but he wanted me to feel a part of it. There were times when I was brutally frank and he might have been put out.'

It soon became obvious, however, that any joy Spurs might have that season could be achieved only through a good FA Cup run, an area where Venables had met with success at Palace and QPR. But they were out to Third Division Port Vale in the fourth round, a serious blow to the side and one, Scholar felt, that had lasting consequences. Venables, as he has done throughout his career, was supplementing his considerable salary with a juicy contract column from *The Sun* newspaper and, in the wake of the Port Vale defeat, he began his column with the words 'Terry Venables is a man in a hurry.' In the interview that followed, he set out his ambitions.

The language was straight, but was always going to be difficult to live up to. 'I've come to Spurs to win the First Division,' he said. 'I need it. I desperately want to do it and I know it has to be next season. I'm supposed to have said it would take three years. That's nonsense. A consolidating sixth is no good to me, I must be right at the top with Tottenham.' He looked ahead to that following season with the assurance: 'It will be my team, my system, my fault . . . I have money to spend and I believe I have enough to build a Championship side. When I leave I would like the next man to come in and find the club in a very healthy state. The Championship would be won, the club strong, the kids coming through and everyone at Tottenham happy. I have six months to start the race.'

The spending started as the results failed to improve, without any of the incoming players really lighting up the First Division. Among his many qualities, Venables will not go down in history as the shrewdest of operators in the transfer market, because for every Archibald there was a Paul Walsh and for every Gary Lineker a Paul Stewart. But Venables was really in a hurry. Walsh and Bobby Mimms were both signed in February 1988. Mimms was another player who was a disappointment with fewer than 50 appearances in almost four seasons at the club.

In the summer, Venables really went to town with the Tottenham chequebook and it was then that Paul Gascoigne came to the club. He also wanted a striker, looking first towards Mark Hateley. When that fell through, Scholar suggested Venables might be interested in re-signing Mark Hughes, who he had taken to Spain from Manchester United. Venables refused, despite his chairman's efforts to make him reconsider. But the need for a new striker was reaching crisis point, for Clive Allen had been sold to Bordeaux. That had been a swift and easy negotiation, with Scholar and Venables meeting the officials of the French club at the Hilton Hotel and agreeing a move for £900,000 in the summer when Allen was out of contract.

Because of this sale they hurried through the deal on Paul

Stewart of Manchester City, though in their desire to sign him they probably paid over the odds at £1.5 million. Venables was now being tagged as an extravagant spender, a label that he resented. He insisted: 'I don't believe I have been irresponsible with the club's money.' Certainly, at that stage, there were no complaints from the Tottenham board, for the desire to improve the club's performances was unanimous. Yet there were other aspects of Venables' personality that had begun already to trouble Scholar, whose interest in the club and its affairs was total.

'He seemed to have a grasshopper mind,' says Scholar. 'He would never spend too much time dealing with any single item. When I persuaded him to join Tottenham, I was clear he was one of the best coaches in Europe. He'd always struck me as a person most at home on the training pitch, working with players. He had a fine reputation even before he went to Spain as being one of the game's leading coaches. I had worked with David Pleat and Peter Shreeves, whose every minute seemed to be devoted to thinking and planning around football. But Terry wasn't like that.' Scholar had been slightly concerned in the very week Venables joined the club about another paid article in which he suggested he wanted to buy his own football club at some stage in the future, 'a fact that had worried me'.

'He had barely got his foot through the door and here he was discussing his intentions for sometime way in the future. The worry that Terry's mind would always wander was a persistent problem.' The need to reach out beyond the instant situation was one that had surfaced in Venables in his early teens. Here he was now, in his forties, with that probing, endlessly restless mind alert to any opportunity.

He had not been at White Hart Lane long when there were suggestions he might be sought as the part-time manager of Wales, and Scholar felt the need to quash that one by telling him that getting Spurs back to their former glories was a full-time job in itself. A letter did arrive on Venables' desk from the Welsh FA asking if they could approach him. He wanted to pursue the matter and he told his chairman he felt he could do both jobs.

There was some appeal in the post to him, since his mother was Welsh. But Scholar was insistent that his total focus must be on Spurs and, having been given that ultimatum, his international managerial ambitions were temporarily shelved. But his interest in international management was never far from the surface, though when Scholar would raise the subject, he would dismiss it as being not a very realistic one.

Certainly, during that initial season at White Hart Lane, it appeared his mind was not totally on the job of running the football club and by the early chill months of 1988, Tottenham's season was effectively over, dismissed from both cups and with a depressing league record. It was Scholar's view, as the man closest to him in the working sense, that part of his fabric was still coming to terms with having ended the Spanish sojourn he had so much enjoyed. Given the clamour for Venables to become England manager in the aftermath of the failure to qualify for the World Cup in the United States, it seems unreal to remember that as his first season at Spurs drew towards its disappointing finale there were actually football fans in North London believing that he was not the coach he had been built up to be. His popularity with the media had always, in a sense, been a pressure, for in placing him on a coaching pedestal that was so much loftier than any other coach in the country, he had an awful lot to live up to. Instead of talking to individual pressmen, he now instituted a daily press conference at the club's Mill Hill training ground so there was a guaranteed audience for his deliberations. These could be quite amusing get-togethers, with Venables always at his happiest with an appreciative audience.

But the sweet talk failed to work with two players whom Venables had been anxious to sign. He missed Andy Townsend when the Irish midfield star decided to sign for Norwich City, while Venables waited to see him the next day. And he also failed to entice Paul McGrath to the club, which was an even crueller blow for he had believed the craggy Manchester United centre-half was the ideal man around whom to build his defence. But McGrath's wife was not keen to move south and he was asking the club for a house, which was against the Tottenham policy. Instead, McGrath went to Aston Villa, because he would not have to move house. Venables then switched attention to another of his old Palace and QPR players, Steve Wicks, now 31 but still capable, he convinced Scholar, of being a great team asset. Yet, within a couple of days, Wicks was himself withdrawing from the deal because of his recurring injuries.

It was ironic that these moves to find a centre-half should be taking place while Venables was preparing to unload Neil Ruddock. Shreeves had taken the big centre-half to White Hart Lane for £50,000 in 1986. But, since his arrival at the club, Ruddock had caused one or two flashpoints with the new manager, who felt he lacked discipline. Venables felt he was a disruptive influence and that it would be better if he moved on. So he was sold back to Millwall for a fee of £300,000. Almost exactly four years later, it was to cost Venables more than twice that to bring him back to White Hart Lane for a second spell. And it was significant that, despite those early disagreements, Ruddock was to become Venables' closest ally in his fight for the football club with Alan Sugar, prompting his move in the summer of 1993 to Liverpool.

Scholar was beginning to learn more about the man who had been such a respected and confident figure in Spain and to realise that there was another, more human, element to Venables. That first season, six months after buying Bobby Mimms, Venables had decided that he was not the dominating goalkeeper he had wanted and he invited Scholar to look at a tape of a Norwegian keeper, Erik Thorstvedt. The two men agreed to meet at Scholar's house in central London to see the video of the Norway v France international.

Scholar takes up the story: 'I was late due to the traffic and arrived to find Terry had already been waiting half an hour for me. This was most unusual since he was very often late for meetings. We talked for an hour and a half during which time Erik's name never came up in the conversation. But Terry was clearly edgy. Eventually, I asked him what was troubling him and he said he had received information from a reliable source that I had been in discussion with Steve Coppell of Crystal Palace and that he would be appointed as Venables' replacement within a few days. I told him no such talks had taken place and that he should know better than listen to tittle-tattle. I had been more than a little surprised to find Terry so nervous, because he always presents to the outside world the veneer of a man with super confidence.'

For all his movement of players, nothing went right for Venables at the beginning of his first full season in charge of Spurs. It had been as dismal a start as the previous one. The side won only one of the first ten matches and even touched the foot of the First Division table. Five wins in November and December had dispelled some of the gloom, but the club was still basically drifting in a limbo. The boast of the previous year that the side would be catching up on Liverpool now looked rather hollow and some fans were beginning to ask whether Venables' reputation as a coach was really a myth.

It was a period of reconstruction for the club, both on the field and off it, with major changes taking place. For while the side struggled on the pitch, there was movement off it, with the club having to change bankers following the £2 million purchase of Gascoigne in the summer of 1988. Barclays had been unhappy with that investment and said they would only support the club if there were personal guarantees from the directors. The board was split on this issue, and it forced the club to move to the Midland, a change that would ultimately lead to dramatic consequences. In this climate, Venables was still seeking money to strengthen his squad.

At the February board meeting in 1989, Venables asked to know how much money was still available to buy players and whether he needed to sell before he could buy. Paul Bobroff, the chairman of the parent company, advised Venables that he should sell to buy, requesting he raise £2 million and spend half of it before the end of the financial year in May. Venables gave his directors a list of 12 players he was prepared to sell, and it is perhaps interesting that on it was Gary Mabbutt, the man who was to become such a guiding force and inspirational skipper. What was more, Mabbutt was almost at the head of his list of players who should be sold first.

Scholar found this staggering. He recalls: 'Ever since Terry arrived at White Hart Lane, it had amazed me that he had developed a complex about Mabbutt and would always pick holes in his game. If ever a result went against us, he would always single out Mabbutt for special private criticism. He would claim he stood too far off the people he was supposed to be marking and point out that he always seemed to be off balance. He was always trying to tell me Mabbutt should be released. At one stage he encouraged a great deal of interest from Steve Coppell at Crystal Palace. They had just been promoted to the First Division and were looking for an experienced central defender to act as linchpin for their defence. Coppell was talking about paying £850,000 and Terry thought this would be a good price. He was convinced Gary's diabetes would get the better of him and told me that his upper body had been getting heavier and was slowing him down a bit. But I persuaded him it would not be a good idea to lose Gary Mabbutt, and he stayed. But the fact the manager wanted to sell the skipper of the club created a strain which we never quite overcame.'

But it was while the board were discussing how much money could be spent that Venables and Scholar had under their hat a deal that would bring to Spurs a player to captivate the imagination, not just of their own fans, but those around the country. The 1988-89 season had been eminently undistinguished with the side finishing in what was really a disappointing sixth place, especially as Arsenal had won the title in a thrilling final match at Anfield with George Graham, who had learned so much from working under Venables, the man to bring the trophy back to London. They, of course, were the ultimate rivals and their success served only to accentuate the problems Tottenham were having in re-establishing former glories. The two men would meet regularly for meals, still firm friends from their days together as players at Chelsea.

In the summer of 1989, however, Venables had excitement on his mind. Since he left Barcelona, he had been carefully chronicling the fortunes of Gary Lineker. The two men had stayed in touch and Venables would visit the Linekers on his own return visits to Spain to check on the land investments he had made there while he was the Nou Camp manager. There had been growing disillusionment between Lineker and Venables' successor Johan Cruyff, with the England striker often finding himself playing out of position on the right wing.

Lineker's agent Jon Holmes takes up the story: 'It was obvious something was going to happen at the end of the 1988-89 season, because Cruyff had tried to sell Gary. There had been all kinds of rumour and, in the end, we got the club to admit Gary could go. We said that was fine so long as Gary could choose where he moved. They said they understood and lined up all kinds of clubs, all sorts of deals. But all the time I kept knocking them down to keep the fee low. The higher the fee, the less there is in it for the player. Eventually, we reached a situation where Barcelona thought there were no clubs bidding at all.'

Holmes talked to Genoa, Fiorentina and Monaco. There was interest from PSV Eindhoven in Holland and Bayern Munich in Germany. At home, the parade was led by his old club Everton, but Lineker did not favour a return to Goodison. Lineker had enjoyed living abroad and learning a new language and culture and he was in no hurry to come home. It would have needed only one of the big Italian clubs from Milan or Turin to make a bid and he would have gone there. So, in the end, Holmes rang Venables and said Gary might be interested in a return home and a meeting was arranged. Venables asked how much Lineker would demand and he promised to put it before his chairman. That call was made to Scholar one Saturday morning that summer and he was told the asking price would be 1.2 million. While Scholar paused, Venables quipped: 'By the way, that's dollars not pounds.'

While Scholar dealt with Lineker's own demands, Venables flew to his old stomping ground to settle the deal with his old director, Juan Gaspar. When he came home, not only had he secured the services of Lineker, he had also negotiated a package to include a young player he knew and admired, Mohammed Ali Amar, known to all at White Hart Lane as Nayim. The deal was approved by the board, with £600,000 cash down and the rest to be paid on 1 August 1990.

Venables at last felt he was building a side to really make the challenge that had failed to materialise in either of the previous two seasons. Not only had he acquired Lineker, but there was also Chris Waddle, who he had felt fortunate to inherit from Peter Shreeves, and Gascoigne - quite a mouth-watering prospect for the new season. Everybody was looking forward to what the season would bring, not least the players themselves. But a phone call from Paris was to put paid to all the blossoming optimism.

Scholar takes up the story: 'We were holding a press conference on the Friday to announce the signing of Lineker. This was due to start at 10.30 and, as I was about to leave my office to face the newspapermen, there was a call came through from a Mr Barin. He was an agent I had dealt with over the sale of Clive Allen to France and now he came quickly to the point. "Chris Waddle?" he asked. "Not for sale," I replied. But he then said he had a client who was very interested.' But, as Scholar persisted in negatives, so Barin started quoting figures, starting at £2.5 million and working upwards each time he said no. Even at £3 million the answer was no.

Scholar discovered during the conversation that Barin was representing Marseille. On his way to the conference, Scholar stopped at Venables' office and told him of Barin's offer and that he had turned it down. Venables proved more flexible, suggesting that for a player who was in his late twenties it might be worth considering. Scholar has his own theory why: 'I knew Terry was not happy that, less than a year earlier, we had committed Waddle to a seven-year contract. I did it because I wanted to secure him. I did like to get players on long contracts, but there was a psychological aspect to it. I knew the bond between Chris and Paul Gascoigne and felt the longer we had Waddle at the club, the easier it was going to be to retain Gascoigne. Waddle really was something of a father-figure to him.'

Venables came up with the idea of doing a deal along the lines of the one Liverpool agreed with Juventus for Ian Rush, where Spurs would receive the money there and then, with the player moving one year hence. And so it was, the two men went into the conference to introduce Lineker and talked happily about the trio of talented internationals they had now brought together. As soon as the conference ended, Scholar was back on the phone with Terry's suggestion. A meeting was arranged at the Carlton Tower between Venables, Scholar, Barin and Bernard Tapie, the high-profile president of Marseille.

Scholar recalls: 'Terry and I met for lunch to discuss our strategy for the meeting. I did not want to sell Waddle and I asked Terry what his valuation was. He said the maximum figure Waddle was worth was £2 million, in his opinion, and we ended lunch agreeing we would put a £5 million price-tag on him. This was way above what he was worth, but by pricing him so high I was hoping to scare the French away. Terry was also thinking about selling Paul Walsh and tried to manoeuvre the meeting in such a way that not only would we be talking about Waddle, but Walsh as well.

'Tapie was candid about why he wanted Waddle. He was buying several players, including French international Manuel Amaros from Monaco and explained how he believed Waddle would fit into this new team of his. It then got to the point where we had to quote a price. I then said to Terry that we ought to go outside for a minute. I burst out laughing and told Terry I was too embarrassed to say £5 million. But I composed myself and went straight to Tapie and said: "The figure is £5 million". Tapie replied: "I'll pay you £5 million for the two players," meaning Waddle and Walsh. I could hardly believe my ears, for I was certain the answer would be no. Tapie had called my bluff. It was my turn to backtrack and I said to him: "Hold on, we can't just agree like this." I was now moving onto the back foot and wanted to delay. Even Terry was shaken. Tapie simply said he had concluded a TV deal the day before worth £5 million and now he wanted to give us the money.'

The clubs parted that day without a deal being struck, but it was obvious they meant business. The sale of Walsh had been removed from the equation and still the French club were prepared to pay Tottenham £4.25 million. Scholar and Venables retired to Scholar's home in Regent's Park and discussed their next move. One of the options was to try to buy John Barnes from Liverpool. Venables was certainly keen to sell, for Tapie was offering twice what he considered Waddle was worth, bearing in mind his age. For certain, they had to put the deal before Waddle himself.

Accordingly, Scholar met Waddle's agent Mel Stein the next day, informed him of the bid, while stressing his own wish that Waddle might not be interested. When Waddle returned from his holidays a few days later, his reaction was not what Scholar had anticipated. He asked for a day to think about it and then announced: 'It's a once-in-a-lifetime chance and I want to take it.' There was nothing Scholar could do about it and within two weeks, Waddle was on his way and Spurs were £4.25 million better off.

Venables believed the lion's share of that fee would come back to him for further investment on new players. He had said: 'I wanted to invest in defenders who I felt could keep us in the top six of the table and maybe might even allow us to challenge for the title. But the money didn't materialise and I felt hard done by. Whether they knew at the time they couldn't spare the money or whether it was bad luck with the bank, I don't know. But they actually slaughtered me because I didn't have Chris Waddle and I didn't have the money. As the saying goes: "I want the player or the money. I don't want the bit in the middle." But that's what we ended up with - the bit in the middle. Irving wanted some of the money for the bank and some money for players, but it didn't happen that way.'

All Venables got was the £1.4 million to buy Steve Sedgley from Coventry City and Pat Van Den Hauwe from Everton. Bobroff had even tried to halt the signing of full-back Van Den Hauwe on the grounds the club could not afford the fee. This, Scholar felt, was the chairman of the public company reneging on his promise that Venables would have the Waddle money to spend, and created a rift between the two men who had bought the club that was not to be healed. Indeed, it was in the autumn of 1989 that Bobroff called a meeting with Scholar and sought his resignation. This, in turn, led to a power-struggle between the two businessmen which Scholar was to win.

Meanwhile, it did not help Venables' frustrations in trying to build a side to challenge not just neighbours Arsenal but the power bloc in the North-West of England. Scholar was keen to help Venables in every way he could, though the purchase of defenders never held the same excitement and buzz for him as the purchase of players in the Tottenham tradition, with flair and imagination. The club finished a very creditable third place in the 1989-90 season, with Gary Lineker turning out to be just the bargain that Venables and Scholar had anticipated he would be. Spurs had finished ahead of Arsenal, always an important consideration, and Gary had scored an excellent 24 goals in 38 league matches. It had seemed that, with the chequebook out of reach, Venables had got down to working with what he had and had made it appear quite successful. Scholar was to say: 'The chequebook was often Terry's worst enemy. He had been presented with it when he took over at the club, yet his best period had come when circumstances had forced us to lock it away.'

That summer, of course, Lineker and Gascoigne contributed to the encouraging performance of England in the World Cup and Gascoigne returned a national hero, a factor that was to prove of some importance in the future of both Tottenham and Venables. The global spotlight brought some problems, for the offers to buy them were coming in from all over the place, and

Torino were certainly interested in signing Lineker. Spurs, of course, were not keen to release him and had the security of a further three years on his contract. But Scholar and Venables did meet the Torino go-between, who was a friend of Venables, and he suggested that if they would pay £5 million for Lineker that would enable him to go to Derby and get Mark Wright and Dean Saunders. Torino, however, were not prepared to bid more than £3.5 million. Lineker's agent Jon Holmes did go to Italy to speak to the club, but Scholar put his foot down, insisting that Gary had had his big-money move and would not be going.

The third-place finish encouraged Venables to believe that the new season might be even more successful if he could supply the one ingredient he felt was missing from his side - a dominant centre-half. He still believed Scholar would find a way of enabling him to invest. He wanted Terry Butcher, but was told he was too expensive. It was perhaps typical that, as the news of Tottenham's financial crisis began to seep increasingly into the public domain, so Venables intensified his focus on the team and their form picked up encouragingly.

Venables had become accustomed to the machinations of football directors during his stay at Barcelona, and he had worked with one of the most astute in Jim Gregory, but he had sensed, too, that the advent of the paid director and the involvement of the City in the game would hasten the day when the old-style English soccer manager would be superseded by the straightforward football coach, as on the Continent. He knew the value in keeping the world of the boardroom and the dressing room distinctly separate and, in view of the events at White Hart Lane, this became not merely advisable but essential if the team were to perform.

In their book *Heroes and Villains*, Alex Fynn and Lynton Guest give some insight into Venables' thinking around that turbulent and uncertain time. He told them: 'I am not worrying about who is supposed to own the club. I'll wait and see what happens.' What was happening was that Scholar was trying to put together a financial package with Robert Maxwell that would have injected £13 million into the club and averted the impending problems. 'I have to be aware of the possibility for new players. At the moment, I couldn't lay out a fiver on a World Cup star.' But he could also see the inherent problems a Maxwell-Scholar team could bring: 'The role of the manager in English football is being diminished by amateur directors who want to play at professional football and if we had Maxwell as well as Scholar we would all move one step down towards the bootroom, myself included.'

But while Scholar was trying to shore up the club, Venables was at last giving the fans a little of what they most wanted - success on the field. The side began the 1990-91 season with ten games without defeat and Venables seemed to have struck a team balance that meant they had conceded four while scoring 17 goals in that soaring start. Venables had given David Howells a role just in front of his back four and this in turn was allowing Gascoigne the freedom to make important forward runs. That season he would match Lineker for goals, 19 apiece. The club was full of optimism on the pitch and on the terraces. They were oblivious to the fact that, behind the scenes, Scholar was in a panic about the £900,000 outstanding to Barcelona on the Lineker deal and which had been due for payment on 1 August.

What was happening off the pitch was putting an ever greater strain on the relationship between Venables and Scholar. Venables had always believed the most important relationship in a football club is that between chairman and manager. It was a comment he made to Scholar just before he signed for Tottenham. But what he had not really understood, when he agreed to join Spurs, was the extent of Scholar's own commitment to the club.

Scholar had been living in tax exile in Monaco when his takeover bid for the club had been successful and, for a year, he was running Tottenham from there. His control was total and he exercised it with an energy that could be overwhelming. No decisions at the club were taken without his authority and, although such dedication was well-meant, it would often leave those in his employ frustrated that they were not allowed to make decisions for themselves. His first manager, Keith Burkinshaw, resigned when he felt his control over team affairs was being eroded and that they were just becoming an arm of a much bigger public company that had been floated on the Stock Exchange. Burkinshaw's replacement was Peter Shreeves, a much easier-going personality who Scholar was able to manipulate in terms of the players coming in and out of the football club. For Scholar, a keen student of the Continental game, this was a natural progression. For years in England, there had been strict lines of demarcation about where directors stood in relation to managers and there was an unwritten understanding that the board did not interfere with the running of the side, while exercising their right, at a whim, to remove the man who was if results were not forthcoming.

Scholar was perhaps the first football chairman in England who conducted the business side of the club, while encouraging the manager to be more of a coach. Other innovations of Scholar's takeover, which are now taken for granted, were to infuriate some of the club's supporters for most were directed at increasing the club's revenue. It is ironical that when one examines where it all went wrong at the club, the enormous costs of rebuilding the East Stand may take second place to the losses incurred by the subsidiary companies of Tottenham Hotspur plc.

The initial idea, when Spurs went public, was to invest in areas outside soccer and use the profits to re-invest in the playing side. Scholar allayed any fears about the possible failure of these subsidiaries with the assurance that it would never affect team matters. Most of the subsidiary companies did not initially perform particularly well, but this had been buried in the accounts so that when the parent company showed a profit in 1987-88, it was mainly due to profit on football operations and the sale of the club's Cheshunt training facility, which brought in £4.5 million. Two other companies, Synchro Systems, a computer-ticket operation, and the Hummel sportswear franchise deteriorated dramatically during 1989. It was a mistaken decision to inject £3 million of football club money to support it. This contradicted Scholar's belief that it was the subsidiary that should support the club.

Paul Bobroff took the opposite view and, as Tottenham was now a public company with a responsibility to shareholders, his was probably the strictly correct stand. This difference led to Bobroff's failed attempt to oust Scholar. When Bobroff discovered that the third major shareholder, Tony Berry, backed Scholar, he resigned himself and offered his ten percent stake in the company up for sale. Scholar and Berry realised they could not buy this stake without having to make a similar bid to all shareholders, in accordance with Stock Exchange regulations. But then the club's merchant bankers insisted on Bobroff's reinstatement. By the summer of 1990, it was clear that two other of the Spurs subsidiaries, clothing companies Martex and Stumps, were also in serious financial difficulty.

With the problems mounting, another cash injection was urgently needed to write off the debts of the subsidiaries and to service the Midland Bank debt, which had touched £10 million and was still rising. On the day of the World Cup final in Rome, Scholar spotted Robert Maxwell being driven through the streets of the Eternal City and felt it might have been an omen. For some time now, he had in mind that the Mirror Group Newspapers owner might yet be the man to rescue his ailing club from bankruptcy. He phoned Maxwell, with whom he had sat on a Football League television committee in 1984, and the two men met on a Sunday morning, 25 July, in Maxwell's office.

Scholar outlined his plan to create a new share issue for the parent company while accepting that in the current financial climate the chances of City investment were small. He felt the help of a major investor would do the trick and wondered if Maxwell would underwrite a rights issue at £1.30 a share. The shares would be offered to existing shareholders on a one-for-one basis. Scholar and some of his colleagues would not take up all their offer and Maxwell would be left with a guaranteed 26 percent of the company, possibly a good deal more if the new shares were not bought. This would have the effect of injecting £13.2 million into the company, thus clearing the £12 million that Scholar now assessed to be the debt. In return for an assurance that he would not sell his shares and would remain to run the club, Scholar had Maxwell's provisional agreement, providing the whole deal was kept strictly secret.

There was also the other matter of the outstanding debt to Barcelona, which Scholar knew would not be forthcoming from the bank. Scholar turned to Maxwell again. He asked the newspaper magnate to loan Scholar's own company, The Holborn Property Company, a sum of £1.1 million which Holborn would then re-loan to Tottenham to pay the debt on the Lineker deal. That way, Maxwell's involvement in paying off the outstanding amount would remain secret, for Maxwell, in turn, supplied the money from a private company, Headington Investments. Scholar offered a block of shops he owned in the Kings Road as security for the loan.

Scholar now had to place his share package before the club's directors without being able to identify the man who would underwrite it. Scholar and the club's financial director, Derek Peter, were given the go-ahead at a board meeting from which the chairman, Bobroff, was missing, having taken a holiday. Although he was unaware at the time, Scholar was now in uncharted waters and was not receiving the soundest counsel about the rules governing the conduct of public companies. The Stock Exchange would look with distaste on a company that negotiates a rights issue and loan without its chairman being present or its shareholders informed.

When Bobroff discovered the plan, he felt it smacked of desperation and he immediately attempted to slow down the deal. Most of the club's shareholders were the fans who stood on the terraces and who would not normally be consulted on the running of the football club. But a public ownership should have obliged the board to inform and consult. This was to have serious repercussions on Scholar and Tottenham within weeks. Maxwell reached agreement with Scholar on the rights issue, but was for the moment unable to proceed because of the rules of the Football League.

These stated quite clearly that no individual could have a financial interest in more than one football club and had been introduced when Maxwell had tried to purchase Elton John's shares in Watford while he was still involved with Oxford United and Derby County. To proceed with the Spurs agreement, he would have to sell in his interest in Derby County and, when the directors there refused to buy his shares, he put the club on the market, blaming the sale on what he described as 'a lamentable lack of support'. And he added: 'They [the supporters] must realise that I do not have a licence to print £50 notes.' His asking price for the Baseball Ground was £8 million, but he was not bowled over in the rush to buy. This was not a climate where buying a football club was seen as a common-sense investment.

It was while Maxwell was waiting for a buyer that the *Sunday Times* newspaper revealed his identity as the man who would underwrite the share issue. This story, by the paper's city editor Jeff Randall, was to send shock waves through the game at large, and through Tottenham in particular. The League were adamant that any such deal could only proceed if Maxwell sold his shares in Derby County and Reading and that his son Kevin would need to relinquish his chairmanship of Oxford United. The PFA made comments about people who chose to use football clubs like Monopoly pieces.

Scholar believed that the story might even have been leaked by Maxwell himself, for he certainly did not deny having a conversation with the *Sunday Times* man and advising him: 'You have a notable scoop'. Maxwell had now advised Scholar the deal was off because he felt he had not been given the fullest detail of just what trouble the club was now in. But Scholar refused to accept he had lost his, and the club's, potential saviour. Yet it was the secrecy surrounding the deal with Maxwell that was to cause as much of a furore as the arrangement itself. Had Scholar kept his shareholders fully informed of the dire straits into which the company was sinking, he might well have evoked more sympathy and certainly prevented official action from the Stock Exchange, who launched an enquiry into the £1.1 million loan from Maxwell which paid off the Lineker transfer. In legal terms, that deal should have been presented to a meeting of shareholders for their approval.

Venables was managing to shield his side from the worst of the behind-the-scenes manoeuvres as they embarked on a very successful early season run of results, little knowing how perilously close they were to seeing the club crumble beneath them. A board meeting on 14 September, squeezed between victories over Derby County and Leeds, had Scholar seeking Bobroffs resignation since their destructive squabbles were threatening the saving Maxwell package. A vote of no confidence in the company chairman was passed by four votes to one, after Bobroff refused to resign, though he could not be kicked off the board without a full shareholders' vote. He refused to resign his directorship, insisting he would stay to protect the interests of the smaller shareholders. Scholar threatened to call an EGM to have him removed while, in the meantime, the club's financial adviser and broker both resigned in protest at Bobroffs sacking.

But, at this stage, Maxwell went on David Frost's breakfast TV programme to say that once the bickering was over he would re-start negotiations. 'I am flashing a yellow card at those involved in the squabbles,' Maxwell had proclaimed, as he used his Mirror sports pages to try to get across his message. 'It is inconceivable that I or anybody else would entertain a rights issue, or become in any way involved in a club, while some of the board are behaving like children.' Privately, he had told one of his Mirror sports staff: 'I want Bobroff to accept me or I want him out of the way.'

On 19 October, the Stock Exchange suspended shares in Tottenham Hotspur plc and would later censure Scholar for the way he had conducted his negotiations with Maxwell. When the board finally tried to explain their intentions in a letter to shareholders, several of Scholar's actions were described as 'ill conceived and inappropriate'. Within two weeks of the share suspension, Scholar had bowed to advice that he should resign from the plc while maintaining his position as chairman of the football club.

Venables may have been shielding his players from the turmoil, but he himself was keeping a sharp eye on the various developments and sensing that this might be his own opportunity to throw his hat in the ring as the man who could lead a move to rescue Tottenham. He had made no secret from back in his QPR days that one of his ultimate ambitions was to own a football club. Here, it seemed, opportunity was beckoning.

Perhaps, given these off-the-field problems, it was not surprising that, after the good start, results began to deteriorate in November. Venables pointed to a squad depleted because of the shortage of money, which meant he could not rest key men and had to select others with niggling injuries. But results were not the only thing occupying Venables' mind at this time. He had been linked to a vacancy at Real Madrid following the departure of John Toshack, even though it always seemed unlikely the Spaniards would allow one British manager to follow another, even if he had once won a championship with Barcelona. Venables was not unhappy that the story was being floated, because his own contract was due for renewal at the end of the season. When talks with Scholar over a new contract began, Venables was asked to sign a new form of deal that was bonus-related but which meant a reduction on his previous basic wage by £25,000 a year. This infuriated Venables, who found the offer insulting. But another bombshell was to fall from the pen of the extremely well-informed Mr Randall in the next issue of the *Sunday Times* that December.

CHAPTER EIGHT
The Bid for Power

IT WAS SUNDAY, 23 December 1990 that Jeff Randall reported news of a new consortium seeking to buy Tottenham Hotspur with, at its head, the well-known boxing promoter Frank Warren. It was said to have involved overseas investors, including pension funds, but, interestingly, they wanted as their chief executive none other than Terry Venables. Warren's profile had been a high one following the trial of Terry Marsh, the former boxing world champion, for his attempted murder in a shooting in Essex. Marsh was found not guilty.

Scholar took this news quite calmly, for nobody could take over the club without his consent as the major shareholder. Venables reacted cautiously to the story while admitting he had been in discussions with a business associate of Warren about the crisis at the club. 'What I am doing is trying to help to solve the club's problems,' he said at the time. 'I think that is the aim of everybody connected with Tottenham at the moment.'

But an indication of the plight they were in came with the announcement of an increase in admission prices halfway through the season. This outraged the supporters, the more so since there had been an alarming slump in the club's results following their ten-match unbeaten start to the season. Since the beginning of November they had dropped 19 points out of 30, and their only avenue for success for the rest of the season was through an FA Cup run. But, as they began their preparations for the third round tie at Blackpool, there were further, humiliating revelations as Southampton threatened court action over a £20,000 sum they claimed was outstanding on items for the club shop under their old Hummel agreement. Likewise, Chelsea were seeking £45,000 over a ticket bill.

Meanwhile, Scholar went to see businessman Ted Bull, who ran a company called Landhurst Leasing and lived in a country house near Crawley. Scholar had already discussed with him, some time previously, a scheme to raise money by creating a leasehold investment out of the boxes at Tottenham, thus providing a steady stream of income over a period. Frank Warren was involved in the general discussion, while the mood of Bull was that he was violently opposed to any deal with Maxwell. During the course of the afternoon, Bull would take repeated telephone calls and it was Scholar's belief that he was being pumped for information on what it would need to persuade him to sell the club.

On the last day of 1990, Spurs held an annual general meeting, as they were required to do, but it lasted just a few minutes. The plc were still not in a position to present their accounts. Scholar recalls: 'As I was no longer on the main board, I stood at the back of the room feeling like a fly on the wall and sympathised with the shareholders agitated by what had happened and by their failure to get answers to their questions. Douglas Alexiou had presided over the meeting, but Midland Bank had made it clear that we needed a full-time executive chairman. The problem was finding one. Our ideal chairman would obviously be someone who cared about the club and had some standing in the City.'

This was how Nat Solomon was appointed to the position. He was a well-known City troubleshooter, an ex-chairman of Pleasurama casino and leisure group. Solomon had met Scholar in 1988, when Tony Berry had introduced him as another Spurs-mad fan who might have helped with the rights issue. Scholar says: 'He had taken Terry and myself to one of the restaurants owned by the Pleasurama, but he made the fatal mistake of trying to prove he knew more about Spurs than I did.' His appointment was approved by both the Midland and the Stock Exchange, who were calling for an administrator to run the club's affairs. The big question Solomon now had to face was who could be found to provide the money to solve Tottenham's problems. Solomon had no easy answers.

Venables monitored the meeting from the club's training

ground, where he was preparing for the third round FA Cup tie, which he knew he needed to win. His record in the competition had been poor since his arrival at Spurs, just one win in four seasons. Scholar had dark forebodings about the match at Bloomfield Road, but he was also superstitious and as a Spurs historian was well aware that Spurs had four times won the trophy when the year ended in a '1'. Paul Stewart did not share the apprehension, suggesting that ex-forwards always scored on their return to their old club. He did and Tottenham progressed 1-0.

With that important game successfully negotiated, attention switched again to the club's predicament and the necessity to attack the debt and have the block on sharedealing lifted. The newspapers were now conducting what amounted to a public auction for Paul Gascoigne, whose sale abroad they knew would make considerable inroads into the £12 million debt. Meanwhile, the bank were agitating for a sale of assets and Gascoigne was the biggest asset the club possessed.

Scholar says: 'Nat Solomon's arrival as chairman changed things somewhat. Although I was no longer a member of the plc board, Nat had requested me to attend board meetings and almost his very first words to me were "I know how you feel but we have to demonstrate to the bank that we are actually making some effort to reduce our debts, so we have to try and get some proposal from an overseas club to show we mean business." What I didn't know at that time was that the Midland had made the sale of Gascoigne one of their conditions of continuing to service the overdraft. They wanted Tottenham to undertake a "marketing exercise" and Nat, in his first public statement as chairman, made it clear Gascoigne might be sold.'

That news was plastered across the back page of the *London Evening Standard* on the day of the Rumbelows Cup quarter-final against Chelsea. Thus far, Venables had largely insulated the players from the chill blasts coming from the boardroom, but knew that their jewel may have to be sold. It upset Venables, whose relations with Scholar were still frosty as a result of the

Frank Warren consortium story. Meanwhile, Gascoigne's sale became a regular item on the agenda of every board meeting the club held. The bank were now pressurising the directors over the issue, and Scholar was warned by co-director Douglas Alexiou that unless he went along with their view, they would be forced to ask him to leave.

Alexiou pleaded that if an alternative means of raising the money could be found, the sale of Gascoigne could be averted. Scholar recalls: 'I attended the board meeting but made it very clear I would be prepared to discuss the sale of Gascoigne only on the basis that the alternative would be putting Tottenham into administration or receivership. If it was a choice of Tottenham going broke or Gascoigne going, then I was prepared to discuss his transfer, although I was still opposed to it and would do everything to stop it Solomon now turned to Scholar to seek advice as to how the club should go about notifying possibly interested clubs of his availability. Scholar suggested the club seek the help of agent Dennis Roach, even though he knew that Roach and Gascoigne's adviser, Mel Stein, could not stand the sight of each other. They had fallen out badly over the sale of Chris Waddle to Marseille to such an extent that they refused to sit in the same room. In a clever way, Scholar reasoned that the bank could not object to a reputable man like Roach, while he would find it difficult to organise a deal with Stein involved. Scholar, in fact, warned Roach that these were not normal circumstances, that normal rules might not apply and that even if he found Gascoigne a suitable Italian club, there was no guarantee the deal would be pushed through.

But one deal Scholar was happy to sanction, and which promised to bring in £800,000, was the sale of Vinny Samways to Aston Villa. The Villa chairman Doug Ellis had agreed the sale in a telephone conversation with Scholar, who had requested the deal was put on ice for a couple of days because Samways was needed for the League Cup replay against Chelsea. The Villa manager Josef Vengios and his assistant Peter Withe attended the game, where Samways performed poorly and was substituted in the second half. The next day, Ellis pulled out of the transfer despite Scholar's belief they had struck a verbal deal. In his autobiography, Behind Closed Doors, Scholar reflects that Venables' substitution of Samways in that game.'put a spoke in the deal'. He reflected: 'Terry had expressed objections about Samways going and felt his true value was £1.5 million.'

Venables, indeed, was on the warpath, fed up with what was happening behind the scenes at the club and the effect that the open publicity was having. A story suggesting he was to be offered a huge salary to manage the United States World Cup squad, whether true or not, made depressing dressing-room reading for the players. Venables, meanwhile, was using his flair for publicity, and his popularity with the press, to launch his own broadside on the Spurs board. 'For heaven's sake, sort this mess out' was his message in bold type.

But it didn't help the side in their League Cup quest and they lost the replay on their home ground to Chelsea. That night, too, Scholar had to be smuggled from the ground after a warning that he would be shot had been telephoned to the police. Now, all that was left for Tottenham was the FA Cup and the prospect that their best player was being hawked around the Continent.

Emlyn Hughes also put the boot in on Venables in his Daily Mirror column in an article which began: 'I've got some advice for Terry Venables this morning. He may not like it but I think it's about time someone told him. Stop moaning about not having any money, mate, Spurs are skint and you have spent all they can afford to give you.' Above the article were pictures and prices of the players he had bought. His only consolation was that it was accompanied by an even bigger picture of Venables with his latest business venture, a new board game called 'The Manager', for which he probably got more publicity than was given to Trivial Pursuit. But playing at really being a manager is no board game lottery.

He was a beleaguered man and badly in need of some encouraging news. It continued to be supplied in the FA Cup with Spurs drawn at home to Brian Horton's Oxford United, who had already disposed of Chelsea at Stamford Bridge with a convincing 3-1 scoreline, but now they came across Gascoigne in his most irresistible mood, as he scored twice and made the other two goals in a thrilling 4-2 success. It was a performance that had Venables purring: 'You cannot compare him to any player from the past,' he said after the match. 'He has Dave Mackay's attitude, a hunger for the game. He has that upper-body strength that helps make Maradona a great player.'

Roach had been busy on the Continent while Gazza was performing his tricks. His own deal was to take one percent of any transfer fee up to £7 million and 1.5 percent for anything over that. He rang Scholar to say that Lazio of Rome were interested and a meeting was arranged. This was the start of the protracted Gascoigne saga, the signal that Scholar was about to lose his battle to keep the club's, indeed the country's, most talented player at White Hart Lane. Gascoigne was helping to build up his own reputation as the Spurs FA Cup run continued on 16 February 1991 with another outstanding virtuoso performance against Portsmouth at Fratton Park, where another two memorable goals carried Spurs into the quarter-finals, where they would face Notts County.

Just ten days later came the club's annual general meeting, and the speculation was building that Venables was going to front a takeover bid for the club, backed by some influential investors. But he was reluctant to elaborate on his plans. At the meeting, chaired by Solomon, the board sat at the top table, with the professional advisers seated to the right and Scholar and Venables to the left.

The meeting was held in the *Chanticleer*, the restaurant run by the football club where the fans eat before the big matches. There was the promise of pertinent questioning from the Tottenham Independent Supporters' Association, which had been formed in the wake of the Robert Maxwell revelations. Scholar knew he was a man under fire and that he was being fingered as the director who had led the club into crippling debt.

It was only partly true, for the blame was a collective one which the board of the plc had to shoulder. That was little consolation to Scholar as he faced his inquisitors. But the reception was less hostile than he had anticipated.

Solomon handled the meeting skilfully, giving the irate fans their opportunity to present their questions, even if the answers to many of them were vague and indirect. Solomon told those who doubted his commitment to Tottenham: 'I have not been a supporter of this club for the last 55 years to preside over its demise.' Amazingly, there were no detailed accounts presented, just the broad outline of the financial position, with debts of £13.6 million and liabilities totalling £22.9 million. Solomon spelled out the plain truth of the position which everybody knew. Either money had to be found or the star players had to be sold. It was as simple and straightforward as that because the Midland were owed in excess of £10 million and the debt could be called in at any moment.

The statement of intent on the big-player issues was clear enough. 'Regarding star players, namely Gascoigne and Lineker, I would like to say very clearly that I speak for the whole board when I say we fervently hope we can find a solution to our problems that will not require them to be sold. Nevertheless, if an offer is received by the board, we will have an inescapable responsibility to look at it carefully in the light of the prevailing circumstances.'

Discussions with three potential buyers of the club were under way and if any of the offers proved satisfactory then the existing board would be prepared to give way. He confirmed that Venables was a party to one of them, that a second was on behalf of financial services company Baltic and there was a third, unidentifiable, offer, though it was in no way connected with Robert Maxwell. The antagonism towards Scholar dissipated when the shareholders were informed that he had taken no financial gain from the loan deal with Maxwell to pay off the Lineker transfer and that he had not cashed his dividend cheques, which had saved the club monies well in excess of £100,000.

There was, indeed, a recognition that although he may have acted ill-advisedly on occasions and although his hands-on philosophy had led him to conflict with Venables on playing matters, Scholar did have his heart and soul in the club.

It was a matter of weeks later that it was discovered who the man was behind the Venables consortium. His name was Larry Gillick, the son of a famous former Glasgow Rangers footballer. He claimed to have the £12 million needed to buy the club lodged in banks in his native Scotland. At this stage, it was uncertain whether Gillick had raised the money himself or was the front man for an anonymous Mr Big. It was in early March that a meeting was first arranged between the Spurs board, Venables, Peter Earl of Tranwood, a small merchant bank who were acting as Venables' adviser, and Gillick. It transpired that Tranwood were already in financial difficulties and these proved so serious they eventually went into liquidation.

But it was Gillick who fascinated Scholar. He says: 'I had never met him before and when I arrived at Nat's office my first impression was that he resembled an out-of-work gangster. Everything from his clothes to his looks suggested that, the dark suit, white shirt, fish tie, the portly, thickset appearance with shortish crinkling hair and a thinning, receding hairline. None of us knew then anything about his background or what he had been doing and we were surprised that he seemed to be presenting himself as principal in the deal. That suggested he had something in the order of £25-£30 million at his disposal. He was to buy Tottenham at 90p per share, which would cost £9 million, plus take on a debt in the region of £12-£13 million, plus putting in a further £5 million for new players. There are not too many people who emerge from nowhere and claim to have £30 million at their disposal.'

Further investigations into 44-year-old Gillick would reveal that his father, Terry, had played for Glasgow Rangers and Everton in the pre-war years. Gillick first became a figure in Scotland when he was the builder and a director of the Victoria Stadium in Ayr, a project in which he invested £100,000 in

1980. But, after a champagne launch at the £430,000 greyhound stadium, things went horribly wrong.

There was never any greyhound racing on the 'ghost track', he became involved in a legal wrangle with his 'partner' Thomas McCool and the local council cancelled the lease on the stadium. Some months later the stadium was damaged by fire and re-opened several months later under new management. Six years later, McCool was jailed for five years at Edinburgh High Court for embezzlement and fraud, though there was no suggestion that these offences were linked in any way to the stadium project. After the failed dog track venture Gillick disappeared from the public eye, surfacing again behind the consortium bid and described as a London property developer.

There were some assurances that appealed to the board, Scholar in particular, for they were insisting they did not want to sell Gascoigne, which he had made one of his conditions for selling his interest in the club. There was also a warm response to the commitment to put £5 million into the club beyond what was necessary to buy the shares and clear the debt. On the other hand, Gillick refused to provide any information about who his backing investors were. Eventually, the board asked the three men to wait while they conferred, and it became clear that some directors were not totally happy with the way the bid had been presented. Scholar suggested that he speak to Gillick alone and Solomon readily agreed.

Scholar relates what happened: 'I took Gillick to one side and said that if he could up his offer to 110p, or even slightly over the £1 at which the issue had originally been floated in 1983, then maybe we could do a deal. He eventually agreed that he could move up to 95p. Bobroff and Berry agreed to go along and that accounted for 44 percent of the shareholding.' The three men then came round the table together and it appeared the deal was on. Scholar patted Venables on the cheek and said: 'Now go and win the European Cup.'

Scholar sat in Solomon's office that night believing that the club had new owners and all that now needed to be done was for the solicitors and financial advisers to write down the agreement. He felt Venables had put a deal together and had the money in place. But, not for the first time, Venables failed to deliver when it came to paying up. It was quickly apparent that Frank Warren was, indeed, involved in the consortium and had in fact set it up. He had introduced Gillick to the group, which also included an anonymous North London businessman who was believed to be providing the bulk of the finance. Warren subsequently withdrew and investigations proved that Venables and Tony Berry, an existing director acting as go-between in the consortium, had known Gillick for only a matter of weeks.

Within days of that first meeting, Berry rang Scholar to urge him to another meeting with Gillick at the consortium's solicitor's offices in Harley Street. Gillick went straight to the point by saying that he was unable to proceed at 95p but was prepared to offer 85p. He promised a banker's draft from Barclay's within two days. Scholar accepted with reluctance, but insisted that this was the final deal and there was no use them coming back in again. There had been a hint from Gillick that the money to finance the deal had come from the Middle East. In fact, it was Sheikh Tanoon Bin Saeed Al Nahiyan, the nephew of Abu Dhabi's ruler Sheikh Zayed, who was the provider, though he insisted on keeping his name secret. The consortium, too, felt this was the wisest course, since the club's large Jewish support might not approve. However, the Takeover Panel, who had to be consulted in the takeover, insisted that the Sheikh's name must be made public under City rules.

They refused a request for a nominee to be used for this purpose, since the Stock Exchange insist on full disclosures and would not put out an offer document which did not contain all the information available as to who was providing the funds, where they were coming from and what sort of people were going to be involved. However flawed it may have seemed, this was the only offer on the table. On 20 March, the Spurs board met again without having any evidence that the money from the Gillick consortium existed or that he could satisfy the regulatory authorities. They had no alternative but to recommend that the offer could not be accepted.

Two days later, the club's advisers told the board to issue a statement making it clear that all talks with the Venables consortium were now at an end. The board held another meeting the next day, prior to their match against QPR. Tony Berry now found himself in an unusual position. He was a middleman for the consortium yet had been at the meeting and voted for an end to the negotiations with Gillick and Venables. Less than 24 hours later, he was relaying messages from the pair, informing his fellow directors that Gillick still intended to bid for the company.

Certainly Venables was not prepared to drop his fight for the club. Immediately after Tottenham's withdrawal from the agreement, he was still insisting that he had the money in place. 'All this talk about not having the money is totally wrong,' he said. 'The money is there and I am optimistic about taking control. The deal will either break down or go through but how can there be a deadline?' It was early April that Gillick was back with another offer. Having shaken hands on 95p and then 85p, he now wanted to offer 80p per share. But Solomon still had no letter of credit in relation to the offer terms and they could still not satisfy the Midland that the loan would be repaid.

There was little doubt Venables was working flat out to win his fight for control and he admitted: 'I have never worked as hard at anything in my life. I come in to take the players training in the morning and then go to meetings afternoon and evening. I am working round the clock to try and save the football club.' If he was a man in a hurry, then Scholar was not and he was happy that the newspapers were clinging on to what, in many cases, was disinformation which made it difficult for anyone to grasp what was truly happening at any given moment.

Scholar was still in a good bargaining position, for the only way he could really lose out was if the bank called in the overdraft. This was an unlikely prospect, since if they did foreclose they would incur some unfortunate publicity and no doubt lose thousands of customers who might have been Tottenham fans. Scholar was buying time. Tottenham had defeated Notts County, as expected, to make the FA Cup semi-final and a lucrative match against Arsenal was in prospect. For the first time, a semi-final game was to be staged at Wembley, a controversial decision in itself. So Venables was preparing a side for that vital derby while pressing forward with his wrestle for power.

Just when the latest bid was under consideration at the beginning of April, however, Scholar had another lucky break. The Scottish *Daily Record* had been investigating Gillick and were able to inform their readers that he had been bankrupt and only discharged three years earlier. In addition, he had been savagely criticised by the chartered accountant appointed as his trustee. These damning facts were to discredit the latest consortium bid more than somewhat and effectively brought another Venables effort to control the club to an end.

But, in any event, all talk of takeovers was shelved while the FA Cup semi-final against Arsenal beckoned. Gascoigne had recovered encouragingly from a double hernia operation and had successfully come through a test on the injury against Norwich four days before the big Wembley date. At Wembley, Venables' side began as the underdogs, their league form was erratic and the club's problems never too deep below the surface. But Venables had prepared his side brilliantly, and his decision to risk Gascoigne was a momentous one.

Gascoigne's free-kick in the first few minutes of the game remains one of the outstanding strikes of a football seen for many years and he then contributed to the second, scored by Lineker, which effectively put the game out of Arsenal's reach. 'That free-kick must be one of the best ever seen at Wembley,' Venables would suggest after the game. 'It is easy to bend a ball without pace or to curl it. But to bend it with power and accuracy is very special, especially from 35 yards.' Alan Smith did pull one goal back just before half time, but there was little doubt this was Tottenham's day as they stroked the ball to feet. Gascoigne was replaced halfway through the second half by Nayim. Arsenal increasingly took risks as they went for the equaliser, as they had to do, and it was to cost them the game as the predatory Lineker scored his second goal.

Spurs, the ailing giant, had made it to Wembley and, with a month to the final, could they manage to avoid more boardroom tremors? The answer, of course, was negative. But at least Scholar was again able to raise the subject of a contract with Venables. His current one was running out and he had dismissed Scholar's earlier attempt to offer him a newly structured contract based on performance which would have given him £25,000 less on his basic salary, but might earn him a good deal more if the club were successful. Scholar now told his manager to name his terms and that would give them a negotiating point, but as Venables went off to celebrate with his father Fred, nothing had been agreed.

In the interim between the semi and the final, Venables and Scholar met again to discuss a contract without agreement being reached and, shortly afterwards, Gillick re-appeared on the scene. This time he did not want to make a bid for the entire company, but instead to acquire up to 29 percent of the shares and refinance the Midland loan together with the loan Scholar had provided to finance the purchase of Lineker. The board were still prepared to talk, with Tony Berry again acting as the middleman. But, by the end of April, Venables was forced to concede that his Middle Eastern backers had withdrawn.

Now Venables had another proposal and this was backed by David Garrard, another property man. It would mean that once Venables bought the club, he would do a sale and leaseback of White Hart Lane and he had already signed a conditional contract to that effect. The deal was intended to raise £11.5 million, with Tottenham paying an annual rent of around £1.5 million and retaining a buy-back provision over a specified period of time. But, once again, when the deal was examined and when money needed to be forthcoming it wasn't there.

The offer on this occasion came from a company named Edennote. The news of Gillick's background suggested that he had now dropped out of all negotiations, and even Venables had spoken of new backers for his latest bid. But Scholar was suspicious and, as it transpired, correctly so. Edennote were listed at Companies House as having just two directors, Terry Venables and Larry Gillick. It was a complicated deal, but basically involved a new share issue of five million shares to be bought by Edennote for £3.5 million. They would then effectively own 35 percent of the club. Edennote had also prepared a schedule to reduce the Midland debt, but they wanted to appoint a new board. There was also a condition that Gascoigne would not be sold.

But there were problems. The Midland had already rejected guarantees from the Gillick-Venables consortium and was unlikely to accept promises to reduce the overdraft over a period. Lazio now had a binding contract to buy Gascoigne and the price of the new shares was set at 70p, which was just over half the amount Maxwell had offered and 21p less than the price at which they were suspended. This latest offer was heard by the board on 29 April, but after five hours of deliberations, the meeting broke up without a decision being taken.

At a further meeting on 7 May, just 11 days before the final, the latest Venables bid was under review, again with Tony Berry pushing hard for it to be accepted over a counter-offer from Baltic. Despite the fact that Scholar had been advised that it would need a package worth £2 million plus salary to keep Gascoigne at Tottenham Hotspur, Berry was still insisting that if Venables was successful in his bid they would keep him. But he could not convince the other directors. They wanted to have proper advice on what the sale and leaseback part of the offer would really mean.

Scholar had his own concerns. He reflected later: 'I just could not see where Terry was getting his money from. I had shaken hands with Gillick on 95p months before, thinking a deal was done, and then found myself in a crazy reverse bidding situation. Now I was being offered 70p by a new Venables consortium. Even if the bidding had ended there and my handshakes were translated into legally watertight agreements, what guarantee was there that Venables would produce the money? He had failed to do so in the past and this failure had become something of a joke, even among the advisers. The sale and leaseback proposal had stated "time is of the essence" and required the payment of a deposit. But even this payment was three weeks overdue, which under such a contract is laughable.'

The deal was not agreed, but it did nothing to diminish Venables' now obsessive determination to take control of the club. It now seemed to have taken him over, and in the week building up to the FA Cup final against Nottingham Forest he combined preparing his players with a round of business meetings designed to have agreement from the board for a takeover before the final was played.

Scholar had begun that day with meetings, too, regarding the exact nature of the Gascoigne move to Lazio. He had made it clear some eight months previously that if Gascoigne was sold then he would leave the club. On a point of principle, he did not believe it was right for the football club to be responsible for financing debts that were not of its making. He believed that player transfers should be approached on the basis of whether it was right for the club and the team rather than whether it suited the bank. He said: 'I had tried everything to stop the transfer and, although the Gascoigne contract had been signed by Solomon at the end of April, it was only during this meeting that I finally came to terms with the fact that his sale was now inevitable.'

Stein had asked Scholar at the meeting if the club was in a position to present a package to keep Gascoigne at the club. That would have had to guarantee him a minimum £2 million net after tax over the first year plus a hefty annual salary. Scholar told him the chances were virtually nil. He knew then that he had lost his battle and, despite it being the eve of a big cup final for the club he loved, Scholar was a sad and depressed man.

But there were other meetings still to come that day. Venables was still engaged in last-minute talks to put together another offer. It was what Robert Maxwell described to Scholar as 'trying yet another pair of knickers'. But here he was, while his players were resting in their rooms at the Royal Lancaster Hotel, with yet another proposal. It was at 4.30 in the afternoon that Scholar took the call from a mutual friend of both Venables and himself to say the Spurs manager had the money in place. Scholar had one last gesture to make, and he said that he was prepared to deal at 80p a share, but if Venables could guarantee to keep Gascoigne at the club, he could have them for 70p. In other words, Scholar was prepared to put £270,000 into the battle to keep Gascoigne at the club.

The mutual friend, Philip Green, went to report back to Venables at the team hotel and the lawyers and advisers got to work on preparing the agreement. Scholar went to join friends for a drink while keeping in constant touch with his own solicitor, Peter Robinson. But, once again, there was to be a breakdown in a Venables deal and by 10pm no agreement had been reached. Venables was looking for 'certain comforts from the Midland Bank', the bankers to the company, and since that made it a conditional deal, Scholar advised Venables they could not proceed. Venables' cherished hope that he would lead his side out at Wembley alongside Brian Clough as the owner of the club could not now be fulfilled.

Venables himself had been spending a good deal of his busy calendar working to keep Gascoigne at the club, stressing: 'I fear for him if he goes abroad. I know it won't be easy for him to deal with. He will have problems on and off the pitch.' Venables had made his own plea to Stein and tried to convince him of the seriousness of his attempts to take over the club and present a challenge to Europe with Gascoigne at the helm. Then might be the suitable time for him to make his big-money move to Italy. But Stein refused to give any assurances and the contract from Italy lay ready for signing.

If the week of the final had been conspicuous for non-football events as far as Tottenham were concerned, the football had not been completely overlooked and there had been a good deal of backslapping between the two managers. Venables had described Brian Clough as 'the greatest manager in my lifetime. I can't think of anyone to compare. He must be doing something right, because he has been doing it consistently well for so long. He has not had the financial facility some of the bigger clubs have enjoyed and yet he has won trophies consistently.'

Clough, in contrast to Venables, who was working 18 hours a day, went for a holiday between the semi and the final and when Nigel Clough was asked on the eve of the match what frame of mind his father was in, he replied: 'We don't know. We haven't seen him all week.' Despite this, Forest were favourites to win the match because of their strength at the back with England internationals Stuart Pearce, Des Walker and Gary Charles. They had, too, one of the brightest young midfield players in the game in Roy Keane and, of course, Nigel Clough himself, one of the game's most astute passers of a football.

Yet Spurs had enjoyed a fine cup campaign and their own passing style would be suited to Wembley's big pitch. And, of course, they had Paul Gascoigne, whose goals against Oxford, Portsmouth, Notts County and Arsenal had brought Spurs to this critical day in their recent troubled history. Clough was typically phlegmatic about the Tottenham star: 'I have not seen much of him, actually,' he said. 'But I think he has a lot of talent and I've asked our coach driver, if he sees him in the Wembley tunnel, to run him down.'

But when Gascoigne was lining up for the presentation to the Prince and Princess of Wales and the Duke and Duchess of York, it was clear that he was once again hyped up. This surfaced in the opening minutes of the match with a dreadful challenge on Garry Parker for which he should most certainly have been cautioned. Just a few minutes later, as Gary Charles supported his attack on the edge of the Spurs penalty area, Gascoigne again lunged in crazily, his leg outstretched, a desperately dangerous challenge which should have brought an immediate red card. But referee Roger Milford merely awarded a free-kick.

But the real damage had not been inflicted on Charles, but on Gascoigne himself. It was bad enough for Tottenham that

Stuart Pearce had driven the free-kick beyond Erik Thorstvedt to put Forest ahead. However, as Spurs restarted the game from the centre spot, so Gascoigne collapsed to be stretchered away, his final finished after just 15 minutes. This had a dramatic effect on the game, because there had been a sense of anticipation in the Wembley atmosphere each time Gascoigne came near the ball.

His popularity in the country was not quite at the fever pitch it had been on his return from the World Cup a year previously, but he was still a talent who could excite and turn a game. The television analysts condemned him for the tackle in their half-time assessments, and there is little doubt Tottenham were lucky not to be contesting most of the match with ten men. So that sympathy for him was tempered by the knowledge that he had brought this injury on himself. There is little doubt that, as a young lad, he had found the pressures on him a burden. His natural humour could quickly be overtaken by a mood of sulkiness whenever he spotted a man with a notebook and pencil. Yet there was a vulnerability about him that made more experienced people connected to the game wish to put an arm round his shoulder to give him advice. Now he was waiting to be taken to hospital for examination while his side battled their way back into the match, re-organising their side and digging in to find the spirit to get back into the game.

Gary Crosby missed a glorious chance to increase Forest's lead, a goal that would almost certainly have broken Tottenham's heart. Thorstvedt made the save, Tottenham survived and, when Gary Lineker found himself one-on-one with goalkeeper Mark Crossley, he was dragged down and a penalty given. Lineker took the kick himself, but Crossley flung himself to his left and touched it away for a corner. This, it seemed, was not Venables' or Tottenham's day. They were one down at half time, but Venables got to work on his players in the dressing room and in the second half they gradually took control. Seven minutes into the half, a move begun by Nayim and carried on by Paul Allen provided Paul Stewart with the opportunity to drive the ball across Crossley and into the net.

From then on, Spurs assumed control of the match, but could not quite produce the winner. When the final whistle went, Venables was quickly in a circle with his players with instructions and encouragement. Clough, in contrast, never moved from his seat except to pass the time of day with a policeman. He left his coaching staff to issue the orders and this was surely an error of judgement on his part. Spurs continued to hold the initiative in the extra half-hour, but the goal that won the FA Cup for them was a cruel stroke of fortune for England's centre-half Walker. A Nayim corner kick, flicked on by Stewart, was heading towards Gary Mabbutt, charging in behind the Forest defenders. Walker sensed his presence, went to intercept but succeeded only in deflecting the ball past his own goalkeeper.

Tottenham had won and the relief and joy were unbounded, for this had been a team performance and one to be proud of. For Venables, it was his first major English trophy and he admitted: 'It would be an understatement to say I was thrilled by the way the lads performed to come from behind. Given the year we have just had, I would say this is my finest achievement as a manager.' While the celebrations continued that night and the next day around Haringey Town Hall, thoughts were spared for Gascoigne who was undergoing surgery on his right knee, a career threatening injury to his anterior cruciate ligament. Venables revealed: 'The boy is pleased for the lads but is devastated by his injury and by missing most of what was the biggest game of his life.'

Despite the problems between them and the rift that had grown, Scholar was generous in his tribute to Venables' part in the Cup success: 'I have never wanted Terry Venables to leave this club,' he told the press afterwards. 'He will be offered a new contract. That is what I want. You only need to look at what he has done for Tottenham. He has won us the FA Cup.'

But even in his moment of triumph, Venables found this insincere. 'I would have thought it was plain to everyone by now that unless I can get the equity, the absolute decision-making authority and the position I want within the club, I won't be staying at Tottenham. Not after all that has happened. There is no way I can continue to manage the club under the frustration I have endured for the last three years. Not only have I not heard anything about a new contract since I told the chairman some weeks ago I could not carry on as manager in the present circumstance, but the propaganda about Tottenham's offer is nothing more than a gimmick to deflect attention from the reality of the situation.'

Venables also stated his intention now to try to finance a takeover himself, without the help of a consortium, an objective that was always going to be over-ambitious. But there was a point of no return, and both Venables and Scholar had gone way beyond it. There was blame to be attached on either side. Scholar was the victim of his own dedication to Tottenham's cause. He was the archetypal fan who made it to the boardroom and he could hardly resist having to be involved in every facet of the club. But if he should have left everything on the playing side to Venables, so the manager was engrossed in his own ambition. He was the kid from Dagenham who made himself a limited company at the age of 17 and, throughout his life, simply coaching a football team was never quite enough to fulfil his own idea of his potential. As a coach he is outstanding, and never better than when he is pitting his own tactical acumen against that of other managers.

Venables' success with the FA Cup only intensified the supporters' belief that he was the man who should have control of the football club. It was a sentiment shared in the dressing room, where Venables was highly popular and well respected. They would not have long to wait. At a meeting on 22 May, the Wednesday after the game, the matter for discussion was how the club continued trading. Could and should the club sell season tickets for 1991-92 while it was felt Tottenham might go into liquidation? What was now the position of Lazio in regard to the Gascoigne transfer?

While these deliberations were taking place, Terry Venables

was taking a telephone call from Alan Sugar which was to give the manager the situation he had dreamed about for most of his working life.

CHAPTER NINE

Venables and Sugar - 'The Dream Team'

ALAN SUGAR BECAME Terry Venables' sugar-daddy. Like a shining white knight he rode to the besieged manager's rescue so that he could escape from the clutches of the fire-breathing dragon in the guise of Robert Maxwell. It was the dream ticket for Spurs fans. Sugar was a man of substance and financial muscle who could secure the financial future of Tottenham, while Venables was the manager who had just lifted the FA Cup. His position at the club would be guaranteed, and Tottenham would be saved from going in to receivership. What more could anyone want?

Those fans, so perturbed at the prospect of the 'ogre' Maxwell taking over, naturally rejoiced in 'the dream team' of Venables and Sugar. They had no idea that it would turn into a nightmare - and so quickly.

The partnership seemed, on paper, to have all the hallmarks of a pairing made in heaven. Venables was something of an institution in the football world, with an outstanding record and an exceptional reputation as a successful football manager and coach in this country and abroad. Sugar was a powerhouse in his field, a wealthy entrepreneur who had built up computer giants Amstrad from nothing. He was the ideal man to sort out the club's finances. Between them, perhaps, they could take Tottenham beyond their North London rivals Arsenal, champions twice in the previous three seasons.

The key man in their negotiations was Irving Scholar. If Venables and Sugar could persuade him that their partnership, and not the offer from Maxwell, was best for Tottenham then he would sell to them. However, Scholar did ask his successor: 'What function will Venables fulfil? Will he remain as team manager?' Scholar says: 'Sugar told me "Venables thinks he's an entrepreneur, I don't. He'll look after the team." On that basis,

I decided to sell to Sugar.' Therefore, it was a huge surprise to Scholar when, not long after the takeover, Venables appointed ex-Tottenham manager Peter Shreeves as team coach while he took a back seat in the dressing room, and was not seen in the dugout.

But there was no criticism of Venables abdicating full control over the players on match days at the time. Instead, there was relief at the Venables-Sugar double act saving the club. Tottenham had experienced crippling financial difficulties. A new stand at White Hart Lane that had been completed at the unexpectedly high cost of more than £9 million was at the root of the crisis, but unsuccessful non-football businesses had also hit Tottenham plc very hard.

To offset these debts, Tottenham had been negotiating with Italian club Lazio to try to sell Paul Gascoigne, whose success in the 1990 World Cup had made him a very valuable asset. In mid-March 1991, the Lazio bid was confirmed at a world record £8.5 million. However, Tottenham, in winning the FA Cup (and thus guaranteeing a lucrative appearance in the European Cup-Winners' Cup), paid a price when Gascoigne seriously injured himself, throwing the transfer deal into the balance and endangering Spurs' financial recovery. For a while, he was as crippled as the club's finances. This injury seemed to have reopened the door to a bid from Maxwell - a move that the fans were vehemently hostile towards.

Indeed, Maxwell had been interested in buying the club for a long time up to the FA Cup final. Venables had hoped to take his seat in the Royal Box as owner of Tottenham, but instead he led Spurs out at Wembley and won the FA Cup final against Nottingham Forest, despite Gascoigne's injury. Maybe the match hinged on Gascoigne's reckless self-inflicted injury - he might have been sent off for a dangerous early challenge on Garry Parker, and almost seemed intent on earning himself a red card as he charged about the pitch. As it was, Gascoigne received his coveted winner's medal in his hospital bed while Venables celebrated his greatest triumph as a manager in English football. It was his first major domestic trophy since he became a manager in 1976, and it was one of the game's most prestigious prizes.

But Venables knew there was still a more significant 'match' to be won - control of Spurs. His failure to put together a package that Scholar would trust before the Cup final had much embarrassed him. He spoke of how it was inconceivable that the two men could now work together as if nothing had happened. Therefore, when Alan Sugar rang, Venables knew he might at least have someone who could definitely be relied upon to put forward the necessary money. Unlike Gillick, everyone knew Sugar had substantial funds at his disposal.

The 46-year-old Sugar had supported Spurs since childhood and watched his football at White Hart Lane. His two sons, 24-year-old Simon and 22-year-old Daniel, supported Spurs; his elder brother, Derek, had been a lifelong fan; his first Amstrad offices were in Garman Road, Tottenham, near the ground. Despite the feeling at the time that the Sugar interest came out of nowhere, the truth was vastly different. He had a longstanding affinity with the club, was familiar with their financial plight, and saw an opportunity to diversify. He also had some previous knowledge of Venables. When Sugar commissioned an advertising company to come up with a slogan for Amstrad hi-fi equipment, Venables was chosen to promote the 'Great Players' theme.

So it was that, 48 hours after Spurs won the FA Cup, Sugar placed his call and asked to speak to Venables. He was not at White Hart Lane, but when Venables heard that Sugar had been in touch he returned the call, and so set in motion the events that were to change his life. However, in the aftermath of his dismissal, Venables even disputed the timing of Sugar's call to him, which he says took place during the week before the FA Cup final. He also maintains that he was in no hurry to contact Sugar because there were many other potential buyers in the running. However, Venables had certainly been involved in a series of failed attempts to buy Spurs, with doubts cast over the credentials of his backers.

Whatever the timing, after the two first spoke to each other, they arranged to meet up on the following day. Sugar was attending a CBI dinner at the Grosvenor Hotel in central London and they met before dinner. Venables brought with him Eddie Ashby, introducing him to Sugar as one of his financial advisers. The conversation centred on Scholar and Bobroff s willingness to sell their shares at 70p and so relinquish control. Venables estimated the cost at £2.7 million. When Sugar enquired about Spurs' finances, he was informed that the company owed the Midland Bank around £11 million. Ashby told Sugar that Venables had £3 million to invest, and Sugar was particularly impressed that his prospective partner would be putting his own money into the club.

That was an important factor for Sugar. However, he told Venables he would consider the proposition to invest his money only if he was going to be chairman and in sole control of the finances. He would leave all the football matters to Venables. When Sugar announced he wanted to be chairman, Venables wondered what his own position would be. Sugar suggested the titles of 'managing director' or 'chief executive'.

The outline of the football side of the company was that Venables planned to employ a coach/manager and give him directions on how to run the team. Venables wanted to handle some of the commercial aspects of the business, although Sugar remained uncertain exactly what that entailed. Sugar was keen to run the marketing side of the operation himself, as he had organised successful departments in marketing in his own business.

At that first meeting, Sugar made it perfectly plain that he considered an investment in Spurs as a 'business transaction' and that he had no intention of being emotional and pouring millions into the club unless it made 'good commercial sense'. Sugar considered that the downfall of many notable and otherwise successful clubs had come through squandering too much on players. Both men left the meeting excited about the prospects for the future.

The next day, Ashby travelled to Sugar's Amstrad headquarters in Brentwood and met Sugar's financial director Colin Sandy and Ken Ashcroft, another of his advisers, to run through Tottenham's financial state of health in detail; Sugar himself was on a four-day break over the Bank Holiday weekend at the end of May. On his return, talks continued between him and Venables.

Sugar had a private and confidential meeting with Spurs chief executive Ian Gray, who ran the club's financial affairs, at Amstrad's offices at 10.30am on 7 June. Ashby and Iac Koumi, representing one of Britain's small merchant bankers, Henry Ansbachers, were present as the deal reached an advanced stage. The next evening, Venables and Sugar met at a hotel near Langan's Brasserie in Mayfair where they agreed to invest £3 million each.

Venables provided an up-to-date analysis of the Gascoigne transfer to Lazio and felt he was still worth between £5 million and £6 million, while Gary Lineker would be joining a Japanese club for £4 million. Sugar questioned Venables about Gascoigne's injury and was informed that the surgeon, Dr John Browett, diagnosed that he would make a full recovery but it would take a substantial amount of time. Venables warned that Lazio were trying to get Gascoigne at a bargain rate as they had withdrawn their original offer because of the serious Cup final injury. Lazio were adamant that a deal would go through only when Gascoigne was fit. The Italians were clearly trying to take advantage of the club's parlous financial state, but the arrival of Sugar helped alter that scenario. Sugar's involvement forced Lazio to make a sensible offer along the lines of Venables' valuation. If they did not, he insisted, there were numerous alternatives such as Marseille, Juventus and other Continental clubs who had shown interest.

After chewing over the details of their agreement, Sugar went to Langan's to dine. There, he was approached by a *Sunday Mirror* journalist, who had heard that he was buying into Spurs, and the next day the story broke in the *Sunday Times.*

Sugar's next high-level meeting took place with Spurs board members Tony Berry and Nat Solomon. They pointed out that after so many false starts with potential backers for Venables, they were glad that a final solution looked likely. The Midland Bank, despite wanting their £11 million back, were being co-operative and on 12 June gave the club a year's extension on their huge overdraft.

Sugar first approached Paul Bobroff, who still owned a large stake in the company, in early June and twice spoke to Irving Scholar. The man who had controlled Spurs for the best part of a decade told Sugar: 'You're the first man of credibility with money.' He also gave Sugar some advice: 'Terry Venables is a good coach - that's it.' It was advice that Scholar repeated several times.

The reason that Venables saw so much hope in bringing in Sugar was that Scholar's favoured option was to sell the company to Robert Maxwell. Venables knew that, with Maxwell in charge, there would be no opportunity for him to run and own Spurs, he would merely be the manager -and Maxwell did not have the reputation of someone who would leave the manager in peace. However, because Scholar was a friend of Maxwell and they had been negotiating a possible sale on and off for the best part of a year, he felt an obligation to give him the first refusal on the sale of his shares. This connection between the two men was underestimated, even by Sugar, as they trusted each other. Furthermore, Scholar believed that the financial clout of Maxwell (one of the ten richest men in Britain, it was estimated) would secure Spurs' position as there had been a strong chance of the club going into receivership. To ensure the survival of Tottenham was Scholar's main aim.

In addition, although a full-scale union had not been reached, Maxwell had dug Scholar out of trouble with a personal loan to the Spurs chairman which had enabled Scholar to make the final payment in August 1990 on the purchase of Lineker and Nayim from Barcelona, just days before the Spanish club could have reclaimed England's captain. It was that transaction, when discovered, that led to Spurs shares being suspended on the Stock Exchange on 19 October 1990, and Scholar being removed from the board of the limited company, although he still attended board meetings and remained chairman of the football club, a subsidiary of the parent company. Despite all this, Scholar still controlled the club even though he had only 24 percent of the shares.

But, with Bobroffs allegiance, Scholar ruled supreme and was a shrewd negotiator. Sugar met Bobroff and spoke to Scholar and found that the pair were denying Venables' assessment that their shares were available for 70p. Scholar had made that offer only on the basis that Gascoigne stayed. Eventually, they reached agreement on a price of 75p a share, with completion arranged for 21 June at the offices of Ansbachers. Bobroff personally assured Sugar that the shares owned by Scholar and himself would then be sold. Sugar accepted in good faith that Venables had the £3 million to proceed. Venables himself, having antagonised Scholar because of his determination to take control of Spurs, sensibly left all the meaningful negotiations with Scholar and Bobroff to Sugar.

Maxwell publicly declared that he was out of the running to buy Spurs through his own newspaper, the *Daily Mirror*. Privately, he had no intention of losing out and plotted to persuade Scholar to sell to him and win over Bobroff to do the same.

The day of completion turned into one of high drama. Colin Sandy, representing Sugar's interests, dealt with the finer details at Ansbachers until 4pm, when he rang Sugar with an urgent warning of a 'hitch'. Maxwell had enormous influence over most City institutions, and Ansbachers were no exception. He had telephoned Ansbachers' directors to inform them that he was going to buy Scholar's shares. Sugar tried to sort out the complication on the phone, but quickly realised that would prove impossible and rushed to Ansbachers. Sugar burst into the room and there was an instant angry exchange with Bobroff.

Sugar confronted Bobroff and accused him of going back on his word and reneging on the deal, but Bobroff warned Sugar that he and Scholar were still considering the matter. It was then that a team of Maxwell's lawyers muscled in on the meeting and tried to scupper the deal. Scholar's lawyers were nowhere to be seen. Sugar was furious, he told Bobroff that Scholar had pulled out so late in the day. With the whole deal on a knife-edge, Sugar told Ashby to summon Venables to Ansbachers in the emergency.

When voices were raised, Sugar's was the one that could usually be heard. There were angry discussions with Scholar on the phone, and eventually Bobroff's resistance broke and he agreed to sell irrespective of what Scholar did. Scholar was, in fact, locked away in his flat in Monte Carlo, negotiating with Maxwell at his offices at Holborn Circus while simultaneously talking to Bobroff and Sugar at Ansbachers. Scholar was still ready to sell to Maxwell, but insisted that there must be an unconditional deal before the night was out. Maxwell agreed, but faced a major stumbling block; Maxwell could not fulfil the Football League regulations by disposing of Derby County. His idea was to put the ownership of the club into trust. But, with the minutes ticking away, Maxwell failed to satisfy Scholar's insistence on an unconditional deal.

As Maxwell had heard from Scholar that Bobroff had lost patience and agreed to sell to Sugar, he telephoned Sugar, realising that Scholar's position was weakening. He was still confident that he would reach a deal with his pal in Monaco, although the loss of the Bobroff shares was a big blow to his aspirations. Therefore, Maxwell suggested to Sugar that he would still buy Scholar's shares and be accepted as a 'passive investor'. As the publishing tycoon put it: 'Spurs will have two sugar-daddies.' Sugar told him straight that it was 'laughable' to believe that Maxwell would be a passive investor in any business, never mind one so high-profile as Tottenham, where he was determined to come out a winner. Sugar advised Maxwell that he was not interested in having him as an investor, but if he was successful in buying control of the club there was nothing to stop Maxwell buying shares on the open market. Maxwell slammed down the phone.

Venables arrived on the scene when most of the drama was over, just prior to the signing of the documents with Bobroff. Much later that evening, Scholar's lawyers arrived, not really sure how to proceed. One of the main problems was the £1.27 million loan by Scholar to Tottenham, money which Maxwell had provided for Scholar to pay for Lineker. Scholar demanded that the loan was repaid immediately; he did not want it left in the company if it was controlled by Venables and Sugar. But Spurs did not have the financial resources to pay back the money to Scholar. So Sugar agreed to pay the money into the company in order that Spurs could reimburse Scholar. But this then caused further complications.

The Midland overdraft was so high the bank wanted assurances before they agreed to such a transaction. Representatives of the bank were also at Ansbachers and they agreed to Sugar's plan, provided the new regime promised to wipe out the overdraft, or most of it, by November. Sugar made it clear to the bank from the outset that he would not be pouring money into the company, but as soon as he was in a position to do so he would involve various financial people in the club to sort out Tottenham's finances and ensure the Midland were provided with regular updates on proposed player purchases. On that basis, they allowed the repayment of the Scholar loan with an 'in and out' transaction that resulted in Tottenham owing Sugar £1.27 million.

At midnight, Scholar finally telephoned the Ansbachers offices and confirmed his decision to sell to Sugar and Venables. Maxwell telephoned to offer Sugar his congratulations. 'Magnanimous in victory' was Maxwell's usual motto, but here he was having to be magnanimous in defeat.

A meeting of the new Tottenham board took place immediately; Alan Sugar and Terry Venables were appointed directors. A draft shareholder's agreement, an issue which was later to become crucial, was drawn up between Venables' company Edennote and Sugar. The proposed agreement restricted the two partners in buying or selling shares in Tottenham without the other's consent. Venables realised that the agreement would enable Sugar to have control over what he did with his shares, and so he changed his mind about it. But, within minutes of the partnership being cemented that night, Sugar first became aware that Venables was borrowing the money.

Ashby had told Sugar that Venables had £3 million to invest, but now Ashby was having to explain a delay in Venables' money materialising; until it did Sugar bankrolled the entire deal. In hindsight, Sugar admits that he was 'naive' to have believed that it was Venables' own money. He recalls his feelings on the night: 'I've been out there performing in true Sugar fashion, banging my hands on the table with the lawyers from Scholar, other lawyers, and throwing the lawyers from Maxwell out, and generally saying this deal is going ahead tonight and we've got the money and let's get on with it. And Ashby calls me to one side casually and says there's a hitch. So, consequently, what I had to do was fork out all the money on the night, on the promise that it would be here tomorrow, his half of it anyway. As it transpired, it did turn up ten days later. I know it might sound stupid, but it was the first time that it really dawned upon me that he was borrowing the money.'

Both men initially held 17.8 percent of the shares in Tottenham. Sugar had bought them through his private company Amshold Limited, and Venables through his company Edennote, controlled and owned by him. Edennote plc had begun its life on 5 March 1991 as an off-the-shelf company designed for the specific purpose of buying shares in Tottenham. Larry Gillick, the Scottish businessman who was Venables' first partner in the attempt to take control of the club, was appointed a director on 12 March. Two months later, with the Gillick deal having fallen apart, he resigned as a director on 17 May. He was succeeded by the late Melvin Jeffrey Pottesman, Venables' solicitor and a partner in Kanter Jules Grangewood, who remained with the company until April 1992. Not surprisingly, Eddie Ashby has been involved in the business too.

But, under City rules, they had to make an offer for the entire company, although Venables and Sugar urged fans not to sell their shares. However, despite their appeal, the two men had to spend another £820,000 on doing so. It was in this original share issue document, published on 3 July 1991 and signed by both Venables and Sugar, that the investors had to declare the full details of their financing. Sugar had no trouble - it was from his own resources. Venables announced that his company Edennote would fund his acquisition of shares in the following way: £1 million was to be provided by Venables to Edennote by way of subordinated debt. This £1 million was from two sources: £750,000 from his own funds and £250,000 from an 'unsecured' loan to Venables from the architect Igai Yawetz. The other £2 million came from a Blackfriars finance company, Norfina, who insisted the loan be repaid 364 days later. (This loan was guaranteed by the Pan Financial Insurance Company, who charged £7,000 for committing to it and a £100,000 premium). Clearly, Venables had stretched his finances to the limit to secure the deal.

However, the problem was to get worse for Venables when it was decided to have a rights issue to raise more funds for the club. This issue took place on 6 December 1991 on a four-for-seven basis. As the merchant bankers would not underwrite the issue, Sugar did so himself with his personal fortune. In total, 5,820,313 shares were available at 125p. Because Venables had few funds available, he took up only 800,000 while Sugar subscribed 3.85 million. As a result, Sugar and family now owned 48 percent of the company while Venables owned just 23 percent. Most of the balance of the shares were held by supporters, though director Tony Berry held about five percent. This meant that the Venables-Sugar equal partnership was now at an end, with Sugar very much in the dominant position. Venables could do nothing about it.

Just how far Venables had overreached himself became

evident when he attempted to refinance the Norfina loan. Norfina agreed a refinancing deal on 9 July 1992 on the basis that Edennote charged 2,361,112 Spurs shares as a first guarantee to Norfina. In other words, Venables had now lost control over these shares. If he failed to repay the money when it was due, Norfina had the right to sell the shares. There was a second charge to Pan Financial which provided insurance facilities as further security for the loan from Norfina. On 10 September 1992, a further 800,000 Spurs shares were charged by Edennote, once again to Norfina and then Pan Financial. The Norfina facility was for one month only. Venables urgently needed new support, as most of his shares were now charged. He was able to do a deal with the Bank of Liechtenstein on 2 October 1992. Security for the new loan was arranged by Edennote with Chubb Insurance and so the Bank of Liechtenstein refinanced the deal. By this new deal, Edennote charged two million Spurs shares to Chubb, who also had authority to take any dividends, plus any of Venables' income paid into Edennote.

Clearly, Venables was having great difficulty in holding on to his shares because of the complexity of his loan agreements. If things had deteriorated, he might have had to sell his stake in the club. Indeed, when he finally surrendered his court action against Sugar and sold out, the Bank of Liechtenstein were already pressuring Venables for the money to be repaid.

Initially, however, Sugar had convinced himself that Venables was putting up his own money because in that offer document Venables declared '£750,000 from my own resources'. Sugar says: 'I was pleased as it is a maxim of mine only to do business with people who have invested their own money into a venture. It means they are totally committed.' Sugar, however, was shocked when he discovered the full extent of Venables' borrowings, for they were even greater than was admitted in that issue document of July 1991.

In September 1991, Venables' company Edennote had borrowed £1 million from Landhurst Leasing, the firm run by Ted Bull, who had had negotiations with Scholar in late 1990.

Landhurst Leasing went bankrupt a year later with debts of up to £100 million, according to the receiver, and the company was being investigated by the Serious Fraud Office. The £1 million loaned from Landhurst meant Venables faced quarterly interest repayments of over £55,000, routed through his company Edennote, on top of all the other crippling interest repayments. With high interest rates on his Norfina loan - repayable within one year - it was little wonder that Venables said that all of his £225,000-a-year Spurs salary as chief executive went to pay the interest on his debts.

These problems also explain why Venables was quick to renegotiate his contract so that £150,000 would be paid upfront to Edennote, with the balance of £75,000 as an annual salary, and a 'signing-on' fee of £50,000 to pay off his loan agreed with Irving Scholar when he joined the club as manager. So it was that Venables, through aides like Ashby and Jonathan Crystal, spent much of his time in his first year as chief executive in renegotiating his Norfina loan.

But, in fact, it was the loan from Landhurst Leasing that cast doubts on Venables' reputation and it was this aspect that was highlighted in a damaging investigation by *Panorama*. Venables insists that the Landhurst money was used to buy two pubs, and for other business interests, including paying off creditors from a previous venture involving his former company TransAtlantic Inns, rather than for buying Tottenham shares. Venables says: 'People have made allegations that I didn't put my own money into the club. But I can demonstrate quite clearly that I did, to the tune of, in all businesses I've been involved in, £1.4 million in the last couple of years. I can show that quite easily.'

Venables used one of his former companies, TransAtlantic Inns, to raise money without the knowledge of his fellow directors Paul Kirby, the FA's representative for New Zealand, David Brown and American Colin Wright. According to the *Panorama* programme, 'he decided to cheat' the company which ran three pubs, leasing them from various breweries but owning the fixtures and fittings within. These assets included the bars, tables, chairs and the like.

Venables resigned as a director of TransAtlantic Inns on 28 June 1991, but two months later, in August, he arranged to sell and lease back to Landhurst Leasing the fixtures and fittings of the pubs: Macey's in the West End, the Cock and Magpie in Epping and the Granby Tavern in Reading. For this, Landhurst agreed to pay £1 million - and they deposited the money into Edennote, Venables' private company, not to TransAtlantic Inns. The money came in three tranches, two instalments of £250,000 and a final payment of £500,000.

Two further issues are raised by this deal. First, there is no evidence that the other TransAtlantic directors knew anything of the sale of their assets and, second, they would have been astonished to hear that Venables got £1 million for them. The maximum value of these fixtures and fittings was just over £104,000, although such disparities are not, in fact, unusual in these type of transactions.

Internal Edennote documents show that £800,000 was paid out of the company to Tottenham Hotspur just six days after the Landhurst Leasing money came in. It was this money alone which enabled Venables to keep his part of the bargain with Alan Sugar to purchase the Spurs shares.

Landhurst were paid a £10,000 arrangement fee for this deal, but they also received another perk from Venables. He instructed Spurs' marketing department to provide Landhurst Leasing with an executive box at White Hart Lane for the entire season. Normally, this would have cost Landhurst £20,000. By these dealings, Venables had achieved his ambition to become a controlling partner in Spurs.

But had he committed a fraud to do so?

The *Panorama* programme, broadcast on 4 October 1993, considered that he had. Whether or not their view can be taken as an authoritative assessment, their conclusion stung Venables: 'Terry Venables' decision to sell property he didn't own, at a vastly inflated price, and then put the money into his own company is unlawful. It hurts both the shareholders of TransAtlantic Inns and those of Landhurst Leasing.'

Both TransAtlantic Inns and Landhurst Leasing subsequently went into receivership. Venables threatened to sue *Panorama* and reported the programme to the police, claiming that their allegations were based on stolen documents. These allegations were completely refuted by *Panorama* and the police could find no evidence to substantiate the accusations.

The magazine *Business Age*, in its November 1993 issue, looked into the Landhurst Leasing deal and was even more critical of it than *Panorama*: 'The money was removed from TransAtlantic Inns without the permission of its directors or shareholders. Effectively, it was stolen - which is even more relevant because TransAtlantic Inns subsequently went into liquidation.'

Even before the Landhurst Leasing deal the company was in trouble. In no way was TransAtlantic in a position to have £800,000 'effectively stolen' from its bank account. In the year to March 1990, TransAtlantic's accounts record net assets of £45,000, while the company's overdraft amounted to £100,000. Those accounts were also qualified by its auditors stating 'there is evidence of cash stolen by a manager at one of the units . . . and no independent procedures to verify whether all cash sales were properly recorded.'

At the time of the Landhurst Leasing deal, Venables was no longer a director of TransAtlantic Inns. According to documents filed in Companies House, Venables resigned on 28 June 1991, yet the resignation was only filed on 5 March 1992. This was potentially important, as *Business Age* pointed out: 'The timing of Venables' resignation is significant. Had Venables completed the Landhurst Leasing deal while a director of TransAtlantic Inns, the legal implications are rather different than would be the case had he not been a director of TransAtlantic at the time.'

This was the astonishing financial background to the setting up of 'the dream team', Venables and Sugar. Sugar believed that he had the right partner in Venables for a venture into football, especially as the manager seemed to be putting so much of his own money into Spurs. As he explains: 'I saw Terry Venables as a lot of people see him on your TV screens, as that kind of very wise football man who knows everything about football - very good entrepreneur. I saw him as a man that owned clubs and pubs and made games and had written books and written articles and Barcelona - all this type of thing. So I steamed in, in the normal Alan Sugar way, head first, without any due diligence. And, look, I've only got myself to blame.'

CHAPTER TEN

The Buying and Selling of Paul Gascoigne

GAZZA EPITOMISED all that is brilliant and bewildering about Terry Venables. Venables has a touch of genius in football management, and there is no better illustration of that than his decision to sign Paul Gascoigne from Newcastle United. He was not George Graham's type of player, for the Arsenal manager had the chance to buy him at a time when the price was only £800,000. Gascoigne was ready to move to a bigger club, for Newcastle were going nowhere other than the Second Division when an approach was made to Arsenal to see if they wanted him. Later, it became a three-club chase for a player who had grown in stature.

But Gascoigne chose Tottenham, and undoubtedly one of the main reasons for his decision to go to the North London club was Venables. Mel Stein, Gascoigne's adviser and confidant, may not get on with Venables, but says: 'It is a fair comment that Gazza was immediately impressed by Terry when they first met in my office to talk about a move to Spurs and that he liked him.'

Although Venables knew he was signing a potentially great player, even he could not have predicted the way in which Gascoigne became a national hero during the World Cup finals in 1990 - a status that was confirmed when he shed a tear on receiving a second booking in the competition in the semi-final against Germany, a booking that would have kept him out of the final if England had won the penalty shoot-out. Not only was he a hero, he was also the highest-valued player to emerge from Italia '90 - and Tottenham had to cash in when their debts mounted.

At the beginning of his Spurs career, however, the fans felt more like wincing in embarrassment as Gascoigne was taunted as 'Fat Boy'. Venables had gambled hugely in spending £2 million of Tottenham's money on the 21-year-old, but he helped to transform him into a £10 million wonder boy. Stein insists that the role of his client in this was the vital factor: 'Paul is a genius and didn't really need Terry or anybody else to bring that out in him. However, he did need careful handling and Terry provided that . . . most of the time.'

But, below the surface, was a murky world of finance surrounding Gascoigne, the club's most saleable asset, from the moment he arrived to the day he left. He had initially earned a modest £225-a-week at St James' Park, but Newcastle offered to up his £12,000-a-year salary to £100,000 in an effort to keep him. However, Tottenham were to pay him £130,000 annual salary. The club tied him to White Hart Lane with a five-year contract, but enticed him to the south, rather than to Old Trafford, with the charisma of Venables and the benefits of two house deals.

Venables was determined to enhance his reputation, building on his success at Barcelona - and to do this he urgently needed to cement his position as heir apparent to Bobby Robson with his first major trophy in English football. Tottenham were undoubtedly going through a transitional period when Venables succeeded David Pleat in November 1987 having gone through seven games without a win beforehand. Venables returned to White Hart Lane as the man who could solve the club's problems, but after going out of the FA Cup at Port Vale in the fourth round, he boldly announced that he planned to take Tottenham back to the top immediately, and began a spending spree on new players to fill the seven gaps Scholar had left in the team when he had first met up with Venables in the United States. Some of his early purchases surprised people, but having spent three years out of the country with Barcelona meant he had to rely on advice. It often backfired, as can be seen by the fact that he signed three goalkeepers in a short period of time.

Scholar, meanwhile, was concerned about Venables pushing up the club's wage bill. We have already seen how he objected to the high salary that was given to Terry Fenwick. It was, he commented: 'A development that made me extremely nervous.'

Scholar describes Venables as a 'hands-on manager' who, as a rule, took the players and their advisers/agents to the Royal Garden Hotel, not far from Scribes, or the Royal Lancaster to discuss terms (ironically where he discussed his England contract with Graham Kelly). Venables would take the agreement to club secretary Peter Barnes for authorisation. Scholar would not always agree with the terms resulting from Venables' negotiations, but explained that there was precious little he could do about it. Once a player had been told he would receive a certain remuneration, he was unlikely to agree to a renewed offer that was less than Venables had arranged.

One such occasion came during the negotiations to sign Coventry City star Steve Sedgley, who joined the club for £750,000 in July 1989. The England Under-21 player was then earning £25,000 a year, and Venables told Scholar he would like to offer him £50,000. Scholar suggested that he should aim for £45,000, and so was horrified when Venables contacted him later in the day to announce that they'd agreed a deal at £75,000. Scholar was livid, but there was nothing he was prepared to do about it. Venables' expensive approach to negotiations damaged the relationship between the two men, as did some of the fringe benefits he offered.

The Saturday prior to the devastating FA Cup defeat at Port Vale, Spurs played at St James' Park on a very heavy pitch. Tottenham had been watching Gascoigne for a long time, although his predecessor David Pleat was lukewarm about buying him. Now Gascoigne was up against Spurs, with Venables in the perfect position to assess him.

Venables was friendly with Jackie Milburn, who was convinced Gascoigne was going to become 'one of the best players in the world'. Milburn raved about this player to Venables and recommended that he should sign him.

Scholar recalls: 'At one moment in the first half Gascoigne collected the ball just on the arc of the centre circle in his own half and strode forward. Fenwick went in very forcibly to try and dispossess him, but Gascoigne, with just a shrug of the hips, shook him off and Fenwick literally bounced off him. Newcastle were rebuilding a certain part of the ground at that time, and we were standing in a large Portakabin by the corner flag with the windows slightly steamed up. As Fenwick bounced off Gascoigne, Terry and I looked round at each other. We didn't need to say anything, our eyes did the talking. Terry was astonished at the sheer power and strength of a player who was still only 20, and I am convinced that at that moment Terry decided that Gascoigne was the signing that we both felt the club badly needed.'

After the end of the season the directors met with Venables over dinner to discuss the manager's requirements for the new season. Venables named Gascoigne as his number one priority. He also needed a centre-forward, with Mark Hateley of Monaco at the top of his list, followed by Paul Stewart at Manchester City, whom he had liked when, as QPR manager, he first saw him play for Blackpool.

Gascoigne's 21st birthday fell on 27 May 1988, and Newcastle's then vice-chairman, Gordon McKeag, demanded a £2.5 million fee for him, but Scholar was sure Tottenham could negotiate the price down to around £2 million. Competition was tough, but Scholar had a trump card in Venables. He says: 'While the race for Gascoigne was tight, there were other things going for us. I knew Terry had an ability second to none to cajole players into signing. He always looked after them afterwards, and his ex-players have always remained very loyal to him - a highly commendable quality.'

Scholar negotiated the fee with McKeag, while Venables spoke to Waddle, who was in Newcastle at the time. On the Sunday morning, Waddle took his Geordie pal for a drink in a local pub and spent more than an hour trying to persuade him that Tottenham was the right club for him. As Venables was on holiday, Scholar met Gascoigne with Allan Harris, Venables' assistant, also present to discuss the footballing aspects.

Stein made no secret that Gascoigne's preference was to

go to Liverpool, but the Anfield club were unable to make a proper move for him. Instead, Stein suggested there should be a condition of the contract that if Liverpool came in at any later date Spurs would agree to release the player. This sort of deal is prevalent in Italy, where a big club 'parks' a potentially top-class performer with a smaller one for their own convenience; for example, Michael Laudrup signed for Juventus, but played a couple of years at Lazio before moving to Juve. Scholar resolutely refused to agree to this arrangement.

Gascoigne was understandably hesitant about Spurs, because the team had finished 13th in the league, five places below Newcastle, and had been knocked out of the Cup by Third Division Port Vale. But Gascoigne opted for Tottenham and, with Venables still on holiday, Scholar presented the new recruit with a fishing rod! Scholar then rang Venables in the States, where he had been waiting patiently by the phone. Scholar recalls: 'I said we had a slight problem. He sounded very nervous. I said: "It's not an easy problem to overcome, but only you can make the final decision as to whether or not you agree to the particular condition he is insisting upon." Terry said: "Yes, yes. What is it?" I replied: "Gascoigne says the only way he will sign is if I play upfront with him in the same team." Terry suddenly realised that his leg was being pulled for a change, and shouted down the telephone: "Just tell him the deal is off!" and burst out laughing. Terry was absolutely delighted and it was left that we would meet again on Thursday morning at Mel Stein's office in Park Street, Mayfair, to sign all the final documentation.'

To sign the best around, Tottenham had to concede the 'right' financial inducements. There had already been a few loan arrangements at the club, without notifying the Football League, prior to Gascoigne's arrival. Gascoigne benefited in the same way - after all he was briefly the costliest player in British football when he signed for Spurs, although the tag did not last long, as Everton signed Tony Cottee for £2,050,000 from West Ham United. While Cottee struggled to justify his price, under Venables' guidance Gascoigne more than quadrupled his value.

While it was Scholar's philosophy that to create a happy dressing room it was important there should be as much equality in salaries among the stars as possible, because he didn't want any 'poor relations in the dressing rooms', he knew that the differences in house prices between Newcastle and London were vast and that Gascoigne would need some help to sort it out. Because the Spurs chairman shared Venables' vision that Tottenham should reach the top, he agreed that the club would buy a third of Gascoigne's new home near the training ground, thus enabling the new recruit to negotiate a mortgage. The club also agreed a £30,000 loan for Gascoigne to fulfil his wish to purchase a house in Newcastle as a gift for his parents. Scholar admits that these two loan arrangements were made.

Stein neither admits nor denies it. Speaking of loans in general, he says: 'It is not our concern whether or not these payments were declared to the Football League or not. We did not enquire whether they had, because there was no need for us to do so. It had nothing to do with us, only with the club.' In a note from Eddie Ashby dated 31 January 1992 to Brian Fugler, Tottenham's solicitor, these two loans remained outstanding and Spurs had 'conditionally agreed to waive both in favour of Paul.'

The loan to Gascoigne was the latest in a series that had been arranged by Tottenham for their players that were not cleared with the Football League, although the former chairman insists that all these payments were declared to the Inland Revenue. However, when the *Sunday People* broke the story of the irregular payments at Swindon Town, Scholar, now realising the breach of the rules had a potential significance beyond a technicality, decided the time had come to stop such loans. When the Football League subsequently demoted Swindon, he knew he had made the correct decision. Swindon were relegated for being found guilty on 36 counts of irregular payments to players. This belated desire to obey the rules was to have an effect on Gascoigne in 1990.

By 1991, however, given Tottenham's growing debts, the sale of Gascoigne was increasingly inevitable. However, Scholar insisted he would quit if Gascoigne was sold. Jim Gregory, once Venables' chairman at QPR and now the owner of Portsmouth, advised Scholar to sell Gascoigne and save himself. But he was special to Scholar, whose fantasy was that under his regime Tottenham would one day win the European Cup. The reality was that Gascoigne might have to be sold to save the very existence of the club.

Nat Solomon, chairman of the plc, had signed the letter of commission for Dennis Roach to try to sell Gascoigne. Scholar suggested him, even though he knew Roach and Mel Stein were at the time mutually hostile. Roach had become a football agent almost by chance when his son made friends with Johan Cruyff's daughter while on holiday in Spain. The outcome of this meeting was that Roach and Cruyff became friends and Roach ended up representing Cruyff's UK interests. The chance meeting changed Roach's life. He has grown into one of the most powerful agents in Europe, a man who can open doors to some of the biggest clubs on the Continent. Among his most spectacular transfer coups have been Mark Hateley's move to AC Milan, Glenn Hoddle to Monaco, Mark Hughes to Barcelona, Trevor Steven to Marseille, Des Walker to Sampdoria and John Toshack as coach to Real Madrid.

Through his close friendship with Hoddle, and Scholar, Roach had been chosen to renegotiate Waddle's contract at Spurs, but it was then that Marseille made an approach to Tottenham for Waddle. Scholar did not want to sell and so put a high price on his player - he was anxious to see him link up with Lineker and Gascoigne. Eventually, Waddle was sold for £4.25 million, but Roach was not told of this deal until the last minute. Roach was furious with Scholar for keeping him out of the picture and accused him of being 'just like all the rest'. There was a subsequent row when Roach released the true price of £4.25 million, when Spurs wanted to convince their fans that it was £4.5 million.

Scholar was very disappointed at having to sell Waddle and believed Venables could have persuaded him to stay. But Venables had felt the price was too good to resist (his own valuation of Waddle was £2 million), and would fund the purchase of more players. In turn, he became aggrieved with Scholar that he did not get to spend all the money, but Scholar's hands were tied by plc chairman Bobroff because of the club's worsening financial position brought on by building the new stand. Venables never forgave Scholar for going back on his pledge, despite the reasons offered. Lineker, too, was bitterly disappointed by the sale of Waddle, but still forged an exciting partnership with Gascoigne, which was to lead the club to FA Cup glory. In fact, it seemed that as soon as Venables stopped spending and concentrated on getting the best out of what he had got already on the training pitch, he was able to succeed.

Roach commented on how he became involved in the moves to sell Gascoigne: 'I was appointed by Spurs to go into the market and examine the possibilities of selling Paul Gascoigne and Gary Lineker because they knew I had the contacts to go to Italy and find out. I came back with two offers, one from Lazio and the other from Milan. The one from Lazio was superior by a long way. We then contacted Lazio and we had a secret meeting in London with their president and secretary, Irving and myself, at a hotel in London which has never been mentioned or recorded, and that was the first time there was even any interest shown in Gascoigne.' This 'secret' meeting took place at the White House Hotel, just off Euston Road.

Scholar recalls: 'Roach rang me in some excitement to say that Lazio of Rome were very interested and a meeting was arranged the first week of February.' In fact, the meeting took place on 20 February 1991 and Scholar adds: 'I have rarely gone to a football occasion with greater misgivings or lack of interest.' The Lazio delegation was led by their president, Gian Marco Calleri, but Scholar made it clear he was not interested in selling. He was, however, prepared to quote a price: £10 million. Lazio responded with an offer of £5 million.

Scholar insists: 'I said: "Thank you very much for your interest. This is certainly not acceptable to me, but I doubt if the transfer can take place." My feeling was that this would be the end of Lazio. I could turn round and say that their valuation was way below a realistic price, and kill any talk of Gascoigne going. I just did not believe that Midland could force us to sell Gascoigne. The board were nervous that they would appoint an administrator, or put Tottenham into receivership or liquidation, but this just did not make sense.' Scholar argued that although the club owed the Midland £10.5 million, the company had assets of £40 million, as the ground had been valued at £19.5 million and Scholar's 'conservative' estimate of the players' worth was £20 million. In any event, what was in it for Midland if they bust us?'

Despite Scholar's reluctance, moves to sell Gascoigne continued. Roach explains: 'From that [meeting] it developed. Their first offer wasn't enough and negotiations started and I continued in these negotiations. There were probably five or six further meetings in London and Mr Stein was not involved until it became time to negotiate Gascoigne's terms.' Various prices have since been quoted for the valuation of Gascoigne before the FA Cup final. Scholar's view was that: 'Tottenham were to receive £6.7 million, which was less than I had previously been led to expect. I decided to find out what it would take to keep Gascoigne at Spurs.'

Scholar kept on stalling, and it was not until later that he learned that the Midland Bank had made the sale of Gascoigne one of the conditions of agreeing to extend their facility. When Nat Solomon went to Italy for advanced discussions in an effort to conclude the deal and end Spurs' financial crisis, Scholar called him back. Meanwhile, Venables was furious with Scholar for being kept in the dark over the Gascoigne transaction, and became suspicious about Scholar's motives. Scholar had, in fact, no intention of selling Gascoigne but was merely allowing the market to be sounded out. Venables thought it odd that Scholar should announce he would resign if Gascoigne went, and yet still continue to negotiate to sell the player behind the scenes. He questioned Scholar in a *Daily Mail* article by Jeff Powell.

Scholar sued; Venables was the paper's star witness, but Scholar was still awarded £100,000 in damages plus costs.

On the day before the Cup final, as Scholar awaited yet another Venables-inspired bid for his shares, talks were still going on with Stein in a last-ditch effort to keep Gascoigne at Spurs. The club had failed to agree terms with Gascoigne - hardly a surprise as Lazio had offered him a mind-boggling £2 million signing-on fee, to be paid immediately, and a £1.3 million-a-year salary, plus extras. If he was to stay, Tottenham had to match Lazio's signing-on fee, with a hefty salary on top of that. This was clearly beyond Tottenham's capabilities, so Solomon was anxious for Gascoigne to sign for Lazio that morning in his office. Neither Scholar nor Gascoigne wanted the deal to be concluded then, because they wanted him to concentrate on the most important game of his young life.

What was to happen the next day was to throw the whole deal into confusion. According to both BBC commentator John Motson, who had interviewed the players beforehand, and Mel Stein, Venables had got Gascoigne hyped up. Stein recalls: 'Terry told him to "get stuck in", and that is about the worst kind of thing you can say to a young lad like Gazza on the day of the FA Cup final.' No one could have predicted the consequences of that advice: Gascoigne was in hospital and the transfer deal hung in the balance. Soon after, the future of the club seemed to be secure as both Maxwell and the Venables-Sugar partnership put in their bids. Scholar felt this opened the possibility of Tottenham forcing Gascoigne to see out his contract. He recalled what happened next in his book, *Behind Closed Doors*: 'I had just walked into the room when Nat [Solomon] came running over to me, holding a piece of paper. He said: "Irving, look at this". It was a proposal by Terry Venables and Alan Sugar, but Nat was pointing to a clause in the proposal and I read it with absolute incredulity. It said that the Sugar-Venables offer was conditional on the sale of Paul Gascoigne for a figure of not less than £4.5 million.

'After I had recovered from my shock I started laughing. For months now there had been any number of stories in the press as to how keen Terry was to keep Gascoigne at White Hart Lane, how if he was allowed to take over the club Gascoigne would actually remain at White Hart Lane, and he would do everything in his power to make sure he did. I was painted as the villain of the piece, the man who said he wanted to keep Gascoigne but was secretly planning to sell him. In contrast Maxwell had made it clear to Nat that he would be very unhappy if Gascoigne were sold.'

At the board meeting of 6 June, Scholar recalls that Lazio's lawyers were examining an agreement produced by Ashurst Morris Crisp which would mean that Lazio would pay for Gascoigne at once and the money would remain there, with the interest going to Spurs, until Gascoigne recovered. Tottenham would have 'something like £5.3 or £5.4 million in its bank'. If he did not recover, then Lazio would have the initial sum returned. Not long after, a new Venables-Sugar bid arrived, this time with no reference to Gascoigne. Scholar is certain that Venables had realised just how damaging the publicity would be if the news leaked that he had insisted on selling the player he had previously said he would try to keep at all costs.

Indeed, although Tottenham's precarious financial position was well-known at the time, what is often overlooked is that the plc chairman Nat Solomon publicly stated the club did not need to be rescued once the Midland Bank had extended their loan facility for a further 12 months. In theory, Gascoigne did not need to be sold, for the time being at least. However, the amount of money on offer from Lazio had become too tempting. His departure instantly turned financial uncertainty into a success story, especially when combined with Sugar's millions.

With Venables and Sugar now installed at Tottenham, Venables decided that he wanted to remove Dennis Roach from the negotiations, thus breaking the contractual arrangement whereby Roach would receive one percent of any transfer up to £7 million, 1.5 percent thereafter. In total, Roach could have claimed £64,400 commission on the £5.5 million transfer, but instead he agreed to £27,500 on 12 September as 'full and final settlement'. This then cleared the way for Gino Santin, a London-based restaurateur, to become the agent for the deal. He was ultimately to receive an astonishing £200,000 for his services.

When Roach discovered how much Santin had been paid, he was furious. Not the least of his reasons was that he had once acted for Venables, and maintained strong links with the new Tottenham chief executive. Roach had bought three houses, at £325,000 each, on behalf of three clients: 3 Oxford Gate, Brook Green, was bought in the name of Glenn Hoddle while he was playing for Monaco in 1987. A second - 4 Oxford Gate - went to Mark Hughes shortly after he moved to Barcelona from Manchester United. And a third in the row - 5 Oxford Gate - went to Mark Hateley after he started playing for Monaco. A fourth house - 6 Oxford Gate - went to Venables, when he was manager of Barcelona - although Roach says Venables bought the house independently. Roach had acted for all three players during their recent transfers, and he also represented Barcelona while Venables was there. Roach pointed out that the houses were all investments. He explained: 'You have to lock some money away for these boys, otherwise they will spend it all.' In an interview with the *Daily Mirror* in 1986, he said he would never see his clients broke - unlike earlier soccer stars such as Tommy Lawton. 'Cash should go into pensions and safe investments. Where is the point in signing for £50,000-a-year when 60 percent will go in tax?' Venables bought his house on 10 July 1987 through Roach's solicitors, and just over three years later raised a £235,000 mortgage against the property.

Given Roach's vast experience of international transfer dealings, as well as these personal links with Venables, it was very curious that Venables should drop him for Santin, a man with much less experience in the football transfer market - especially as Santin was eventually to present Tottenham with such a large invoice. This cited work carried out by the Anglo-European market research & consultancy Company regarding the transfer of Paul Gascoigne. The £200,000 requested was to be sent to a PO Box number in Zurich [see document 1, page 331].

The invoice was sent on 2 September 1992 and, five days later, on the insistence of Venables, Sugar and finance director Colin Sandy signed the cheque. However, it was not long before the club issued a statement: 'Mr Santin's involvement in the transfer of Paul Gascoigne is now a matter on which the board is refocusing its attention.' The reason for this change of heart was that it was not clear how Santin had earned this money, nor whether it was justified. Clearly, there could also be concern over the fact that the money was not sent to Santin's up-market restaurant in Belgravia, or to his home address, but to a PO Box in Switzerland. Sugar now suspects he was taken for a ride, especially as the cheque was made out to cash, guaranteed by Credit Suisse. Still more unusually, the address to which the cheque was sent actually belongs to another company, Commercial Treuhand, which acts as a mailing address for others. Perhaps it was not surprising that Santin looked so nervous when he was quizzed about it on television, commenting: 'I was advised by my accountant to set it up to allow me to do similar deals.'

Claims that Santin's knowledge of the Italian football scene and language were crucial to the deal can, in part at least, be refuted, because when Nat Solomon was involved in the negotiations he did not need to speak Italian, as the Lazio general manager spoke perfect English.

Venables explained at a Tottenham Hotspur plc board meeting that Santin had to be paid or the deal was in danger of collapse. He told his colleagues: 'He went to Italy several times. He knew all the right people there and persuaded them to raise the offer to £5.5 million. Gino made all the difference.' Part of the invoice referred to 'legal advice', yet Santin has no legal expertise, and unless he sought advice from an Italian lawyer, as Spurs had Jonathan Crystal on the board, that part was particularly hard to justify.

However, the real key to why Venables justified, and

continues to justify, the payment is contained in his comment that Santin 'persuaded them to raise the offer to £5.5 million'. According to Venables, the original price, before Santin skilfully increased it, was £4.8 million. It was that claim, accepted by the Tottenham board, that finally persuaded them to agree to the payment. But, since the sacking of Venables as chief executive and the subsequent court showdown, Spurs have conducted a thorough internal probe into all invoices. In so doing, they were astonished to find that a solicitor's letter exists, dated 20 June 1991 - well before Santin's involvement in the deal - confirming that Lazio had already offered £5.5 million [see document 2, page 332].

This letter, from Lazio's London solicitors Allen & Overy, to the lawyers representing Tottenham at that time, Ashurst Morris Crisp, is a vital, illuminating, and mysterious item. It was sent at 12.26pm by John Campion, from Lazio's lawyers, to James Perry, representing Spurs. It reads:

> In view of difficulty in achieving satisfactory insurance arrangements, our client requires that the fitness test to be taken by the player will be along the lines of the draft 'perfor[m]ance warranty' which has been previously faxed to you. On this basis the client would be prepared to pay a price of £5.5 million. I should be grateful if you could obtain your client's instructions on this proposal.

That fax was copied by Ashurst Morris Crisp as for Irving Scholar and the then Tottenham Hotspur plc chairman Nat Solomon. Scholar left for his Monte Carlo home the following day feeling totally frustrated and weary, as the sale of his shares and those of Paul Bobroff was due to go through, and give the Venables-Sugar partnership control of the club. The fax had arrived a day before the takeover and may well have been temporarily overlooked in the confusion and emotion of the big event. Indeed, as Sugar put it: 'Terry should have gone to the club lawyers for any information he wanted.'

Venables said: 'Scholar had been dealing with the transfer, so I presumed he knew what was going on.' Venables claims that Scholar never replied to three requests for his Tottenham files, specifically those relating to the Gascoigne transfer. However, Scholar disputes Venables' version: 'I went abroad, but two or three months later I handed over my Tottenham files through my solicitor Peter Robinson. I received a bland letter from Jonathan Crystal requesting the files, there was no specific reference to Gascoigne.' And Scholar's secretary, Paula, confirmed: 'We first received a letter from Terry on 4 July, but Irving was on a world tour at the time and we wrote back on 8 July saying that Irving would deal with it when he returned. Then Crystal wrote on 14 September that he was disappointed that we had not responded. I sent him on 17 September a copy of the letter we sent to Terry Venables, and suggested that he contacted Irving to make arrangements for a driver to collect the files. Once Irving got back the files were sent via Peter Robinson at Berwin Leighton to Terry's solicitors Fugler's on 28 September, and I can only assume arrangements were made by Crystal or Terry for their collection.'

Sugar had no intimate knowledge of the complex Gascoigne transaction prior to his arrival at the club, while Venables had been largely excluded from the negotiations before the takeover. However, in his new role as chief executive, one of the priorities for Venables should have been to acquaint himself with the latest stage of the deal. Had he done so he would have found the letter from Lazio's lawyers. Certain Spurs directors feel that he made only a scant reconnaissance of the previous detailed negotiations, preferring to do it his way. And his way alone, for he wanted Sugar out of the picture to establish, right at the outset, his philosophy of the partnership - that he was running all aspects of the football side of the company.

There have been attempts to cast doubts on the validity of the faxed letter. Some have even suggested that it didn't actually exist at that time, and was only produced 'like a rabbit out of the hat' to discredit Venables in the two television documentaries in autumn 1993 which highlighted this transaction. Paul Foot, in *Private Eye*, posed the question 'was the letter a fake or a mistake?' Foot approached Britain's biggest solicitors firm Allen & Overy to ask whether it was 'in any way a forgery'. He felt that a section of the media had rushed to judge Venables 'with documents provided exclusively by supporters of one side of the argument'. Certainly the figure of £5.5 million quoted in June cannot stand by itself without an understanding of the circumstances in which it arose and, in particular, of the fitness warranty which the Italians would have required.

Jeff Powell, in the *Daily Mail*, a close personal friend and confidant of Venables, raised the same issue when he wrote on 9 October 1993: 'Venables has also instituted a legal investigation into *Panorama's* sudden production of a solicitor's letter claiming that the price for Gascoigne had been set at £5.5 million as early as 20 June 1991, by extraordinary coincidence the day before he and Sugar completed their Spurs takeover. Seen in chronological sequence with several other key documents, Venables insists that the *Panorama* letter - previously unknown to him and apparently a surprise also to Sugar and which preceding Tottenham plc chairman Nat Solomon appears unable to verify - is mysterious in the extreme.' But the letter should not have been a mystery to the *Daily Mail* in particular, for their lawyers had sight of the letter a year prior to the controversy as part of the libel action successfully brought by Scholar against the Mail and Powell for an article, ironically over Gascoigne. Scholar was awarded damages of £100,000, plus costs, despite the fact that the chief witness for the defence was Venables.

Clearly, then, there can be no valid argument that the letter did not exist on 20 June 1991. This, however, does not mean that Venables, or his ally Powell, ever saw it. But Venables should have seen it so that he could be clear as to what had been proposed.

Venables also gained support from the *Sunday People*, and Brian Glanville in particular. Glanville prides himself on his reputation for exposing corruption in Italian football, yet the vastly experienced and respected columnist, having spent 90 minutes with Venables in Scribes West, wrote on 3 October: 'I left convinced that, in the immortal words of Al Jolson, we ain't seen nothing yet. Venables came across as a bitter man, more sinned against than sinning, and comprehensively outmanoeuvred. "Alan Sugar said to people he'd dance on my grave," he said. "And he's done it." ' Sugar vehemently denied making this last comment, saying: 'I never, ever said this and this is not from my vocabulary. Venables has made it up or heard it from someone else.'

The core of Glanville's article was Venables' determination to justify the £200,000 payment to Santin. As Glanville wrote: 'Santin himself is said to be incensed by the way he's been slurred and is determined to prove his point with chapter and verse. At the moment, you pays your money and you takes your choice. I know that I've made mine.' He then produced a letter from Lazio, which he claimed vindicated Venables, but it was far from conclusive in doing so.

After his article, Glanville received a letter, written on 6 October, from Sugar in which he explained that the payment of £200,000 to Santin had gone through in the normal way. He continued: 'I was asked to participate in the Channel 4 programme and approximately three or four days before its transmission, the producers of the programme made me aware for the first time of the existence of a letter from Lazio's lawyers to Ashurst Morris Crisp [the lawyers acting for Tottenham] which indicated that Lazio were prepared to pay £5.5 million. This letter was dated 20 June 1991, one day before the completion of the Sugar-Venables takeover of Tottenham. This information shocked me and led me to ask my staff to carry out a full investigation into the Gascoigne transfer.'

Sugar concluded: 'I would like to say at this juncture that Tottenham has never accused anybody in relation to this Gascoigne affair of any illegal act, but Tottenham has the absolute right to demand to know what Mr Santin has done for the money that we paid him. Prior to the investigation recently carried out by us and prior to the television programme we sincerely believed Mr Venables. We have the absolute right to check into these matters . . . the only person that makes the suggestion that some form of impropriety has gone on is Mr Venables himself.'

After the programme had been transmitted, Santin contacted Sugar several times, anxious that his name should be cleared. He wanted Sugar's help to exonerate himself, pointing out that he had papers in his possession which he might pass on to the newspapers. Sugar suggested that he worked with the club's lawyers to solve the problem, and to help with the club's own internal enquiries, but Santin declined to do so.

When, the day after Glanville's article, Sugar was interviewed on the same subject by *Daily Express* writer Charlie Sale, he became concerned by the slant on events put by Sale, so he contacted the newspaper's sports editor, David Emery, saying: 'I was left with the feeling that if Mr Sail [sic] did write an article, it could possibly be that some of the information within it would be inaccurate and potentially damaging . . . The purpose of my letter to you today is merely to ask you to please ensure the accuracy of the contents of any proposed article. Please feel free to contact me if you require any further information.' He then sent Emery a faxed transcript of his conversation with Sale, as well as all the relevant documentation to illustrate his side of Santin's involvement in the Gascoigne deal. But Sale went ahead anyway, claiming that 'Sugar has made [Venables] ill'.

The *Daily Mail* and Jeff Powell were next in the line to support Venables. Powell quoted Venables as saying: 'We've identified more than 80 errors in the *Panorama* programme. They have this reputation for accuracy which I know has been crucial in making a lot of the public wonder whether I'm guilty. But they even talked about me winning the European Cup in my first season at Barcelona when in fact it was the Spanish championship. If they can't get that simple fact right, how about the rest of it?' However, the *Daily Mail* reported how Spurs had lost the 1991 FA Cup final 2-1.

Powell's view was that Venables had been subjected to a

'media witch-hunt ignited by his bitter feud with Alan Sugar'. His article concentrated on the Santin invoice, yet the most damaging aspect of the *Panorama* investigation was the £1 million 'fraud' involving Landhurst Leasing. The article also commented that a writ was 'ready to be served' on *Panorama*. But no writ ever arrived, despite the seriousness of the allegations.

Venables' own interpretation of the question of the Santin invoice was: 'Of course, I realise that the intention of the letter which was fed to Panorama was to make it appear that I had lined my own pockets through Santin. The truth is that I ploughed a great deal of my own money into Tottenham and, thank heavens, I never took so much as a bag of crisps out of the social club, never mind a dodgy penny.' He continued: 'I am convinced there is a conspiracy against me. There has been a lot of criticism also of my financial man, Eddie Ashby, but he is nothing if not meticulously thorough. Thanks to his diligence I have copies of everything.'

Venables' angry defence of Santin is perhaps understandable, because at the first board meeting under the Venables-Sugar regime, 26 June 1991, no one remembers the figure of £5.5 million being mentioned, instead the general understanding was that Lazio had offered £4.825 million. As one member of the board has commented: 'Someone was negligent if it wasn't mentioned.' But the fax certainly explains why Santin was able to get a price of £5.5 million - Lazio had already agreed to pay that sum! What seemed to Venables to be a great achievement was, to Lazio, a reconfirmation.

The fact remains that Sugar had taken Venables on trust in the early part of their relationship and never fully questioned the Santin payment. He does now. Once the fax was produced, he searched through the Tottenham files where it was discovered in the files sent on by the Scholar regime. Santin has tried to justify his enormous fee, pointing to a fax he received during his part in the negotiations where Lazio referred to the fee of £4.8 million. But, perhaps significantly, there is no letterheading to the fax. Similarly, Sugar 'in my ignorance' had sent faxes also referring to the price of £4.8 million.

The chronology of the Gascoigne deal went as follows: in the aftermath of the FA Cup final, Lazio dropped their price for Gascoigne. On 17 June, Lazio's London lawyers sent a fax to Tottenham's lawyers, Ashurst Morris Crisp, stating the fee as £4.825 million. One clause of this contract agreed that Tottenham would keep the interest on the payment. Three days later, the fax quoting a fee of £5.5 million was sent. The takeover was then completed on 21 June.

On 26 June, a party from Lazio arrived at the Hyde Park Hotel, hoping to clinch the deal and, according to Venables, there was no mention of the improved £5.5 million offer as the talks revolved around £4.825 million. Venables, in Sugar's absence, threatened to call the transfer off as he felt Spurs could get more money. Spurs director Tony Berry warned Venables: 'Sugar will go mad'.

On 5 July, while Venables was on holiday, Sugar faxed Lazio director Maurizio Mancini saying that if Gascoigne was not fit by 31 May 1992, Lazio would get their £4.825 million back, plus half the interest earned. He wanted to finalise the deal on 10 July. Clearly having heard nothing, Sugar contacted Mancini again on 8 July wanting a decision by 10am the next day and stating that another club had offered £5.5 million, but that Mel Stein was anxious Gascoigne should go to Lazio.

To explain the background for his first involvement in the Gascoigne saga, Sugar points out: 'We had one of our first board meetings with us in control and Venables advised the board that the money on the table at the moment from Lazio was in the region of £4.8 million and the difficulties were in getting them to pay it considering that Gascoigne at the time was injured and, like anybody with half a brain, they are not going to part with money unless they're sure that the goods are in first-class condition.' Sugar explains that his negotiations had nothing to do with the price, which he believed had already been set.

On 10 July Gian Marco Calleri, Lazio president at the time, confirmed the price to be £4.825 million, conveniently, no doubt, forgetting their previous £5.5 million commitment. While on holiday, Venables contacted Sugar telling him to leave the negotiations to him and Santin.

Perhaps the best people to comment on the role of Gino Santin are Lazio, and they are quite specific about Santin's involvement. While they maintain that he kept the deal going at a crucial stage, they also insist he did not raise the original price. Some even claim that the deal could have been jeopardised without him and top Lazio officials have commended Santin on his intermediary skills, but they confirmed that they had already offered, subject to the fitness warranty, a £5.5 million deal on 20 June. Lazio then sent numerous faxes confirming they would pay £4.825 million. But the club's financial director, GianCarlo Guerra, has stated that the 20 June fax was authentic and that the fee could not be increased because it was part of a closed agreement.

While the argument over whether Santin actually increased the basic price of the fee will doubtless continue, Venables took another slant: 'Italian restaurateur Gino Santin did make sure Tottenham earned £1.8 million extra from Paul Gascoigne's departure to Lazio. In the first place, he was instrumental in raising the original fee from £4.8 million to £5.5 million. Secondly, he made sure he got the money upfront, which enabled us to claim £500,000 in interest when Gascoigne made it through the first year. Thirdly, he helped negotiate two matches against Lazio which earned £300,000, plus a £200,000 deal with Sky to screen the first game - Gascoigne's debut in Rome.'

However, a letter of 24 May 1991 from the Tottenham lawyers to Lazio director Maurizio Mancini confirms a 'proposed Agreement relating to the playing of the two friendly matches'. This negotiation had been undertaken by Nat Solomon long before Santin's arrival. Similarly, the £200,000 fee for television rights for the two Tottenham v Lazio games was negotiated by Sugar and Sam Chisholm, Sky's chief executive. Jonathan Crystal completed the contractual formalities - but Santin played no role in this part of the deal. Finally, the deal whereby Tottenham kept the interest, actually worth £470,000, had been part of Solomon's original negotiations.

Santin himself was aware of some internal debate between Venables and Sugar about his involvement. However, Sugar agreed because, he claims, Venables told him that Santin would do it for 'a drink'. He recalls how he'd queried Santin's expertise, which Venables said was good, especially as 'he knows what makes them tick'. Venables explained to Sugar how people liked to do things so as to get involved in the high life of football. 'You won't believe it. I know you're cynical, I know you won't believe it, but people do things for no money.'

At one stage, however, Santin claimed a full five percent of the transfer fee, a figure which came as a shock to Venables also. Sugar says that Venables admitted that he and Santin had not discussed a fee for his services, a point Venables conceded. So it was left to Venables to negotiate a fee with Santin, after the Italian had threatened to scupper the deal. The board minutes of 12 September 1991 state that Venables was 'given authority by the board to negotiate further with Mr Santin. It is hoped that the fee can be limited to approximately £150,000.' Eventually, on 7 September 1992, the invoice for £200,000 was approved, the board having been fully aware of the scale of fees to be expected.

After the *Panorama* programme, which questioned Santin's role in the Gascoigne transfer, his lawyers issued a writ against the BBC. However, with the wealth of evidence outlined in this chapter, while Panorama are defending the proceedings, Santin seems quite prepared to put his position to the court.

Given the catalogue of injuries suffered by Gascoigne since the 1991 FA Cup final, including a shattered kneecap after a nightclub incident, perhaps Tottenham did well to sell him when they did. After comparatively few matches for Lazio, the rumours began to circulate late in 1993 that Gascoigne could be on his way back to England. But, by February, he had made yet another spectacular and successful comeback, coinciding with Venables' appointment as England coach. However, rumours of a return to English football will never be far away. For all concerned, it is to be hoped that the next transfer will be more straightforward.

CHAPTER ELEVEN
Venables and the Agents

HAVING SOLD ONE WORLD CUP star in Paul Gascoigne, Tottenham went on to sell their second, England captain Gary Lineker, to Japanese club Grampus Eight. This deal was to be one of the major causes of the split between Venables and Sugar and, although Lineker played on until the end of 1991-92, it was agreed much earlier and shows just how quickly the mistrust developed between the two partners.

The transfer meant that Venables was confronted with yet another major examination of his managerial skills. It was all very well cashing in on the team's England stars to refinance the company, but the fans would quickly lose their conviction without adequate replacements. He understood that they wanted glory, not balanced books.

Venables urgently needed a goalscorer of repute and, having tried and failed to lure an appropriate striker to the club, Spurs began the 1992-93 season without a recognised goalscorer. Venables wanted Teddy Sheringham, but Brian Clough was proving as elusive as ever.

Venables put out the usual feelers through the club's 'scanner', Ted Buxton, who knew Sheringham from their Millwall days together, to Ron Fenton, Brian Clough's assistant manager. Venables says: 'Ron Fenton suggested a minimum figure of £2 million. About halfway through pre-season training, Sheringham came to London and made contact with me through Graham Smith, a partner with Frank McLintock in First Wave Management.

'I met Sheringham at the Royal Garden Hotel. Sheringham said Nottingham Forest were willing to let him go and he would be interested in joining the club. He then returned to Nottingham. There followed periods of uncertainty during which Nottingham Forest appeared to have changed their minds. We were able to conduct further negotiations. I tried to speak to Brian Clough, but he would never take my calls. I knew that during this period Graham Smith and Frank McLintock were trying to push the deal, because Sheringham had decided he definitely wanted to move.'

Sheringham kicked off the season scoring against Liverpool at the City Ground on the opening day - his only goal for Forest in 1992-93. But Venables persisted and eventually got a striker who, after a five-month spell where nothing much seemed to go right, blossomed into a Golden Boot winner and England international with a transfer value which soared beyond the £2.1 million Spurs paid for him.

Venables explained how he got his man: 'It was not until quite well into the season that the club went ahead with the purchase of Sheringham. By that time, Graham Smith had reverted to me to say that Brian Clough was not going to sell for less than £2.1 million. The reason why the price was pushed up by £100,000 was that Nottingham Forest wanted to get their money back on Sheringham and had overlooked, in initial negotiations, an engagement fee of £100,000 which had been paid for him. I had no direct contact with Brian Clough, since all my negotiations at that time were conducted with Fred Reacher, the chairman of Nottingham Forest. Neither Smith nor McLintock was involved in the negotiation of the transfer fee. Eventually, the fee was finalised between myself and Reacher at £2.1 million. I kept the board informed of what was happening throughout, mainly through Sugar.'

Soccer agent Frank McLintock, who describes himself as a 'sports consultant, TV/radio summariser', makes no pretence about his role in the Sheringham transfer. McLintock has known Venables for 30 years, having played for Leicester City, QPR and Arsenal, captaining the Gunners' double-winning side of 1971 and was club skipper for six years. He also managed Leicester City and Brentford, as well as being assistant manager at Millwall and coach under Venables at QPR.

McLintock says: 'I knew Teddy from our Millwall days. I have only dealt with Brian Clough once and that was when Nottingham Forest wanted Teddy to join them. Clough tried it all when I went up to see him. He even put a bottle of brandy on the table. But I made sure no quick decision was made. Teddy and I stayed overnight to give Teddy time to think things over. He then joined for £2 million.

'In the summer of 1992 I was contacted by Ronnie Fenton, Clough's assistant at Forest. He said Forest were unhappy about certain aspects of Teddy's play, which surprised me greatly.' In his season at Nottingham, he had hit 20 goals (the club's top scorer) in all competitions. It was a strike-rate that justified his high fee.

'I was and still am a great Sheringham fan. Fenton said Forest would be prepared to let him go provided they got their £2 million back. I made discreet enquiries and eventually had Chelsea, Aston Villa and Tottenham keen to sign him. Teddy wanted to go to Spurs, there was no question about that. The transfer fee was tricky. All three clubs were prepared to go to £1.5 million, but Forest weren't remotely interested at that price.

'I kept in touch with Terry Venables and later he agreed to go to £2 million. This took a minimum of three months, but at this stage Teddy was playing well, so it was a good valuation. I got back to Fenton and he then told me: "No, the gaffer's not happy. We want another £100,000."

'I was furious. It was beginning to make me look stupid. Forest wanted the extra £100,000 because they had just had to pay Teddy another signing-on fee for the start of the new season. I contacted Terry and he was furious. He got on to the Forest chairman and finally thrashed out a deal. I feel I've done Tottenham a great service.' It was a fair comment. In 1992-93, Sheringham was the Premier League's leading scorer.

Venables had needed Sheringham desperately, but not desperately enough, he maintains, to provide a sweetener to secure his services. But Frank McLintock submitted a notorious invoice, and took £50,000 in cash, plus VAT, as the transfer was about to be completed.

The invoice, dated 27 August 1992, came from First Wave Management [see document 3, page 333], and was for the attention of Eddie Ashby, who was effectively acting as general manager at the club, even though he was not entitled to be involved in any senior executive role because he was an undischarged bankrupt.

The invoice, number 0053, describes in graphic detail why Frank McLintock was handed £58,750, authorised by the signature of T.F. Venables, and 'received cash with thanks by Frank McLintock 27.8.92'. The invoice reads:

> For the assistance in arranging a distribution and merchandising network on behalf of Tottenham Hotspur Football Club in the United States to include travel and all consultancy work involved in the project.

Clearly, it was a bogus invoice, and was not for the work specified, but in reality for McLintock's involvement in the £2.1 million Sheringham transfer from Forest to Spurs, in which McLintock had played such an important role. What was even more difficult to explain was why such a large sum of money was paid, in cash, just 24 hours before the Sheringham deal went through.

Alan Sugar later revealed where he thought the money had gone. During his High Court battle with Venables, the Spurs chairman's affidavit claimed that Venables had told him that Brian Clough liked a 'bung', although there is no evidence that the £50,000 was passed on to Clough. As with the negotiations to buy Tottenham, Venables and Sugar had significantly different memories as to what had happened, failing to agree even on the non-controversial issues. Sugar believed that Sheringham was unhappy to have left London, while Venables claimed he pursued the transfer for so long because he rated the player so highly.

Whatever the background, Sugar's affidavit explained:

> [Venables] told me that Mr Clough 'likes a bung'. He explained that Mr Clough wished to receive a payment personally for selling Mr Sheringham. I told Mr Venables that it was absolutely out of the question. I had never heard anything like this before and it was certainly not the way Tottenham Hotspur or I would conduct my business. I believed Mr Venables mentioned this to me once more and told me what usually happened in these cases was people would meet Mr Clough in a motorway café somewhere and Mr Clough would be handed a bag full of money. At this I told Mr Venables I did not wish to discuss the matter again, and that he should not even mention it to me again.

Venables' response came in his affidavit:

> The allegation that I told Mr Sugar that Brian Clough 'liked a bung' is untrue. I never used that expression, I have never used those words or words to that effect to Mr Sugar. As to what I am alleged to have said to Mr Sugar about Mr Clough meeting people in motorway cafés to collect his bags of money, that really is a lot of nonsense. I certainly never said any of that to Mr Sugar, he is either making it up or he is repeating something he heard from some other source.

Brian Clough vigorously denied the accusation and challenged Sugar to repeat it outside the privileged confines of the court. Clough said: 'I phoned Rick Parry [Premier League chief executive] at his request and made it absolutely clear that I know of no reason, no reason whatsoever, why Terry Venables should not be made England manager. What reason could there be? Sugar's allegation? Garbage! There was nothing improper about the Sheringham deal, nothing dodgy. A bung? Isn't that something you get from a plumber to stop up the bath? I read about Sugar's claim. All I can say is that my lawyers and I would love him to say it again, only this time beyond the protection of a courtroom, then we would sue. I told Parry there was nothing for the FA to worry about. There was no impropriety. I said the same things in writing, once it's in writing, it's on record for evermore. I ended the letter by saying I hoped they'd employ Venables as England manager - immediately.'

However, perhaps the most unusual and surprising part of the controversy relating to the Sheringham transfer was that the £58,750 should be paid in cash, a point raised by the judge at the hearing. Sugar, Sandy and insiders at Spurs were just as surprised as the judge that the payment had to be made in that fashion. Sugar recalls that shortly after Venables explained that Clough wanted paying, he stumbled across a curious meeting.

'I saw the door closing on what appeared to me to be a secretive meeting held in Venables' office at Tottenham, attended by Venables, Ashby, McLintock and one other person who I could not identify. Afterwards, I queried with £5,000 and drove back to the ground with a security guard by his side. On his return, he handed the money over to financial director Colin Sandy. Shortly after the cash arrived at White Hart Lane, McLintock was handed the money still wrapped up in its package in the offices of Eddie Ashby. He drove off with the money on the front seat of his car. The next day, 28 August, Sheringham was a Spurs player.

Given the widespread unease about dealing with such large sums in cash, it is surprising that Venables denies that he wanted the payment to be in cash, even more so when McLintock insists he didn't request it in cash. Who was so keen for the money to be in cash? McLintock's version is that he was given cash because he had asked Venables for a quick payment after waiting nine months without remuneration for services rendered on behalf of Spurs, but other forms of payment would be just as fast. What was more, he felt uneasy with so much cash and he admitted: 'I felt happier when it was stored safely away.'

He also commented: 'I believe Terry was as surprised as me

when I was paid in cash. I can only assume that there was a misunderstanding between the various parties involved.' Yet, according to Sandy's affidavit, there was no misunderstanding. Ashby insisted on cash only. Sandy commented: 'I did not believe that this could be for a proper purpose.'

McLintock threatened to call off the deal if the money wasn't paid quickly, although he had previously submitted £40,000 in numerous invoices over a period of time (none in cash) for precisely the same sort of deals and had been paid without delay ever since being 'signed up' by Venables on 6 January 1992. He explained: 'Just before the Teddy Sheringham deal was being concluded, I felt it was time to get some money for all our efforts, plus a fee for acting as the go-between for Sheringham.

'I said to Terry: "We don't fancy doing the Sheringham deal until we get paid. We have done everything possible to benefit the club." I have no idea about Tottenham's accounting procedures, but Terry said he would sort it out. I then got a phone call summoning me to White Hart Lane. When I got to the Spurs ground there was a cardboard box containing bank bags. It was £58,750 in cash. I didn't ask for cash, as people seem to suggest. All I wanted was my money and I wasn't going to argue. It was there.'

The next twist in the Sheringham saga came when £8,750 was returned. Venables insists it was because McLintock had been overpaid. He says: 'It was £50,000, including VAT, they paid more, and I went mad with Frank afterwards, which he'll tell you. Frank then took the VAT back, and gave it to Peter Barnes, who put it in the [safe].'

McLintock backs Venables' story: 'Two days later Terry got back to me. He was angry when he realised how much we had invoiced for. I apologised. Graham Smith [McLintock's partner] was in Japan and I didn't see the invoice before it was sent. We had agreed £50,000 inclusive of VAT, but we had invoiced for £50,000 plus VAT. As soon as we saw the error I returned to Tottenham by car and gave the £8,750 cash back to Terry. I made sure Tottenham gave me a receipt' [see document 4, page 334].

This raises yet another question: why was the 'extra' payment returned in cash, and not by cheque? If there was such a huge cashflow problem at First Wave, given the urgency of the request, why hadn't that money been banked straightaway? It seems clear, from McLintock's comments, that the cash was still lying around two days later when Venables rang. Had it been banked, then the relevant bank statements would clear all the doubts about McLintock's role in this. Yet, despite an impassioned plea of innocence in the *London Evening Standard*, there was no such documented evidence to prove conclusively what actually happened to the £50,000.

However, McLintock's partner at First Wave Management for the last four years, Graham Smith, explained during an interview at the company's Biggleswade offices that he and McLintock had split the money between them. McLintock had put his share into an electrical franchise business, while Smith had spent £11,000 of his cash on buying carpets and curtains from shops in St Ives and Charteris in Cambridgeshire. The balance of his money he claims to have used to pay a builder who was working on an extension for his house.

Tim Roberts, the builder, received a total of £28,128 in cash from Smith - a fact that alarmed him so much that he consulted his bank about being paid in this way. He received the money in three payments: £10,625 on 6 May 1992, £7,148 on 18 May and £10,355 on 24 June. Perhaps the most remarkable aspect about these payments was that the last one was made more than two months before McLintock invoiced Tottenham on 27 August. Clearly, then, wherever this money came from, it was not from the Sheringham deal.

Smith is no stranger to controversy, as his company was paid £300,000 when Aston Villa signed the brilliant young goalkeeper Mark Bosnich. Villa and their chairman Doug Ellis, who also happens to be on the FA's finance committee, were charged for making this payment. The club was found guilty and fined £20,000. This precedent has come in useful for Venables during the three-man Premiership enquiry to investigate Venables' and

Tottenham's financial dealings following the various allegations that have arisen since Venables was sacked in May 1993.

Even before the enquiry was over, Premiership chief executive Rick Parry was advising the five-man FA selection committee to choose the next England manager, after Graham Taylor's resignation, as to whether Venables would be indicted. It seems that the Premiership committee will advise the FA not to charge Venables. This was an important issue when Venables was being interviewed for the England post, a meeting that took place at the Football League's London headquarters so as to ensure maximum secrecy.

Meanwhile, the £8,750 VAT payment remained in a sealed envelope in the safe of secretary Peter Barnes, where it stayed by order of Venables, rather than being paid back into the club's client account. Spurs are still searching for satisfactory reasons why this should have been done. Indeed, two weeks after Venables had been sacked as chief executive, and nine months after the Sheringham transfer, Sugar discovered two bundles of cash worth £8,750 in the Spurs safe.

McLintock's comment that the money ended up 'stored safely away' seems surprising. Why was it not put into his company's bank account? Or, if it was deposited in their bank, why has no evidence yet been forthcoming to prove it?

Neither McLintock nor Venables made arrangements to issue a replacement invoice or a credit note so that the correct payment could be recorded in Spurs' accounts. Indeed, Sandy, who had insisted on the VAT invoice in the first place, had no knowledge of the reduced payment until the matter came to court some months later.

However, perhaps the most searching question regarding the whole deal is that if the £50,000 was a genuine payment for the Sheringham transaction, then why did McLintock also get paid by the player as well as by the club?

Sheringham signed a four-year contract worth £125,000 a season, with a £200,000 signing-on fee spread over the duration of the contract, split in four equal portions. He would earn a personal £10,000 bonus if Spurs were to finish in the top five in the table, plus £200-a-game appearance money and a goal bonus of £25,000 each time he tops a total of 22 goals in all competitions. For negotiating this contract and for his services in successfully getting him to Spurs from Forest, McLintock charged Sheringham £5,000 and the star striker paid by cheque. So it would seem that McLintock was paid both by the player and by the club, if one accepts that the £50,000 was not for any third party, which must comprise a conflict of interest for the agent. Did Sheringham and Venables both know about his dual role?

In a similar double role, McLintock openly admits that he arranged for Venables to sign Andy Gray for Spurs. Once again McLintock was paid twice: he invoiced the club for £10,000 plus VAT on 2 March 1992, yet on 24 March Gray's wife Karen withdrew £6,000 from the Halifax Building Society in Croydon. She kept £1,000 for spending, and Gray put £5,000 in cash into a sealed envelope, took it to the Spurs training ground at Mill Hill and presented it to McLintock in payment for his services for the transfer from Crystal Palace to Tottenham.

Venables has made no secret of the fact that he broke FA rules by paying his old pal McLintock a fee for the £2.1 million Sheringham deal, but he maintains that paying soccer agents on transfer deals is 'commonplace in the Premier League'. He argues that FIFA and FA rules are wrong to ban the activities of agents in transfer deals, and that there was nothing untoward in McLintock receiving such a large sum for his part in bringing Sheringham to Spurs.

However, after the accusations of corruption in French football, with the European Cup-holders Marseille in the front line, the FA and the Premier League were alarmed that Venables suggested that a fundamental principle of soccer legislation is being blatantly and often breached. Such payments may be soccer's worst-kept secret, but the FA was not happy to hear them being so openly discussed.

McLintock has since claimed that the original invoice for

£50,000 plus VAT also included much more than the one transfer deal. He explains that this is why there was so much urgency to be paid. Venables agreed: 'This is why we had the £50,000 for the Sheringham deal. That invoice, it was a combination of many other deals; before that we had not paid him. I'd put him off and put off, until the final day and he said, if you don't pay, Teddy don't sign.'

Because the signing of Sheringham has proved so successful, Venables feels totally justified in the deal he did to bring him to Spurs. He reckons Tottenham could now sell him for 'another million' on top of what they paid for him, and that the club had benefited from the signing. Is that an excuse for breaking the rules?

The issue of what happened to the money remains unresolved. McLintock admits to breaking FA rules, admits that he picked up £58,750 in a cardboard box from Tottenham, but he completely denies the money was for Clough. He insists: 'During the High Court cases there were suggestions that this £58,750 was in some way a "bung" to Brian Clough. This is ludicrous. I read somewhere that I was supposed to have met up with Brian Clough at a motorway café. If someone wanted to give any football manager a bung all they'd need to do would be to get a banker's draft, pay it in to their own account and, at a later date, pay the manager a share of the money. This is money we earned. Why should I give some of it to someone else?'

McLintock insists that the £58,750 was for work in connection with a number of transfers, including Paul Stewart's move to Liverpool, Neil Ruddock's from Southampton to Spurs, and Andy Gray's from Crystal Palace to Spurs. He says he even travelled as far afield as Borneo to fix up a match! Yet, McLintock invoiced Spurs separately on many occasions for a number of players' deals, totalling £40,000.

McLintock elaborated on why he deliberately never mentioned the true nature of his services when he submitted invoices to Spurs, notably the one for £50,000 which he now admits was for the Sheringham deal. 'I am not allowed to simply submit a bill for services rendered because that would cause embarrassment to the clubs.'

McLintock says he is trusted by clubs because he can work discreetly on transfer deals. To earn his £50,000 he maintains he worked with Tottenham for 18 months, especially with Venables, and became such a regular at the club that he even had his own parking space. Venables brought him in, he says, to help ensure that Paul Stewart stayed at the club as there were rumours that he was homesick and wanted to return north. For a while, the problem was solved. But, as McLintock recalls, 'within six months, the same problem came up again. This time Terry was worried what the fans would think, so soon after Paul Gascoigne's departure to Italy. He was worried what the reaction would be. So he asked me to take care of the matter for him and to discreetly look for potential buyers. Terry knew I was not the kind of agent who would go straight to the tabloids and start rumours. Secrecy was the absolute key, so I started making discreet enquiries with other clubs to see if I could I quietly arrange a move for Stewart. I was working for the benefit of the player and Tottenham. Manchester United, Aston Villa and Liverpool were the three who expressed immediate interest. Eventually, I put Tottenham in contact with Liverpool and Stewart moved for £2.5 million.'

McLintock's next work was with the signing of Andy Gray from Crystal Palace - a deal for which he was paid both by Tottenham and Gray. The signing of Neil Ruddock from Southampton on 23 July 1992 for £750,000 was another McLintock-inspired deal. Ruddock, a Spurs fan as a boy, was keen to come to Tottenham and knew McLintock from their days at Millwall when the latter was assistant manager. Putting together the deal took three months, including a tribunal, and was another very worthwhile signing by Venables as Ruddock finally fulfilled his potential in his season at the club.

'In addition to these deals, my partner Graham Smith and I have spent nine months travelling to Australia, America, Germany, Holland, Spain and even Borneo on behalf of Tottenham. The cost of all this travel to my company was £69,000 without any guarantee of a return for our time and trouble. I brought over a Russian international for a trial at Spurs and a Yugoslav player, Predrag Radosavlijevic, who for obvious reasons has become known as Precki and now plays for Everton. I paid the air fares and expenses for these players because Tottenham wanted to keep their costs down. They only picked up the hotel bill while the players were having trials. I watched them train at Tottenham, went on the team coach with them for practice matches. I even went to Borneo to fix up a game for Tottenham over there. They get guaranteed crowds of about 25,000 people and there is about £30,000 to be made for clubs bothering to go over there.'

McLintock has listed many other activities he carried out on behalf of Tottenham, not all of which would go down well with the FA, but he insists: 'We have not broken a law of the land, just some outdated Football Association law. But I haven't contravened football's laws either. They don't recognise people like me, so far as I'm concerned I'm outside their jurisdiction.'

FA officials launched an investigation into Spurs' signing of Sheringham as soon as they heard the contents of Sugar's High Court affidavits. Since then they have broadened their brief to include the £5.5 million sale of Paul Gascoigne to Lazio and many other contentious issues. Graham Kelly set up meetings with the chief executive of the Premier League, Rick Parry, and the Football League to look into individual allegations made against Terry Venables. The reason for his concern was that Kelly was determined to enforce FA rule 18 (c) which states:

> 'No payment in respect of the registration or transfer of registration shall be made to an agent.'

So, although McLintock claimed the £58,750 invoice reflected 18 months' work an FA spokesman confirmed that the only money an agent is entitled to 'should be paid by the player for representing his interests'.

Venables' opinion was undoubtedly that, following the loss of Gascoigne at the end of 1990-91 and Lineker after 1991-

92, Tottenham needed to strengthen their squad with quality players. He believed his efforts were in the best interests of the club, even if he had to resort to using agents such as McLintock and Eric Hall to do so. Had these dealings not emerged to haunt him, he might have felt vindicated. Instead, Spurs are still threatened with disciplinary action which could cost them their place in the Premiership.

Venables had a small network of trusted soccer agents. Besides McLintock there was Eric Hall, who describes himself as an 'East-End Jewish hassler' and puffs on a Lord Grade size cigar. His 'calling card' is the motto 'monster, monster' after his answerphone message. Disliked with a passion by fellow agents, he tries to put on a showbiz style having learned his tricks on Tin Pan Alley. By his own admission, his Spurs clients have included Justin Edinburgh, Steve Sedgley, David Howells, Vinny Samways, and former stars like Paul Allen, Paul Walsh, Mark Bowen.

Close friends and associates of Venables have often told him to get rid of Hall as one of his chief aides. But Venables stuck by Hall in the same way he has refused to distance himself from Eddie Ashby. Indeed, it was Hall who organised the press conference at Scribes West the day Venables announced the sale of his shares in Tottenham. With a touch of the comical, Hall opened the door for Venables to face the mass media, TV arc lights and cameras, but he did not appear at first. When Venables did emerge, he told Hall to sit down and keep quiet.

Hall, just like McLintock, claims to be acting in the best interests of the players he represents, yet he too has been paid by both club and player for the same negotiations. As with McLintock, all the invoices he submitted to Spurs are under close scutiny. He says: 'My players are happy. I always get them more than they could do for themselves. What's wrong with that?' But were those same players still happy when they discovered the fact that Hall was being paid by Tottenham for his role in negotiating their salaries?

Hall submitted an invoice for £20,000 plus VAT to Spurs on 26 October 1992 for 'public relations and commercial activities on the Club's behalf. In reality, the invoice was for negotiating contracts for Justin Edinburgh, Paul Moran and John Hendry. Moran and Hendry were to pay Hall £1,000 each, but Hall has yet to receive any payment from them. However, he did get cash in hand from Edinburgh of £5,000. Edinburgh and Moran did not realise that Hall was also claiming payment from the club. Venables wanted to pay Hall £20,000 to convince the three players that the contracts the club were offering were 'substantial and worthwhile'. Perhaps they were and Hall acted honourably, but it would be easy to understand if the players lost faith in the ability of Hall to push up their salaries and improve their conditions when he was also being paid by the company he was negotiating with on their behalf. His dealings raise the same questions that were considered with McLintock.

The reason that the soccer authorities are extremely worried about the activities of agents and have set up regulations against their being paid any money on transfer dealings is that, if they are paid for such dealings, it is in their interests to provoke transfers by making players unsettled at one club and 'touting them' to others. Clearly, such behaviour cannot be in the football clubs' interests as it causes both salaries and transfer fees to escalate. Yet Venables was happy to pay considerable sums to McLintock and Hall. While it would be difficult to find a player in the Premiership who does not have an agent, or one who would agree to a transfer without consulting him, the key question is whether the agent abuses the system and the rules.

Hall has now been banned from Tottenham Hotspur because of his involvement with their players. Yet, Hall concluded in a *Today* article on 21 October 1993: 'I have still dealt with their three recent transfers, involving Paul Allen, Pat Van Den Hauwe and Neil Ruddock. Who doesn't need agents? I have earned around £90,000 from Tottenham in earlier deals when Irving Scholar was the chairman. There were invoices and there was never any trouble. There has never been any trouble. More clubs than ever are ringing me. I don't wait for the phone to ring, I make it ring. They know I do business. I make the poor rich and the rich richer.'

But Tottenham found it necessary to launch a full-scale investigation into all of his dealings with the club after Hall had shot himself in the foot by instigating court proceedings to recover £23,500 when the club refused to pay up. Hall had invoiced the club for that sum, claiming it was for 'public relations and commercial activities' but in reality he was involved in negotiations with a player. When the case came initially before the court on 15 November 1993, one of the arguments raised by Tottenham was that the agreement for payment was illegal. The court agreed that this was arguable and Hall's solicitors wrote to Spurs saying they were discontinuing the action.

Hall had thus lost his fight to be paid, and his court action rebounded as Spurs initiatied a full-scale internal probe into all of his invoices. Tottenham also announced that they would 'vigorously pursue our costs, estimated to be £15,000'. The club is also considering taking action 'to recover substantial sums already paid to his company during that period for alleged services rendered, but for which the company can find absolutely no record.' This referred to the money Hall had received from Tottenham during Venables' period as chief executive.

The most startling aspect of the Tottenham statement, and one that made little impact at the time because of Graham Taylor's resignation as England manager and the constant media interest in who would be his successor, was the reference to the Prevention of Corruption Act. It was the first reference, after so long, to the fact that corruption may have taken place inside White Hart Lane involving Hall and, by implication, Venables himself.

The current Spurs board are deeply concerned about the validity of three invoices worth nearly £50,000, two submitted by Hall, and one from McLintock. They were clearly phoney invoices, at least in this sense: the true nature of the work done was not revealed. These invoices go some way towards explaining the decision of the Tottenham board to dismiss Venables as chief executive.

On 2 June 1993, Tottenham's in-house lawyer, Mr Ireland, wrote to Venables asking for a written explanation of the invoices, and why they were paid:

1. A payment of £20,000 to Eric Hall which you have asked to be paid to him in the last couple of days without further delay.

2. The sum of £10,000 plus VAT to Eric Hall in August/September 1991.

3. The sum of £15,000 plus VAT to Frank McLintock in August/September 1991.

Alan has spoken to Bobroff and Scholar, Ian Gray, Tony Berry and Douglas Alexiou. Those are all people who were directors before the takeover by Mr Sugar and Mr Venables.

None of them know the reasons for payments 2 and 3. Accordingly please ensure that your written explanations are before the Board meeting on Thursday.

Venables received the note on the Tuesday, according to the High Court evidence, while he was 'preparing the final preparation of his evidence' for the case. Venables responded to Sugar's demand for an explanation through his solicitors, who claimed that 'Messrs Sugar and Sandy are privy already to the reasons for the itemised payments.' They believed that the reason Sugar wanted this information so urgently was related to the impending High Court case. That being so 'you ought to first make an allegation. Does Mr Sugar wish to make an allegation in regard to these payments?' They then suggested that a forensic accountant was brought in specifically 'to investigate player transactions'.

Venables' QC promised, before the court, that once the High Court action was over, his client would provide a full explanation, but he clearly did not like being 'harassed' for this information. As yet, however, there has been no satisfactory explanation from Venables. Indeed, there has been no explanation at all.

When the Spurs board did look more closely into the invoices, especially the second and third ones mentioned above, they noticed certain uncanny similarities in the payments to Hall and McLintock. Worth a total of £29,375, they were both submitted after the Venables-Sugar takeover for work done before the change of ownership of the company. And, they had another similarity, apparently: no one in the former regime knew anything about them. Ex-chairman Irving Scholar, ex-chief executive Ian Gray, former directors Nat Solomon and Douglas Alexiou, and ex-merchandising manager Edward Freedman all knew nothing of the work supposedly carried out for them. Indeed, McLintock had never submitted any previous invoices to the former board, nor was he ever approached to do any sort of work for them. Hall's previous dealings were to act on behalf of his extensive stable of Spurs players at that time, and to run the Players' Cup Final Pool of 1991, and he had also submitted at least one similar invoice before the change of ownership, which had been paid. A point which suggests he was not entirely dependent on Venables.

Venables has been asked by the club on a number of occasions to provide detailed reasons in writing for these two invoices. But Venables says: 'They have had them, and they write again, and they've had them from me and my lawyer. I have documentation for all these so-called allegations, which are pathetic.'

Invoice 0001 was submitted by Frank McLintock Sports Management in Winchmore Hill, North London, on 10 September 1991 for £10,000, plus £1,750 VAT. It was marked for the 'attention of Mr T. Venables'. Venables personally signed the invoice and there is a handwritten note 'no VAT number'.

The payment was 'in respect of commercial consultancy carried out on behalf of Tottenham Hotspur FC season 1990-91 to include all expenditure re fax, telex, telephone, travel and accommodation. This consultancy refers to feasibility study carried out on own-brand merchandising and the exploitation of all commercial opportunities at the Club.' In September 1991, no one queried it, but since the boardroom split between Venables and Sugar there has been an internal review of all invoices (some 13,000 in total), and the club became highly suspicious.

Eric Hall's two invoices, as mentioned in the letter of 2 June 1993, also aroused suspicion. Hall had the distinction of being elevated to the title of vice-president at Spurs under the Venables regime, and he had previously run the Players' Cup Final Pool in 1991. However, a handwritten note at the bottom of his invoice [see document 5, page 335], dated 29 August 1991, stressed it was 'nothing to do with Players' Pool'. The fee 'as agreed' was £15,000, plus £2,625 VAT, and was for his work on 'the 1991 FA Cup Final . . . payment due re commercial and public relation activities in connection with the above.' He was paid.

Sugar clearly feels that he has been duped by Venables, and it may surprise many that a top businessman like Sugar could have been caught out. However, initially there was no reason for any suspicion, but it was not long before Sugar became aware that something was wrong. These invoices were part of the reason.

It was Venables who set up the administrative structure at Tottenham once he was installed as chief executive which enabled Hall and McLintock to submit their invoices. He simply brought in all his own men. Chief executive Ian Gray was sacked and replaced by Eddie Ashby, an undischarged bankrupt, who virtually assumed the role of general manager of the club. Ashby had been involved in 43 companies, nearly all of which had failed. He had become Venables' financial guru only after a chance meeting in the Royal Lancaster Hotel.

Gray was contacted by Sugar in June 1993, and Sugar also had a drink with ex-chairman Irving Scholar in a hotel in the south of France as Spurs began their investigation into these invoices. Gray says: 'I was asked if I knew anything about invoices that had been submitted to Tottenham by Frank McLintock and Eric Hall for work allegedly done during the period when I was chief executive, and these invoices had subsequently been approved by Terry Venables. Work of the nature that these invoices described would ordinarily have been discussed at board level and approved in advance. No such authorisation was given for that work, and I doubt if the board, at that time, would have felt it necessary to have that work undertaken.'

McLintock admitted during a television documentary that he was paid money for his services in arranging the Neil Ruddock transfer, and not for the bogus reasons on his invoice. This, he insisted, was why he was paid £10,000. His frankness in admitting breaking FA rules seemed admirable, but his reply raised more questions - not least because Ruddock did not sign for Tottenham until the following summer. Secondly, McLintock had also claimed that his payment at the time of the Sheringham transfer was for the Ruddock deal among many other transfers.

It remains Venables' view that Sugar systematically tried to discredit him to justify the decision to dismiss him. Venables says: 'He has got lorry-loads of lawyers looking for things that he feels may or may not have happened, "may" have happened, "could" have happened. Let's throw the mud, let's see if it sticks. I have had it up to here with it all really.'

Sugar's opinion on these matters is vastly different, as one might expect. However, it is clear that Sugar gave Venables many opportunities to put the club on a regular footing. That is vastly different from Venables' view that he was beaten in a battle of egos by a man who had the financial muscle to ensure that he won. Sugar felt that his chief executive should not be involved with so many shady dealings.

Once Venables was ousted, Hall was stripped of his title as Spurs vice-president, and banned from the club. After possessing a large stable of Tottenham stars, the new boss Ossie Ardiles refused to allow Hall anywhere near the club and certainly did not tolerate him representing any of his players.

Hall remained very active on behalf of Venables during the period when Venables was ousted as chief executive but still remained on the board to fight his court battle for reinstatement. He would wait outside White Hart Lane, intercepting players as they went into the club to see the new manager, Ossie Ardiles. Ardiles could see this from his second-floor office window overlooking the forecourt. The usually unflappable Argentinian was furious, but he has kept a diplomatic silence and has refused to discuss what he considered to be Hall's uncalled-for interference. The situation was made even more complicated because the footballer who had been Hall's first-ever soccer client was Steve Perryman, in 1983. Perryman has become Ardiles' number two. But Hall clearly resented the dismissal of Venables, as his earning capacity within Spurs was bound to be affected.

When Venables was sacked, many Tottenham players were deeply upset because they had developed a great loyalty to him and they did not view Sugar as a true footballing man. One of the most outspoken critics of the sacking was Neil Ruddock, so new manager Ossie Ardiles had a difficult job in trying to agree terms that would keep him at the club. However, his task was made impossible by the behind-the-scenes involvement of Eric Hall, who openly admitted in *Esquire* magazine that he had helped the player to draft his transfer request. This led to further angry confrontations between Sugar and his deposed chief executive Venables, who was still part of the company at this time, and remained on the board.

Sugar sent Venables a memorandum on the subject, dated 23 June 1993 [see document 6, page 336]:

You will have seen in the press that we have not yet finalised negotiations with Neil Ruddock over revisions to his terms of employment. Ossie Ardiles is dealing with this and he thought after his discussions with Ruddock on Monday that terms had been agreed, but then Ruddock called him to demand more. Apparently, Ruddock claims that the offer we have made is less than one he had agreed with you at the end of last season.

In his memorandum to me of 7 June, Peter Barnes stated that you had discussed doubling his salary (from £75,000 to £150,000) and the previously agreed signing-on fee of £50,000 was to stay the same.

Our offer is no less than that.

Could you please confirm that your offer to Ruddock was as I have reported above. It would obviously help Ossie Ardiles in his negotiations if he could say that you have confirmed that and that you believe that Ruddock should accept the offer.

Clearly Sugar was testing Venables' professed continuing loyalty to the club and the company over Ruddock's contract negotiations, especially as the court had ordered that the two warring factions should work together until the issue was finally resolved. But there was little sign of the court's order operating, as was shown when Venables telephoned Sugar the following day at 11.55am, part of which is quoted below:

> Venables: Hello, Alan. I am ringing you in reply to your fax yesterday regarding Neil Ruddock. What you said here is correct. The £75,000 went to £150,000 and the signing-on fee was going to be £50k per year, but we didn't agree that because of the fact it was £200,000 or £250,000, because I was saying I wanted five years and he wanted four. Have you got that?
>
> Sugar: Yeah.
>
> Venables: Are you alright?
>
> Sugar: Yeah, I'm OK. I got it. I would prefer, you know, to have something in writing on this thing really.
>
> Venables: OK that's fine. OK then.

However, Venables failed to live up to his part of the bargain in this conversation. So, when Sugar failed to receive anything in writing as promised, there followed another memo from him to Venables on 25 June 1993:

Further to my memorandum dated 23 June and your telephone conversation with me on 24 June, I enclose a transcript of my understanding of our telephone conversation.

As you are aware, I requested that you confirm to me in writing the arrangements that you had discussed with Mr

Ruddock in the past. Would you please take note of the enclosed transcript and confirm in writing whether you agree with its contents or not.

Just three days later, Sugar was furious at a *Sun* article headline 'Ruddock in rage at £2.8m exit fee', with a sub-heading 'Plea to leave Spurs'. The article claimed that Spurs had put a £2.8 million fee on him (£2 million more than he had cost the club only a year before) to scare off potential buyers when he wanted to leave. It quoted Ruddock as saying: 'I have it in writing I can leave. Alan Sugar has told me I can go if we did not agree terms. Ossie has also come out and said he doesn't want to keep players who aren't happy. I was offered a good contract when Terry Venables was chief executive and then that was withdrawn. So they have gone back on their word once and that means I suppose they can do it again. Yet I hope they allow me to go. I just want to get on with my career.' Hall has subsequently revealed that he was behind this article.

Understandably, Sugar was perturbed about the effect those comments would have on the public perception of the talks. He was particularly upset that Ruddock stated that Spurs had reneged on an agreement over his contract. Sugar fired off another memo to Venables, dated 30 June 1993:

> Further to my previous correspondence with you and our telephone conversation in which you confirmed to me the offer you made to Neil Ruddock whilst you were chief executive, you will see that Mr Ruddock insists on reporting to the newspaper that the offer recently made by the company is not as good as that which you proposed. As you know, this is totally incorrect.
>
> We made Mr Ruddock an offer to increase his salary to £150,000 per year and, in fact, we also agreed to increase his signing-on fee from the current £50,000 per year to £60,000 per year. This means that the offer we have made is in excess

> of that which you made him.
>
> As a non-executive director of the company you will realise it is your duty to have the best interests of the company in mind and I ask you to immediately contact the *Sun* newspaper and ask them to print a retraction of their allegation. Will you please send me as soon as possible a copy of the letter that you will send to the *Sun* newspaper asking them to correct this wrong information.

Venables finally responded to Sugar with a 'private and confidential' fax, undated:

> When I spoke to you last week, I was halfway through explaining the situation relating to this player when you told me you did not wish to discuss the matter further.
>
> You were therefore not aware of the matters I discussed in principle with the player and his father-in-law, and the player's view of his worth to the club.
>
> I am well aware of my responsibilities to the company. I am, however, unable to comment on any offer you have made to the player, because I have been excluded from your discussions with the player, as I have been excluded from decisions you have taken relating to the introduction of Ardiles and the dismissal of staff.
>
> I certainly do not consider it in the best interests of the company to correspond with the Sun about matters on which I do not fully have the facts.

That same day, Sugar sent Venables yet another fax, in reply to the one received from Venables at 12.51:

> The conversation that you had with me last week has been well documented in a transcript, which

you have been sent. I listened to all that you had to say and when you finished I asked you to put it in writing, which you have not done as yet. In that conversation (as per the transcript), it states that you agree with my memo dated 23 June which outlined the broad terms offered by you of £150,000 per annum salary and a £50,000 signing-on fee. You said that the only disagreement that you had was that you wanted a five-year period and he wanted a four-year period. Apart from this, you have advised me of no other offers that you have made to the player.

On the basis of this, the offer which I have advised you in my memo dated 30 June is indeed £10,000 per year higher than you had discussed. It is therefore definitely in the best interests of the company that you correspond immediately with the Sun newspaper about these facts. The facts are that you have confirmed that you offered Mr Ruddock £150,000 per year as well as a £50,000 signing-on fee. The company has since offered Mr Ruddock £150,000 a year plus a £60,000 signing-on fee and, therefore, the article printed in Monday's edition of the Sun (28 June) where it states the Mr Ruddock was ' . . .offered a good contract when Terry Venables was Chief Executive and then that was withdrawn. So they have gone back on their word,' is absolutely inaccurate and you have the facts available to you to inform the Sun newspaper of this.

Once again, I ask you, in your capacity as a non-executive director of the company, to ask the Sun to correct their mistakes. Will you please send me as soon as possible a copy of the letter that you will send to the *Sun* newspaper correcting this wrong.

Sugar did not get what he wanted, as Venables refused to budge on this issue. Indeed, the debate even sparked another disagreement when Sugar noticed that faxes from Venables had been written at Crystal's chambers - Venables perhaps having decided it was better to have a legal mind behind his replies. When confronted about this by Sugar, Venables replied: 'I wrote these memos, not Eddie.' But that was not the suggestion in the first place.

Ruddock, however, took the unusual step of writing to the club chairman. Sugar received a handwritten letter from Neil Ruddock from his Hornchurch home address, dated 1 July 1993. In the letter Ruddock denied that Ossie Ardiles could ever have been under the impression that he had agreed terms with him, as stated in Sugar's memo of 23 June, for when 'our negotiations on 21 June broke up I told Mr Ardiles that I would discuss the situation with my wife and then give him my answer. I did 3 hours later in a phone call to Mr Ardiles, my answer was I would not be signing.'

Ruddock insisted that the accusation he had 'demanded more' was a 'complete fabrication'. He stated that the offer of a pay increase from £75,000 a year to £150,000 a year, plus £50,000 a year signing-on fee had been 'subsequently rejected' and further discussions took place at which 'a new agreement was reached in principle'. There is no record as to what this was.

Even the increase in the signing-on fee to £60,000 per year did not satisfy Ruddock. He commented: 'I told you that I had lost £50,000 in removal and relocation expenses when I moved to Tottenham. You told me to write down what I had lost and you would make sure I was not out of pocket. It now transpires that you are not proposing to reimburse me but to increase my signing-on fee by £10,000 a year over 4 years on which I would pay 40 percent income tax, which means in effect I will only be recouping £24,000 after this loss. To add insult to injury you are now trying to portray this as a wage increase.'

These comments, from a man who had earned £125,000 in his first year at the club and was now being offered a total of

£210,000 a year, as well as claiming £50,000 removal expenses a year on, might not be seen by Tottenham fans as adding 'insult to injury'. He ended his letter by querying his transfer valuation of £2.8 million when his contract offer was so low.

When the Tottenham board next met, on 8 July, it was agreed by all directors to tape the meeting. When they came to discuss the Ruddock situation, Venables commented on the fact that the telephone conversation with Sugar on 24 June had been taped. The transcript of this part of the meeting is quoted below:

> Venables: I didn't finish this conversation [of 24 June], You since sent a letter explaining what I said. Now it was taped that call, and I didn't know that. I was then told.
>
> Sugar: I don't know how . . . Who told you it was taped?
>
> Venables: You sent me a transcript.
>
> Sugar: That doesn't mean it was taped.
>
> Venables: You said it was taped.
>
> Sugar: No! No! No! Who said it was taped?
>
> Venables: You told me you tape all your phone calls.
>
> Sugar: No, who said that phone call was taped?
>
> Venables: I just assumed it was taped.
>
> Sugar: Ah! You have assumed it was taped.
>
> Venables: Yes . . . Can I, can I just tell you also that I know it was taped because you then played it to Ruddock and his father-in-law.
>
> Sugar: Ah! That's precisely what I want to hear. You've had a further dialogue with Mr Ruddock ...
>
> Venables: Yes. I'm not denying anything. His father-in-law rang me and he said that you played him a

> tape without my permission. You showed him a fax of mine which had private and confidential on. Yes or no?

The conversation then continued with Venables recalling how his initial offer had been £100,000 plus a signing-on fee of £50,000, but he ended up increasing the salary to £150,000. The whole tone of what was said clearly reflects the mutual hostility between the two men, and the mistrust.

Neil Ruddock was finally sold to Liverpool for £2.5 million, but he was on the receiving end of a stinging attack from Sugar who publicly branded Liverpool's expensive purchase 'a greedy, money-grabbing wimp'. It was one of the most devastating attacks by a club chairman on one of his former players. He continued: 'Ossie Ardiles used his best endeavours to get Neil Ruddock to stay. Ossie was very, very patient with him. He was even told that he would be a potential future captain. But time and time again he negotiated with Neil Ruddock only for his wife to tell him what to do. That was not the only time I found this big, strapping centre-half to be a wimp. He was shaking in my office when I played him a tape of my conversation with Terry Venables.' However, as Ruddock has pointed out, after watching the *World in Action* programme detailing interest-free loans involving Spurs stars, why should he be accused of being greedy?

Sugar pointed out that this was what annoyed him most: Ruddock had alleged that Tottenham had gone back on their word, yet the taped conversation with Venables clearly disproved this. Sugar explained: 'I got hold of Ruddock and his father-in-law and told them straight that I am not interested in how much he wants to earn, but I did not want him continuing with his claims that we had reneged on any agreement. When I played the tape, Ruddock started shaking like a baby unable to say much at all. He tried to say that he had not made any such claims, but then I handed him a newspaper article with his comments and it was there in black and white. He apologised.'

Despite widespread threats from the players at the time of Venables' sacking, Ruddock has been the only defection since Sugar took sole control of Tottenham. Sugar was convinced that he was the victim of 'sniping' from Venables and Ruddock's agent, Eric Hall, in this matter. He felt that Venables' admission in the board meeting of 8 July that he learned of the taped conversation through Ruddock, combined with his refusal to counter publicly Ruddock's claims in the *Sun*, showed that Venables had ceased to act in the best interests of Tottenham, but was more anxious to discredit Sugar. There can be no doubt that Venables' actions in this issue do him and his reputation no credit. His only excuse can be the deep hurt he felt at having been ousted from the position he had so long worked for.

CHAPTER TWELVE
Venables the Businessman

SCRIBES WEST INTERNATIONAL is Terry Venables' other club - a £600,000 drinking club in the bowels of Barkers, the department store, in High Street Kensington. There is a plaque in the main lounge to commemorate the lavish occasion of its opening: 'Scribes West International. Opened by Prime Minister The Right Honourable Margaret Thatcher FRS, BA, in the presence of Viscount Rothermere. 11th January 1990.' There, in the most stylish of surroundings, the boy from humble Dagenham roots entertains his clientele with renditions of Sinatra songs on a karaoke machine he has installed. Once it was the haunt of Prince Philip and Prince Edward, now Gazza would love it!

At first, it was owned by Geoffrey Van Hay, when Scribes moved from its traditional home opposite the *Daily Mail* in Blackfriars, but it did not prove a financial hit. So, in April 1991, Venables began his involvement to help revive the club. However, despite using Venables' name to attract soccer stars and other big-name celebrities, Scribes continued to lose money. It opened its doors to the white stiletto-heel set, and Venables' second wife, Yvette, became the manageress.

Van Hay, Scribes' managing director, saw Venables as the last chance to ensure the club's survival, as he knew that Venables was keen to expand his own business empire. Van Hay commented: 'Mr Venables saw Scribes as a launching pad in his business world. I think he thought that having such an elegant premises would attract the right people. He loved being Mr Venables, Scribes West International.'

Two senior members of Scribes, Gavin Hans-Hamilton and Noel Botham, soon discovered that Venables wanted to take control of the club. Venables promised to invest £50,000 and appointed Eddie Ashby as finance director. Key Scribes accounts were then moved to the offices of Glenhope Management, the company set up to promote Venables' board game, *The Manager*, which he ran in conjunction with Paul Riviere, a longstanding business associate.

Botham recalled how he was told by Van Hay and Hans-Hamilton that the promised £50,000 had gone, not into the club bank account, but into another account. They believed the money was being paid into that second fund, but could not confirm it because they did not have access to the account details or to the cheque book. So it was that the old guard was swiftly excluded from the financial running of Scribes, which was now handled by Venables and Ashby.

However, during the summer of 1991, the Scribes shareholders were shocked when they received a document that showed the latest development in the business life of their finance director, Eddie Ashby. It announced Ashby's bankruptcy, and Van Hay knew it was illegal to have a bankrupt on the board of a company. Ashby had to resign from the board, but that did not end his involvement with Scribes as he continued to sign cheques and control the finances of the club. It seemed to the old guard that this was done with Venables' consent.

Paul Riviere, another Scribes director brought in by Venables, learned that, despite Scribes' poor financial situation, Ashby had been taking money out of the company to pay the wages of the print company that had been manufacturing *The Manager* board game. Further 'intercompany loans' were made from Glenhope to the printers, in which Ashby had agreed to invest a six-figure sum. By these money transfers, sometimes paid in cash and handed over in lay-bys, Ashby tried to create an illusory business empire and thus raise substantial loans. Perhaps his experience at doing just that was what appealed to Venables when he had to raise £3 million to buy into Spurs.

But Venables had financial headaches with Scribes, as the Ross Benson Diary in the *Daily Express* related on 1 November 1993: 'A cascade of writs have landed on its doormat.' One was for £26,529 for service charges and unpaid rent issued by landlords, the House of Fraser. A spokesman for company owner Mohamed Al-Fayed said: 'We only resort to law with some reluctance. We've been on the point of sending in the bailiffs on several occasions, but each time they settled at the last minute. We've got nothing against Mr Venables, we just wish he'd pay up.' Venables' version of the story was entirely different: 'It's an ongoing argument. They've tried to up my service charge from £6,000 to £56,000 when the rent is only £75,000. There's no justification. I've paid £7,000 over the £6,000 in good faith and I'm fighting the rest.' Yet, at the same time, Venables was also facing legal action from a firm of lawyers, a public relations consultancy he used at the time of his sacking as Tottenham chief executive and throughout his High Court case, plus a drinks company.

It's not surprising that Venables' financial position was a little delicate, to say the least, because of the phenomenal costs in fighting Sugar in the courts, following on from the crippling repayments on the huge loans he had had to take out to buy his stake in Spurs. But Venables always managed to keep his head just above water, paying off his most urgent debts at the last minute.

For this he had to thank his financial adviser, Eddie Moses Ashby, the cornerstone of his most recent business 'empire'. But it was Ashby who was to do as much as anyone to bring about the break-up of the relationship between Venables and Sugar. Indeed, while Ashby seemed to Venables to be doing so much to help him, in fact he was unintentionally leading Venables towards financial disaster. Yet, remarkably, Venables shows a great reluctance to dump Ashby, a constant companion in Scribes before, during and after the Spurs bust-up.

Venables' choice of associates has been criticised by friend and foe alike. A chance meeting between old school chums led Ashby into the path of Venables. Paul Riviere was a close Venables aide, an integral member of the Venables entourage until Ashby arrived on the scene. It was Riviere who brought Ashby and Venables together, yet it was he who ended up as an outsider.

Riviere bumped into Ashby in the Royal Lancaster Hotel, and the former school friends caught up on what had happened to the other in the intervening years. Riviere felt sorry for the out-of-work Ashby and decided to introduce him to Venables. Ashby's influence grew on Venables, particularly as he was involved in setting up the finance for Venables to purchase his shares in Spurs, and he quickly superseded Riviere as Venables' trusted ally and financial adviser.

Riviere and Venables had begun working together in 1989 on the development of a new board game, appropriately called 'The Manager'. It was a diversion for Riviere from his usual work, running a highly successful financial services company selling pensions and other policies. As a football fanatic, he had met Venables and together they had devised their game, which was an attempt to recreate the excitement of running a football club. Perhaps surprisingly, the object of the game was to finish with the most money, not to win the championship. Riviere spent 15 months developing the game and then formed a company to promote it, Glenhope Management. Its two other directors were Ashby and Venables. The game was launched in Harrods before Christmas 1990 and, according to Riviere, 'got off to a very good start'.

He recalls: 'We sold virtually all with the big departmental stores and I think we sold 25,000 by the beginning of the next year, taking into account the Christmas sales, and looked to be running at a pretty good profit.' After working for so long on the project, Riviere was short of money, therefore he decided to make his first substantial withdrawal from the Glenhope bank account.

He says: 'I remember that we thought there was probably about £34,000, but the guy who obviously controlled the purse strings and dealt with all the financial side was Eddie Ashby and when I asked him to tell me what actually could be taken out of the company, because I was experiencing cash-flow problems, I found to my horror that there was no money there.'

It was claimed in a television documentary that Ashby had transferred the money out of Glenhope and into another company. Paul Riviere's comments to *Panorama* were highly critical of Ashby, and he deeply regrets introducing him to Venables, for Ashby's business record has emerged as being consistently bad. In total, he has been a director of 43 companies, of which 16 ended in receivership, eight in liquidation, 15 struck off, and there are no details of the remaining four. With such a commercial history, it was not surprising that Ashby's bankruptcy was filed and advertised in the *London Gazette* on 18 June 1991. Clearly, Ashby was not the man to lecture at the London School of Economics! Yet he had become a fixture of Venables' financial dealings.

Scribes West was the cause of the split between Venables and Sugar in another way, however, when it was found that Venables was using the Tottenham company to help Scribes. Details of Venables' questionable transactions involving the two clubs were made public to the Spurs shareholders in the annual report that dropped on their doormats on 10 November 1993. It was then that some of his more exotic dealings inside White Hart Lane finally entered the public domain when the annual accounts were published.

The annual report disclosed the following unusual payments:

1. £8,683 plus VAT by Spurs to Venables' drinking club Scribes West Limited, some of it built up on a Spurs credit card, part of it for celebrations for reaching the FA Cup semi-final in 1993. This is described in the accounts as 'an arm's-length transaction'.

2. £4,199, still unpaid, for items bought by Spurs for Scribes on Venables' behalf.

3. £2,727 of Venables' personal bills, paid for by the club, still outstanding.

4. £1,725 paid by Spurs to Glenhope Management for Venables' board game 'The Manager'. Also described as an arm's-length transaction.

5. £4,000 invoice to Spurs from the Venables-linked company

Venables Venture Capital Limited. This invoice is not disputed by Spurs but remains unpaid.

However honest Venables' intentions were to see Tottenham properly paid for these items, they displayed a cavalier attitude to the companies he was concerned with.

The first of the payments listed above aggrieved Sugar because he had no knowledge that such sums were being run up on the club's credit card. The Spurs chairman had at first insisted that Venables' expenses would be authorised by him, but, in practice, they went directly to the club's accounts department for payment.

All financial transactions had to be disclosed in the annual report, including loans by directors, and they referred to Tottenham purchasing goods on behalf of Venables and Scribes West. Spurs invoiced these sums to Venables and Scribes at cost. Venables paid Tottenham the full £2,316 he owed, but the money outstanding from Scribes, at the time of the report, amounted to £4,199 (see No. 2 above). This was because Venables made a peach of a deal for Scribes!

The Portuguese linen for Scribes was ordered through the football club. Venables wanted a cut-price deal and Tottenham's executive in charge of marketing at that time, Edward Freedman, ordered it through his merchandising company at White Hart Lane, Stardare. Freedman wrote to the manager of Scribes on 15 January 1992 to confirm that the peach and white table linen had arrived. His letter was copied to Venables. It was not until seven months later that Spurs sent Scribes an invoice for £4,199.54p for the tablecloths. Four months later, Spurs had still heard nothing. The club sent a memo to Eddie Ashby, with a copy to Venables, dated 5 January 1993 chasing payment. Venables' then solicitors, Fugler's, claimed the money had been paid, but Spurs had no record of it.

Early in 1994, Venables commented on the various outstanding claims that Tottenham were still making, totalling some £7,000: 'I am very sad that this sort of thing should be broached at such an important time for me. Once again, I am forced to defend myself when, in reality, I have done nothing wrong . . . These allegations are nothing new. They appeared in the court documents during my case against Spurs in the summer and became public knowledge then ... It is absolute rubbish to suggest I owe Tottenham anything. The only reason there are any bills outstanding is because they owe me money . . . When you balance everything out, they owe me £7,500.'

But there were other potentially lucrative spin-offs for Venables and Scribes because of his involvement with Spurs. General Portfolio national sales manager Bob Patmore promised Venables good business for Scribes in return for his company winning the race for a contract at White Hart Lane. Although Spurs did not appear to be losing out on the agreement with General Portfolio, it was obviously in Venables' interests to see that they won the contract, rather than Legal & General who also bid for the same business. There was a distinct possibility that a conflict of interest could arise for Venables, who had to balance what was best for Tottenham and what was best for Scribes.

Patmore wrote to Venables on 19 October 1992 outlining 'the common aim of increasing Scribes' clientele and generating business for Tottenham Hotspur and General Portfolio'. He intended doing this by selling charity books to Tottenham box-holders while asking if they would like to spend an evening at Scribes as a non-member, thus giving the Scribes staff the opportunity to persuade them to become members. He encouraged his people to hold meetings at Scribes. He also suggested that any fan who completed his company's financial planning analysis would be able to enter a draw to join a team of Spurs fans to play a game of football against former players. Finally, he suggested reducing Tottenham's commission split to 40 percent so that General Portfolio could offer 10 percent to any Spurs staff who wished to do business with his company. On the letter were scribbled agreements to all these points, except the last, by which there was a question mark.

Talks continued between Patmore and Venables, with

their agreements confirmed in writing with a letter dated 3 November. Patmore was also keen to utilise Eric Hall and the leads that he could generate. When Spurs announced the 'partnership' between Tottenham and General Portfolio on 19 November 1992, Venables signed the press release, part of which read: 'Money is not the prime motive behind this partnership. Over the past twelve months or so I have discovered, and now understand more than ever, the importance of quality advice on financial matters. This does not only apply to me and Tottenham Hotspur, but it applies to all of us as individuals. I believe that by signing this agreement we have opened up to you the opportunity, should you want it, for good quality advice.'

If only Venables had heeded his own comments, his troubles in 1993 would not have come about. As with any field of life, there are plenty of people willing to give advice - but it's the quality that counts. Venables' belief that he was receiving sound financial and business advice from Eddie Ashby, an undischarged bankrupt, was clearly misguided. So was his decision to ignore the advice of Sugar, a multi-millionaire, to get rid of Ashby.

Venables' outward confidence in his business acumen, coupled with his great personal charm, were seen as being an ideal combination to promote Richard Branson's Virgin Airlines. In what was a witty and ironic comment on his then financial situation, Venables appeared in a television advertisement in which he is seen reading a book called *How to Succeed in Business.* But he was probably too late in starting to read such books, even though they could have saved him a great deal of trouble.

Having started young with setting up his own companies, Venables continued in the same way. Companies House lists his complete range, some of which have been struck off. Among them are: Terence Venables Limited, with net assets of £47,000 in its last declared accounts filed on 30 June 1992; Terence Venables Holdings Limited, for which there are no accounts filed, as is the case for Venables Venture Capital Limited.

Clearly, none of these companies has generated particularly large revenues - certainly not enough to bail out his more high-profile businesses like Scribes West and Edennote, both of which have faced severe financial difficulties.

As well as the series of unpaid bills mentioned earlier, there was a winding-up order on Scribes West, first issued by Vincent Isaacs, chairman of General Portfolio, in early December 1993. It came very close to being put into action after two High Court hearings. The third, due to take place on Monday, 17 January 1994, would have probably seen the club closed down. However, on the previous Friday, Venables contacted Isaacs to persuade him to resolve the matter out of court. Owing some £150,000, Venables is thought to have settled the matter by paying £50,000 over immediately, as well as General Portfolio's legal costs, with the balance to follow. As he commented afterwards: 'I came to an agreement with Vincent Isaacs and there are no more creditors.'

However, the threat to Edennote still remained, as Tottenham continued to chase their outstanding legal fees. The club presented a petition to the High Court on 12 January 1994 to wind up Edennote. On 26 January the taxing master agreed that the bill should be £336,000. As one of only two directors of the company, along with his wife Yvette, if the winding-up order succeeds, there is a chance that Venables might be disqualified from being a director of limited companies. As the *Independent* commented before he got the England job: 'The FA is a limited company and the Insolvency Act states that a disqualified director cannot "in any way be involved directly or indirectly in the promotion, formation or management of a company" and defines management as "having influence over the internal or external affairs of the company". In that situation, the FA may have to ask the court for a ruling on whether Venables' duties as England manager would breach the law.' This potentially tricky situation may well have been one of the reasons why the FA delayed so long in appointing Venables and eventually made him only the coach.

As early as the hearings for the cost of the trial, on 29 July 1993, it was suggested that Edennote was insolvent and would have great problems in paying the legal costs of Tottenham. How

Venables would have raised the money needed to buy out Sugar, as well as offering for the entire company, was hard to see, unless he could have found himself another sugar daddy.

CHAPTER THIRTEEN
The End of the Dream Team

IT WAS THE MEN with whom Venables chose to surround himself that were the main reasons behind his downfall at Spurs: Eddie Ashby, the undischarged bankrupt who became Venables' financial guru; Jonathan Crystal, a leading libel lawyer detested by Sugar; and three agents, Gino Santin, Frank McLintock and Eric Hall, who were the middlemen in a series of soccer transfers. In their very different ways, they contributed to the behind-the-scenes bust-up and Sugar's decision to sack Venables. We have already seen the controversial role of the agents in previous chapters.

Sugar gave Venables the chance to heal the rift, but the price he demanded was too high: he wanted Venables' aides out of Tottenham, and he had many reasons for wanting this to happen. But Venables continued to back Ashby and the others, much to Sugar's annoyance and surprise. It cost Venables everything.

A series of disagreements over a computer base for Spurs was one area of contention. Venables' handling of transfer dealings involving Paul Gascoigne, Teddy Sheringham, Gary Lineker, Gordon Durie and Andy Gray cast doubts in Sugar's mind over Venables' business acumen. Then, there were disclosures over interest-free loans involving several players, with £325,000 written off in the club's balance sheet. These loans had been recommended by Venables in his capacity as manager and authorised by former chairman Irving Scholar and the previous board. Sugar was determined that the financial mess should be cleared up and the club run on a professional basis.

Finally, it came down to a fight for ultimate power. Venables lost.

The fans were oblivious to the growing chasm between the two major shareholders. It seemed to be the perfect partnership: on the one hand was Sugar's enormous personal wealth, his financial flair and formidable business background; on the other there was Venables' vast experience and great skills in the football world. They seemed to complement each other, but it was remarkable how quickly the splits began to appear. Undoubtedly, Tottenham Hotspur suffered as the relationship deteriorated into bitter warfare, first in private, and then it exploded into the public domain.

Clearly, both Venables and Sugar are forceful, strong-willed, determined men. On occasions they can be touchy. Misunderstandings and disagreements arose over the respective roles and spheres of operations involving Sugar, Venables, his personal assistant Eddie Ashby, director Colin Sandy, nominated by Sugar, and fellow director Jonathan Crystal, nominated by Venables. Perhaps these battles were inevitable as there were bound to be areas where both Venables and Sugar (or their close associates) thought they had the final say. Obviously, Sugar would not contradict Venables about football tactics, while Venables would leave Sugar to deal with the club's massive debts. But finance and football would inevitably overlap in transfer dealings, salary negotiations and so on.

Not surprisingly then, board meetings became increasingly confrontational, even violent. By May 1993, the acrimony had reached the stage where, in practice, it had become impossible for these two talented men to work together any longer as chairman and chief executive. There were many key issues that brought about the final breakdown, but they can be divided into two main areas: Sugar's concerns about the way Venables handled his transfer opportunities and pay negotiations, in other words, his business dealings with the players; and second, the way both men grew suspicious of the other's business connections and operations.

★

PART ONE: VENABLES AND THE PLAYERS

The Sale of Paul Gascoigne

Eddie Ashby's role included preparing business plans to help reduce the club's debt. The easiest way to set about this was to sell the club's most saleable commodity. Gascoigne may have been damaged goods, but he could still command a £5 million-plus transfer fee, a much lower fee than had originally been offered by Lazio before Gascoigne's horrendous injury in the FA Cup final that year. There had never been any doubt that this would be the quickest way to solve Tottenham's financial worries, in addition the terms on offer to Gascoigne would have made it almost impossible for Spurs to have kept him anyway. The arrival of Venables and Sugar strengthened Tottenham's negotiating position with Lazio, as they did not need to sell as urgently as had been the case under the previous regime.

Given that, and the complexities of the transfer deal, Sugar's main complaint was that Venables was reluctant to allow his chairman to become involved. In fact, even though developments were often delicate, Venables told Sugar in no uncertain terms that he did not want him engrossed in negotiations. Venables insisted that he would open talks with Marseille and put the screws on Lazio, but he denies that he told Sugar he would threaten them by telling the Italians to 'go to hell' if they continued to be awkward over the price. Venables was trying to force Lazio to stop stalling on the deal and to make them increase their price by presenting them with opposition in the form of big-spending Marseille. In reality, the player would have had the final say on the transfer, and Mel Stein, lawyer, adviser and agent to Gascoigne, contacted Sugar to make it plain that the player did not want to join Marseille and had resigned himself to going to Italy.

Sugar maintains that Venables' opposition to him being involved in the Lazio deal was a sign that he wanted to show everybody else connected with the club that he was the boss. Otherwise, there was a danger that the reverse would be seen to be the case. To avert Sugar's involvement, the Spurs chairman received a phone call from Venables warning of 'some confusion' with Lazio and suggesting that the restaurateur Gino Santin became involved because he would 'get a better price', and do it almost as a favour. Almost immediately, then, there had arisen a case where the boundaries between the two men's spheres of interest had overlapped. New to the business, Sugar agreed to give Venables the chance to conclude the deal.

Venables' estimate of Santin's fee was very wrong. It was then that Sugar realised that Venables' previous advice that Santin's price would be a 'drink' proved nonsense. However, he trusted in Venables and so approved the payment of £200,000, happy that it had been negotiated down from Santin's original demand for £275,000, and believing that Santin had played a vital role in the deal.

Sugar's suspicions that Venables possessed little or no grasp of financial matters increased when his chief executive 'wasted' his time in trying to work out an insurance policy to resolve the problems in the Gascoigne transaction.

Tottenham wanted the Lazio cash deposited into their bank account immediately so as to reduce the overdraft significantly, pending Gascoigne's return to fitness. Interest rates were extremely high in 1991 and with the overdraft at such a level the club faced heavy interest payments. Understandably, Lazio were suspicious that once they deposited the money with the Midland, they would never get it back if Gascoigne failed to recover fully.

To get round the dilemma, Sugar suggested to Lazio that they could have a guarantee if they deposited their money - a charge over White Hart Lane. Sugar knew that, if the deal went wrong, Lazio would get their money back, and there was no question of ever losing the stadium. However, Venables and Ashby suggested Lazio could have a guarantee in another form, an insurance policy. But Sugar told Venables he 'must be dreaming' if he could find a company that would take on such an insurance policy, and so thought the time spent and cost of such advice was all wasted.

Venables did find one insurance company, but they wanted a premium of £475,000 and added in so many provisos 'that it was worthless' in Sugar's opinion.

It was because of these dealings that Sugar became aware of Venables' lack of business acumen and common sense. As yet, there was no rift, but the Gascoigne deal made Sugar more anxious to have his say in the big-money dealings of the club - an area Venables believed he had established as his own with his handling of the Gascoigne transfer. Perhaps it was then inevitable that conflict would follow between the two men. Indeed, Venables could be justly proud about his success with Gascoigne, a high-risk, record £2 million signing in 1988 who he had helped to become one of the best players in the world and then sold on at nearly three times the price he had paid. But perhaps it merely emphasised that Venables should have stayed with what he knew best.

The Signing of Gordon Durie

However, Sugar seriously questioned Venables' appreciation of how his transfer dealings must be related to the financial position of the club. Venables was privy to the pledges made by the company to the Midland Bank, one of the cornerstones of which was the club's restraint of transfer spending. Indeed, the Midland had been promised that there would be no more spending until the debts had been reduced. But, just days before the start of the 1991-92 season, Venables was anxious to find a strike partner for Gary Lineker as the FA Cup-holders were due to embark on a European campaign for the first time since 1984-85.

With Sugar in Italy on business, Venables wanted to rush through the signing of Scottish international striker Gordon Durie from Chelsea for an initial fee of £2 million, with an additional payment of £200,000 after 35 games because of the player's susceptibility to injury, Sugar was shocked that a company that had yet to resolve all of its financial headaches was just about to embark on a club record transfer. Venables placated

Sugar with the explanation that the money for the sale of Gary Lineker at the end of the season was imminent and that there would be other outgoing deals to balance the transfer account. With the deal in an advanced stage, and Venables insisting that the transfer was essential, Sugar reluctantly agreed, but found himself in an embarrassing position with the bank. Spurs had spent £2 million in blatant disregard of Sugar's assurances to the Midland. Sugar had to quell the concern of the bank by promising that he would personally put money into the business, if necessary, until the rights issue raised the funds to pay off the overdraft. Sugar began to realise that he needed to keep a careful eye over Venables' spending, because of his failure to notice the financial constraints in situations such as this.

Interest-Free Loans

The significance of the scandal of the interest-free loans to 12 Spurs stars never became fully apparent until the end of 1993, and so was not a central issue to Venables' sacking. However, the subject was raised very soon into the partnership and caused Sugar much concern, especially as it gave further indication of Venables' attitude to regular financial management.

Boardroom minutes illustrate that Venables was asked by Sugar to sort out the mess of why so many players had received these loans, and that Crystal was assigned the task. This extract from minutes dated 7 August 1991 comes from Crystal's legal report:

Players loans and benefits - It was resolved that all payments of benefits provided to any players must be written into the terms of the contract and before execution must be reviewed by a lawyer or Mr Crystal. Mr Crystal and Mr Ashby were instructed by the board to look at all current matters and to report back at the next meeting. A discussion ensued as to whether the loan monies were irrecoverable and who should have known of their existence. It was decided that Mr Gray should have been aware of them if only from an audit point of view.

Clearly the interest-free loans had not been declared to

the soccer authorities, the Football League. A major reason for such breaches of the rules was the burning desire of those at Tottenham to create a powerful football team. To do this, they felt they needed to compete with their fiercest rivals in terms of the arrangements that were made with the players - and these included interest-free loans. One such deal was with Paul Stewart for £75,000. No interest was to be paid on the loan and, if he saw out his contract, he would not have to repay it. On top of this, any tax payable in respect of the loan would be handled by Tottenham not Stewart. Paul Stewart wrote to the club confirming the details, which were signed and approved by Venables on 12 June 1988 and countersigned by club secretary Peter Barnes. Stewart wrote:

> Dear Sir, I write to confirm that you will loan to me the sum of £75,000 interest free, for the period of my contract with the football club.
>
> The loan will not be repayable at the end of my contract, provided that I do not request a transfer during the period of the said contract.
>
> In addition, the club will bear the responsibility of my tax payable, gauged on the interest level of tax, of whatever nature, by me, in respect of the said loan, or notional interest thereon, both during, on or after the expiry of the said contract.
>
> The loan and the waiver of repayment, and the reference to tax, in this letter, are made in consideration of my entering into a contract to play for Tottenham Hotspur Football Club (PLC).
>
> The loan will be made to me no later than July 31st 1988.
>
> Kindly sign to indicate your agreement.
>
> Confirm that £25,000 loyalty payments per year, can be paid into a policy or pension fund of my own choice.

Clearly Stewart did not produce such a detailed, wordy letter alone - and it didn't stop him finally signing for Liverpool.

Although not illegal, as the loans were declared to the Inland Revenue, they are 'irregular' payments in defiance of Football League rules. Scholar claims that the intention was for the loans to be repaid, but Venables told Sugar that they would not be. That was why Tottenham were forced to write off £325,000 worth of 'loans' from the company's books. There was no way these loans could any longer be described as assets. An internal probe into the loans was ordered to make sure the money would not be returned. When it was clear that the club was not going to be repaid, writing off the debts was the only solution, as it was clearly an 'unsavoury' course of action to sue the club's players.

Sugar has commented: 'Terry Venables was appointed chief executive to run the day-to-day show and that's what he supposedly did . . . while I focused my attention on reducing the debt. One or two months into the takeover, at board meetings I started to get down to report and accounts and I realised there were certain assets in our balance sheet that related to players' loans. I started to ask: "Are we going to get the money back?" The only person who could answer that was Terry Venables. His answer was "no", but he was the one who initiated these loans as the manager.'

The previous board understood that the majority of loans were always going to be repayable and, in most cases, the letters of agreement specified they would be. In many cases, this is precisely what did happen. But Stewart's £75,000 interest-free loan clearly specified 'the loan will not be repayable at the end of my contract, provided that I do not request a transfer during the period of the said contract'. While the club's hierarchy were the men motivated by the hope of bringing success to Tottenham, their actions, once discovered, could land the club in a great deal of trouble. Sugar is hoping that, by cooperating fully with the footballing authorities, he will be able to absolve the current regime (since he took sole charge) from these past misdemeanours.

A further extract from a Tottenham Hotspur board meeting, dated 12 September 1991, deals with the continuing concern about the loans:

> Players' loans and benefits - The board's view that the loans were never going to be recoverable was reiterated and it was confirmed that the auditors have provided for these loans in the accounts of the Company for the year ended 31 May 1991.
>
> Mr Sugar is very clear that a report must be sent to the appropriate authorities.
>
> In this connection the board instructed Mr Crystal and Mr Sandy to meet with leading Counsel to consider the resulting ramifications of disclosure and any actions that can be taken.
>
> Once Mr Crystal and Mr Sandy have discussed with Counsel they are to report their findings to the next board meeting when it is likely a decision will be taken as to how to proceed.
>
> Mr Berry [director] and Mr Solomon [ex-chairman] confirmed that they were unhappy about the existence of these loans and that the first they were aware of them was when they were declared at the last board meeting.

Despite this record of the meeting, it was to be two years before the football authorities began to look into the club's curious loan systems. There is a mass of correspondence in the files at White Hart Lane relating to 'loans' to many players for varying amounts and with differing terms of repayment. The threat to Tottenham's status in the Premiership is very real, for Swindon Town won promotion to the top division in 1990 only to be sent back down to the Second Division for widespread irregular payments. However, after discussing the matter with legal advisers, it was believed that, as Tottenham had left the Football League to join the Premier League, their position was safe.

However, it is still possible that the FA may wish to take up this issue.

The £325,000 in loans that were written off was made up as follows: £75,000 to Paul Stewart, £55,000 to Paul Allen, £50,000 to Erik Thorstvedt, £30,000 to Nayim, £25,000 each to Paul Walsh, Terry Fenwick, Gary Mabbutt and Mitchell Thomas and £15,000 to Bobby Mimms.

The question of loans even embraced Venables. We have already seen how, on becoming chief executive, Venables' contract was altered so that his salary was split £150,000 upfront to his company Edennote and £75,000 in salary to himself, with a £50,000 'signing-on fee'. He then used that £50,000 'signing-on fee' to pay back Spurs the £50,000 interest-free loan given to him by Scholar when he joined Tottenham as manager after being sacked by Barcelona. Sugar admitted that he had done nothing to prevent this arrangement from taking place, but he was keen that from then on everything should be more closely scrutinised.

Indeed, Venables' involvement in the loans question goes even further than that. For, after Scholar called a halt to such payments at the end of 1988, Venables revived the practice when he became chief executive - including one deal that was struck after the Premier League started in August 1992.

The three players to benefit were Terry Fenwick, Paul Walsh and Nayim (whose full name is Mohammed Ali Amar). The last of these arrangements was with Nayim in a letter sent on 21 October 1992 by Jonathan Crystal [see document 7, page 337], more than two months into the new league's first season.

Prior to that, Venables had renegotiated loan arrangements with Fenwick and Walsh. Fenwick's original loan of 30 December 1987 stated that his interest-free loan of £25,000 would be repayable 'on demand or at the expiration of your current contract, or any extension thereof. If he left the club, the money was repayable within seven days. The revised agreement of February 1992 [see document 8, page 338] was much better for Fenwick as it stated that: 'In the event that TF requests a transfer he shall be liable to repay to THFC the loan of £25,000 made to him by THFC.' However, if he did not ask for a transfer before the end of his contract 'THFC agrees not to seek repayment of the loan'. The repayable loan had become non-repayable.

The agreement with Walsh, signed by both the player and Venables, was worked out on the same basis.

The Sale of Gary Lineker

England captain, superstar, Mr Clean, and one of the world's top scorers, Gary Lineker was sold off for just £850,000! When Lineker and Gascoigne returned to Tottenham after Italia '90 after England just missed out on the World Cup final, beaten by eventual champions Germany on penalties in the semi-finals, their value on the transfer market soared. The then Spurs chairman Irving Scholar rejected a near £5 million offer for Lineker from Torino, £3.5 million in cash plus a Yugoslav striker valued at between £1 and £1.5 million. Gascoigne was priceless, Scholar felt, even though Lineker would be 30 in November 1990, he was worth keeping - and made his views plain to Lineker's friend and agent Jon Holmes.

Scholar says: 'Jon Holmes went to Italy for talks and Lineker himself indicated that he would be interested in a move to Italy if the club were agreeable. I was not agreeable and, to be fair to Terry, he too was annoyed with Holmes. In fact, there were murders because I told Holmes that he had no right to negotiate in Italy without the club's permission. Lineker was under contract and he would have to honour it. I have a lot of sympathy with players in this country because salaries are so vastly higher abroad, and it is hard to stand in their way. But Lineker had already made his pile from a move abroad with Barcelona, so I did not have so much sympathy. Gary and Terry were always very close, but I didn't sense that Gary turned against me because I had blocked a move to Italy. Once I had put my foot down that was the end of the matter, we never discussed it again.'

Jon Holmes agrees that there was considerable interest expressed in Lineker during and after the World Cup and that he referred this interest to Tottenham. However, he says, most of the clubs would clearly not have been able to offer enough for Spurs, with the exception of Torino. Holmes told Scholar that he had spoken to Torino, and at the end of the World Cup the Italian club made an appointment to meet the agent. Holmes indicated that Torino should approach Spurs direct, and that the offer needed to be a good one. However, he heard no more from them after that.

Holmes assumed then that Tottenham would keep Lineker, but he subsequently learned that the club had asked Dennis Roach to sound out various clubs on the Continent during the following season, and insists that neither he nor Lineker was informed of this. Indeed, neither man was aware of any anger from Venables or Scholar at the time because of the speculation about Lineker's future at the club.

Sugar was unaware of Lineker's valuation in 1990, only a year before an agreement was made before the 1991-92 season to sell him to Grampus Eight for just £850,000 at the end of the year. Venables' argument was that Lineker had reached the wrong side of 30 and had two years left on his Spurs contract at the time the deal was made. He considered it a good arrangement, but Sugar was deeply disappointed that Tottenham received such a small sum.

The reason for Sugar's reaction was that in his second meeting to buy the club, his prospective partner Venables had told Sugar that Lineker would fetch £4 million. Once the pair were running the club, Sugar questioned why Spurs had got only £850,000, referring to their original conversation about Lineker. Venables explained that, given Lineker's age, he was unlikely to fetch much more than £1 million on the transfer market. Lineker, personally, would stand to make £4 million in salary and signing-on fees - but not Spurs.

Sugar describes this as one of the 'misunderstandings' that began to creep into his relationship with Venables. Sugar relied on Venables' footballing knowledge, being a novice to the game, but would no longer make such a mistake. His suspicions about Venables' ability had increased, perhaps justifiably, for £850,000 was certainly cheap for Lineker, as an earlier £2 million offer from Blackburn Rovers, which had been rejected out of hand, showed. Sugar was further concerned because a fee of £1 million had been mentioned. But Venables explained that the 'balance' was made up by Lineker waiving a cash payment of £166,666 as the final part of his signing-on fee that was due on 1 August 1992. However, as Lineker had asked for a move, Spurs would not have been liable to pay it anyway.

Venables was pleased with the deal he made with Japanese club Grampus Eight, because he got cash upfront, kept Lineker for another year before he moved on with his age approaching 32. Indeed, had he insisted that Lineker saw out the final year of his contract, to the end of 1992-93, Tottenham would have received nothing for the sale. But, as a result of the Lineker transaction, Sugar insisted that Venables keep him informed in the future of all major transfer dealings.

Spurs intended to keep the details of the deal with the Japanese club under wraps for the entire season, no doubt not wanting to risk the wrath of the fans so soon after the departure of Gascoigne. But the news leaked to the press, and so it became public.

This issue was dredged up again during the court hearings. On 10 June 1993, Venables' QC, Mr Mann, pointed out how Sugar's affidavit gave the impression that 'Mr Venables' integrity has been questioned. We are, ourselves, questioning Mr Sugar's integrity.' This was because Sugar mentioned in his affidavit how Venables led him to expect over £1 million, but in the end the club received £850,000. Worried by this, Sugar wanted to have direct access to the people in Japan because of his long dealings with that country through Amstrad. He also wanted to reassure himself that the full sum Grampus Eight was paying to sign Lineker was being disclosed. The implication from Sugar was that some money was being paid to a third party, a suggestion that infuriated the Venables camp.

Venables also pointed out that Tottenham had signed Lineker for £1.2 million, so 'he was obviously worth considerably less aged 31. The effect of that transaction was that Tottenham was getting their money back for him. The alternative would have been to have let him serve out his contract and get nothing at the end. It is absolutely incredible that Mr Sugar should state that his faith in my business acumen has declined as a result of this purchase.'

Jon Holmes, who had been Lineker's agent and personal adviser for more than ten years, backed Venables' understanding of the situation. He, too, rubbished Sugar's estimate for Lineker of £4 million. He also criticised Sugar's fears that the Grampus Eight agent, Christian Flood, was hiding something from Tottenham. Like Sugar, Flood had plenty of experience in dealing with the Japanese, having negotiated tours of the country by Margaret Thatcher. The other important fact was that Lineker wanted to make the move and if he was kept on against his will then his motivation at Tottenham would have been sure to decline. Sugar's lawyer was quick to state that there was no question mark against either Lineker or Holmes in their dealings with Grampus Eight.

That accounts for Lineker's and Holmes's positions, but not all the facts of the deal emerged in court. Flood and his Japanese partner Yoshio Aoyama were approached by Grampus Eight, backed by Toyota, and given a sum with which to negotiate a deal to sign Lineker, with the money to be split between Lineker and Tottenham. Although the precise sum is confidential, it is in the region of £5 million. For concluding the deal, Flood and Aoyama received a commission of £100,000, plus the lucrative rights to market Lineker's Japanese deals in England. All payments, other than the commission, went direct from Grampus Eight to Tottenham or Lineker and his agent. It was Flood who initiated the deal because he understood how popular Lineker would prove in Japan. He remains convinced that both parties got as good a deal as was possible given the sum of money available.

Therefore, we can see how, within the first few months of the Venables-Sugar partnership being set up, there had I been three big-money transfer deals, involving Gascoigne, Durie and Lineker in which Venables had tried to minimise the role of Sugar in the negotiations, even insisting that he I did not get involved. Yet each of the deals disappointed Sugar in one way or another, giving rise to his concerns about Venables' business acumen. Had Venables involved Sugar more closely there would have been less chance for misunderstanding and suspicion.

Paul Stewart

After his signing in the summer of 1988 for £1.5 million, Paul Stewart for a long time seemed overpriced, and Venables might have accepted £800,000 for him until Stewart's heroic efforts in the 1991 FA Cup final raised the price tag on him to the £2 million mark. Liverpool moved in for Stewart and Venables pushed the price up to £2.25 million. It seemed as though this was a great achievement, but he did not realise that any sale above £2 million would enable Manchester City to claim a cut.

The Maine Road club were entitled to ten percent plus VAT on any sale for any deal of £2 million or over, provided he was sold before the end of the 1992-93 season. The £2.25 million fee gave City a £225,000 cut plus VAT, which meant Tottenham received less than £2 million. As Spurs were then pursuing Liverpool's Dean Saunders, Sugar could not understand why Venables hadn't simply worked an exchange with Liverpool, Saunders for Stewart, with each player publicly valued at £2 million, although Saunders also went for more (£2.2 million) to Aston Villa.

Venables felt he had been let down by club secretary Peter Barnes. He suggested that he had every right to expect that Barnes should have notified him about Manchester City's cut as he countersigned the contract. Venables also pointed an accusing finger at Sandy, because there existed a similar arrangement in the Gascoigne contract, which meant that Newcastle received a percentage of the fee. Venables felt that Sandy should have investigated the Stewart contract. However, as the man who had signed both players in the first place, perhaps he too could have avoided these mistakes. Once again, a transfer deal had caused recriminations.

The Sale of Nayim

Mohammed Ali Amar had joined Tottenham from Barcelona at the same time as Lineker, being a makeweight in the deal. After a struggle to establish himself at White Hart Lane, Nayim, as he is known, became a popular figure at the club. His greatest triumph came in the quarter-finals of the 1993 FA Cup when he secured victory over Manchester City by scoring a brilliant hat-trick. Performances like that meant he was widely valued at £1 million on the transfer market. It seemed to be another Venables success story as a coach, until the time came for him to be sold.

Offers had come in from many Spanish clubs, to where he was anxious to return, but in the end he was sold for just £420,000 to Real Zaragosa. Not only was this lower than the expected price, it was lower than the price quoted by the Daily Telegraph, whose contacts in Barcelona are excellent. On 9 April 1993, they stated that the price would be £500,000.

The general disappointment at Tottenham about his departure was replaced with another emotion when they tried to re-sign him less than six months after he had left -and found that the fee had more than doubled to £1 million. Sugar has been alarmed at the fee the club received and has commented that 'we're looking at that one very closely'. It was the last in a series of Venables' transfer dealings that had caused concern at the club.

PART TWO: THE FALL-OUT

The Origins

Venables and Sugar completed the deal to buy Spurs on 21 June 1991, with both men instantly becoming directors at the first board meeting at the offices of their merchant bankers. Seven days later, at a board meeting at White Hart Lane, Sugar was voted chairman and Venables chief executive, with the previous chief executive, Ian Gray, becoming managing director.

On 7 August Sugar's trusted aide Colin Sandy was appointed a director and secretary of the company, with Jonathan Crystal becoming a non-executive director. Douglas Alexiou and Frank Sinclair resigned from the board. Sugar and Venables had installed their allies. But, prior to the formation of the new board, there was a crucial gathering at Scribes where the political infighting began -just weeks into the Venables-Sugar union. Around the table were Venables, Sugar, Berry, Crystal, part of the time, and Ashby.

On the agenda was the plan to oust Ian Gray from any internal influence within White Hart Lane. Ashby accused Gray of being 'uncooperative' because he had been put out by his change of job title and now wanted a pay rise on his £50,000-a-year salary. Ashby volunteered to perform the same role Gray now carried out, managing director, for the same salary. Sugar raised no objection at this stage, as long as Venables was happy. However, he suggested a separate finance director, a position that Sandy was to take. Gray was forced out, and later successfully sued for compensation. Ashby assumed a 'managerial' position in the company, without being given any specific title. Sugar had no perception of Ashby's murky financial past, let alone that he was an undischarged bankrupt. He now states that had he known about this, Ashby would not have been permitted to assume such an influential role within the administration of the club. In fact, Ashby assumed Gray's role of preparing business plans, but the dealings with the Midland Bank were left to Sandy. Their combined role was crucial, as the Midland were still very deeply concerned that there was no money to pay off the £11 million overdraft, and they were demanding to see Spurs' business plans.

As we have seen, the first part of the business plan was to sell Gascoigne, the second part was to set up a rights issue which would generate the necessary funds to clear more of the Tottenham debt. The 6 December 1991 rights issue meant that Venables was now in a comparatively weak position, as Sugar had 48 percent of the company, Venables 23 percent. From that moment there could only be one real, effective boss. However, Venables argued that he and Sugar remained equal partners, basing this assertion on the agreement outlined in the share offer document, a pledge to Spurs fans, countersigned by both men. 'Our short-term objective is, of course, to resolve the financial difficulties of [the company]. Going forward, we believe that, with the combination of Terry Venables' expertise in football and Alan Sugar's experience in financial matters, we can put in place a plan for the company to be profitable on a longterm basis. Alan Sugar has already been appointed chairman of [the company] and Terry Venables has been appointed chief executive. Now firmly on board, we are both confident that we can fulfil our objectives.'

But there was a crucial meeting prior to the rights issue in December at the Grosvenor House Hotel, and it was on this that Venables' claims in court that the partnership remained on an equal footing were based, despite the clear disparity of shares the rights issue would inevitably bring as Venables did not have the money to take up his own rights of shares. Venables raised the issue with Sugar that they would no longer have equal voting power. Sugar replied: 'Trust me, even if I pick up all of the shares we have a shareholders' agreement.' It was on this statement that Venables based his entire prolonged court action against the Spurs chairman. However, there was no written shareholders' agreement, only a draft one prepared on the night of the takeover, and then it was only appropriate when the pair held equal shares. Even though Venables conceded, on advice, that it was not legally binding, he still went ahead and fought his case, because of Sugar's comment that the agreement would continue. No written agreement was in existence until after the rights issue, and then there were just draft arrangements. Venables wanted Sugar to vote on 'one half of his shares 'for the time being' in excess of Venables' shares, and for Sugar to 'use his best endeavours' to transfer his excess shares to independent shareholders over a period of five years. That was rejected out of hand by Sugar in a conversation with Ashby, who related Sugar's views to Venables early in 1992.

Venables himself admitted that his relationship with Sugar 'deteriorated progressively' from September 1992, even though he felt that he had 'played a substantial part' in turning around the company's performance from a loss of £2.8 million in the financial year ending 31 May 1991 to a profit of £2.8 million the following year, with anticipated profits beyond £5 million in the year ending 31 May 1993.

Amstrad and the Tottenham Computers

Venables complained bitterly that Sugar was plotting to exclude him from his management rights within the organisation, with the premeditated intention of wresting complete control. According to Venables, Sugar's method was to introduce a sophisticated computer system, Kilostman Interform, linked to Amstrad headquarters in Brentwood, without 'adequate consultation'. Venables and Crystal felt this was one of the most contentious issues, and the second most important move by Sugar, after the rights issue, to gain full control.

Sugar called in an expert from Amstrad, Richard Simmons, for advice on bringing in the best equipment to monitor stock and buying requirements for the merchandising division. This also raised the question as to who should control the merchandising arm of the company. At a board meeting on 29 October 1992, it was agreed to link the computer system to Amstrad's central computer at Brentwood, with the hardware at White Hart Lane and, at the board meeting on 25 February 1993, it was agreed that £75,000 would be spent on hardware. But

Venables contacted a separate consultant to do work that Sugar felt had already been done by Simmons. Venables felt there was a serious conflict of interest for Sugar in this deal, but Sugar didn't accept Venables' view that he was not acting in the best interests of Tottenham. The Venables consultants wanted £5,000 before they would conduct a proper evaluation. Venables agreed to pay, but, on Sugar's advice, gave them the cheque with instructions not to cash it until they had completed their task. However, they ignored this and when it was discovered that they had banked the money, the company had to stop the cheque.

Sugar had originally informed the board that he estimated that the cost to Spurs to install the computer system would be £200,000, but, because of 'our efforts', it cost only £105,000, a saving of £95,000 on the original estimate. But Sugar felt it was 'offensive' and 'idiotic' that Venables and Crystal should think installing the Amstrad system was of benefit to Sugar's company. The cost of the link to Amstrad's headquarters in Brentwood was £25,000 - hardly a share-jerking amount for a company of Amstrad's size, argued Sugar.

Sugar's answer to the criticism that Amstrad was benefiting from the link with Tottenham was that his company paid £115,000 plus VAT to Spurs on renting executive boxes and ground advertising at 'normal going rates'. In return, Amstrad supplied the club with £22,000 worth of computers 'at trade prices' and the company runs the computer system at Spurs for the annual fee of £25,000. Given a turnover of £300 million, the Spurs dealings were clearly not important for Amstrad.

Sugar and Sky

Venables felt that Sugar's links with Sky TV was another area for personal benefit, an accusation which angered Sugar no end. Venables pointed to agreements between Tottenham and BSkyB in 1991 and 1993 which were made without 'any prior discussions' with him. Venables was adamant that these deals were of more benefit to Amstrad, who provided satellite dishes, and actually harmed Spurs.

The Fiorucci Tournament was one such occasion which ignited yet another bitter internal row. Inter Milan and Real Madrid were the star attractions for a three-cornered competition at White Hart Lane. In March 1993, Venables successfully negotiated the tournament, whereby Spurs would keep all the gate receipts and the cash from British television rights in return for providing live television coverage in Spain and Italy. Venables contacted ITV and Channel 4, but neither station was interested in buying the rights. According to Sugar, it was Venables who actually suggested that Sugar should contact David Hill, head of Sky Sport. But he wasn't interested either, as the dates of the tournament clashed with an England Under-21 match they were committed to screening. Sugar suggested highlights later that evening. Still Hill would not agree, as there was no budget for it.

Sugar informed Venables that he couldn't pull off any deal with Sky. Venables rang back saying the tournament was still on, but that Tottenham still had to provide a television link to Spain and Italy. Sugar went back to Hill suggesting he would accept £20,000 for the rights, a knockdown price as Spurs would have expected nearly £100,000. Hill pointed out it would cost Sky another £25,000 to £30,000 for a crew and there was still no budget for it. Ten days later, Sugar was in Hanover when Crystal raised the subject again, suggesting to the Spurs chairman that the sponsors foot the bill for the camera crew. It was a sound plan and an agreement was signed with Fiorucci.

But, on the Sunday prior to the tournament, Sky publicised the games and the next day Venables rang Sugar, who recalls Venables' protest: 'Have you seen what those bastards Sky are doing? They have screwed us.' Venables was furious because Sky were planning highlights on the same night as the tournament, so soon after the event that it could affect the gate, thus diminishing the receipts that would go totally to Spurs. Venables insisted that such an arrangement had never been agreed and that Sky should pay Spurs. Sugar was astonished by this outburst, feeling that all the issues had been agreed beforehand. When he tried to explain again, Sugar observed: 'He didn't appear to listen and continued to curse.'

Venables considered that the entire episode was 'bizarre', and, worse, he felt it was 'concocted and entirely inaccurate'. Venables had wanted the highlights screened at a later date, not on the same evening. There was a chance to put right the misunderstanding when Sugar discussed the issue with Venables and Crystal, because it was Crystal who had suggested the final agreement.

Sugar was furious and he later realised that Crystal was the one who had signed the contract with Sky, and Crystal, in his own handwriting, had altered the contract at the particular point which allowed Sky to show highlights on the night. This handwritten alteration was initialled by Crystal himself. Sugar's frustration was over the fact that Crystal seemed frightened to tell Venables, in such a mood, that it was he who had made the arrangement. Instead, he allowed Venables to continue accusing Sugar.

The suspicion has always existed that Sugar got involved with a Premier League club to influence the television negotiations when Sky beat off the challenge of ITV. Clearly, his company stood to benefit by selling more satellite dishes. The top clubs like Arsenal, Manchester United, Liverpool, Aston Villa and Spurs normally voted together on the key issues in football, and they had been hostile to Sky. However, when Spurs broke away from the rest of the 'Big Five', there was much annoyance from the others.

Sugar has explained that it was his Tottenham connections that persuaded him to come to the club's aid, rather than his desire to help Amstrad by helping Sky. However, there can be no doubting his key role in the biggest television deal in the sport's history. Sam Chisholm, BSkyB chief executive, contacted Sugar to ask his advice on whom he should talk to in the Premier League. Sugar suggested Venables. A meeting was arranged at Scribes with Chisholm, Crystal, Venables and Sugar in attendance. Asa result, Chisholm took up discussions with

Rick Parry, the chief executive of the Premier League.

Sugar's next involvement in the negotiations was when the Premier League chairmen were summoned to a meeting at the Royal Lancaster Hotel on 18 May 1992. David Dein, Arsenal vice-chairman and majority shareholder, is a leading light inside the 'Big Five' and he was in favour of ITV's offer, because it would protect lucrative shirt and perimeter advertising deals that relied heavily on regular live television coverage on terrestrial channels with a far wider audience. The smaller clubs had less exposure, and were being offered more television appearances with Sky, albeit to a relatively small viewing public. The North London rivals on the field began their television battle off it. Dein alleged that Tottenham had a vested interest. Sugar admitted that to be the case and asked to abstain from the vote. However, a vote was taken that allowed Spurs a vote. Sugar could not avoid such accusations as were made by Dein, and many others, but he showed the right way to behave when such conflicts exist, as they undoubtedly did here.

Sugar and His Salary

The internal rows rumbled on, the next one coming in the third week of December 1992 when Crystal went on holiday to Mauritius. Crystal felt he was in charge of reviewing all contracts at Tottenham and 'preferably' preparing them, but while he was in Mauritius, on 17 December, Sugar was employed by Spurs at a £50,000-a-year salary. Crystal raised the point at the next board meeting on 28 January in a 'heated' discussion and claimed that Sugar was 'offensive' toward him. Sugar emphasised that his contract had been signed by Sandy before being ratified by the board, and pointed out that Venables was not granted any prior board consent for his own 'two' contracts, nor for those of Ray Clemence and Doug Livermore. Sugar had not been paid during his first 18 months at the club, but he started taking a salary only after consultation with Venables. Venables took the opportunity to discuss having a pay rise himself - from £225,000 to £400,000.

Ernest Saunders

Sugar continued to be amazed by some of Venables' judgements. Although Sugar never made this an issue in the court case, he was astonished when Venables suggested that Ernest Saunders, convicted in the Guinness scandal, should work at Tottenham. The former chairman of Guinness was jailed after a sensational share scandal when he was found guilty of artificially inflating Guinness's value during the takeover of Distillers. He received a five-year sentence, but had served only nine months at Ford Open Prison when it was announced he was suffering from Alzheimer's Disease and so was set free. Astonishingly, once free, Saunders made a remarkable recovery and found work as a marketing consultant and after-dinner speaker, as well as benefiting from a £65,000-a-year pension. He also received a tax-free £150,000 payment after being released from jail.

Venables first met the Austrian-born Saunders when he was manager at Queen's Park Rangers. Guinness were the big-money sponsors of QPR at the time. Now Venables suggested that Saunders could be employed by Spurs in a marketing role.

Venables twice brought Saunders to White Hart Lane with a view to him meeting Sugar and thus arranging some work for him. Sugar stressed there was none for him to do. But, again, Venables was showing flawed judgement in his associates. While possibly admiring his generosity in forgiving Saunders for his involvement in such a big scandal, one must also question whether such an employee could ever be in the best interests of Tottenham Hotspur.

The Final Breakdown

However, seven days before that acrimonious board meeting, on 21 January, Sugar wrote to Venables with an offer that showed Venables what Sugar now wanted. He pointed out that when they had bought Tottenham, he 'did not for one moment imagine that you would need to go to the lengths that you have to fund the transactions'. Venables' financial difficulties were now obviously well-known to Sugar.

The letter continued with a stinging criticism of Eddie Ashby: 'Nothing that he has done . . . has been done in a professional manner . . . His commercial judgement, in my opinion, is bad. If I speak very frankly, I observe that there is somewhat of a comfort factor of you having Eddie around in your life.'

Sugar then points out how, in public, he has not criticised Venables and his running of Tottenham. 'But I am afraid to say that I do not believe that the organisation is running properly and I think we have a long way to go to professionalise it.' He is particularly alarmed at this because roughly 50 percent of the money spent by Venables belongs to Sugar. 'When you go out and spend money on players . . . in most cases, I know nothing about it. I think, up until now, I have been pretty damn reasonable in allowing a completely free hand.'

Sugar is concerned that anything 'that implies that I am more senior than you in the company seems to annoy you and seems to be taken very personally'. Therefore the only other approach is 'to discuss alternative plans for each other ... I am not going to carry on in the way that we are at the moment.' If Venables will not privately recognise Sugar's seniority, then the only possible outcome is 'one or other of us departing from ownership of Tottenham, which I for one do not wish to'.

The effect of Sugar's ultimatum to Venables was to provoke an angry response from the chief executive. On one matter they could agree, he wrote: 'We cannot continue as present.' Venables pointed out that the imbalance in their stake in the company was brought about because Sugar had insisted on a rights issue 'rather than raising finance on the properties. You knew that I did not have the extra money.' As we have seen, the valuation of Tottenham property was £19.5 million, easily enough to cover the debts with the Midland Bank - but only by transforming one type of debt to another.

Sugar had complained that Venables did not seem to work hard enough, but he replied: 'I need to be at the training ground' as opposed to White Hart Lane, because 'that is where the football product is' during the week. Criticism that there was 'no direction' in the commercial and administrative departments was due to Sugar 'relying on Colin Sandy for your information'. Venables insisted that he himself worked a seven-day week.

As Sugar criticised Ashby, so Venables listed the failings of Sandy, including: 'The computer system for stock control is still not up after 14 months . . . management accounts are never on time . . . board minutes are at the last moment ... no reconciled merchandising accounts since May.' There were other accusations of Sandy going beyond his role - 'he cut across my actions' - while his behaviour with regard to Sugar's new contract was 'at best disgraceful'.

Venables pointed to Sugar's angry response to newspaper speculation that the club was to sign Paul Wilkinson of Middlesbrough. Clearly, Sugar had wondered why he had heard nothing but, in fact, the story was merely speculation: 'If you asked me, I could confirm that.' He concludes: 'I will sit down with you to look at alternative ways forward, The sooner the better.'

As the struggle between them was clearly drawing to its climax, Sugar insists he embarked on a policy of reconciliation, inviting Venables to his Chigwell home for a one-to-one, heart-to-heart chat to resolve their personal differences as discussed in the correspondence above. In a relaxed atmosphere over a private lunch, away from the him-or-me environment of the boardroom power game, Sugar explained the reasons why the club should adopt the Amstrad computer system. Venables listened intently and then raised the subject of his salary: 'I'd like £400,000 a year, no strings.' This claim was not rejected out of hand, but Sugar wanted to increase bonuses so that salary was linked to the club's success. They also discussed Ashby, whom Sugar was anxious to see go. If Ashby were ousted, and replaced by John Ireland, the board would then re-negotiate Venables' salary. But Sugar also made an offer to buy Venables out, with a cash settlement on his contract. If he was going to continue as chief executive, Sugar felt it was appropriate to discuss Venables' salary once the season was over. But Venables raised the subject again after the Chelsea match on 20 March when they were unwinding at Scribes. Venables justified his claims for a massive pay rise because his close pal George Graham was earning more than him. Venables, according to Sugar's version, compared himself to Graham, and pointed out that Graham once worked for him at Crystal Palace where he had taught him much.

Venables also justified his claim because of his role in turning around a deficit into huge profits, but Sugar refused to accept the transformation had a great deal to do with his business expertise. The year ending 31 May 1992 showed a substantial increase in income from television, with Spurs involved in the European Cup-Winners' Cup - an area where Venables certainly had made an enormous contribution because his success in winning the FA Cup enabled the club to qualify. But the £3 million profit from the sale of Gascoigne and the enormous influx of money from the new Sky television deal were the real reasons for the 'success' in turning a loss into profit. In fact, the general trading income from the company declined on a like-to-like basis. For example, attendances were ten percent down in 1991-92 and did not improve in 1992-93.

All these issues had been building up, so that by the board meeting of 6 May 1993 'matters came to a head', according to Crystal, with Sugar in a 'volcanic mood' at this meeting. The reason was that Crystal had accused Sugar of 'altering board minutes to suit his position', while the computer issue came to the crunch. Venables presented the report he had commissioned relating to the 'advisability of containing Spurs computer information at Amstrad'. Sugar 'became very angry' at the contents and, according to Crystal, swore at him and accused him of 'arselicking Terry

Venables' in front of the entire Spurs board. Crystal feared that he would be physically attacked. Sugar maintains that he kept his self-control and never threatened Crystal. Then, according to Crystal, 'he emptied the contents of his briefcase over the table and threw a letter at Terry Venables and stormed out, roaring "You'd better read this." '

The letter demanded that Venables should leave the company and offered Venables a pay-off, of just under C million (the price he had paid) for his shares, plus £450,000 as a full and final settlement of his cancelled contract. Sugai later apologised for his behaviour to fellow directors Berry and Yawetz, but not to Crystal or Venables. When Crystal did receive a call in his chambers the next day offering an apology, Sugar emphasised that he stood by every word he had said. Just as he would not make suggestions on footba! tactics, he did not expect Venables to advise him on computers. The split between Venables and Sugar was no* irreparable.

On Monday 10 May Venables received notice of a board meeting for that Friday - and Venables knew that that would be the day he would be kicked out of Tottenham.

The next day, at Highbury of all places, there was a highly controversial and contested Spurs board meeting. Venables and Crystal arrived together at Arsenal for the North London derby at 6.35pm. Venables headed for his 'work' place in the dressing room, while Crystal went to the Gunners' boardroom. Berry, Sugar and Sandy were already there. A share in the football club had been transferred from Ian Gray to Colin Sandy; the effect of this was that the plc now controlled all the shares in the football club and could call board meetings of the club without the usual notice requirements. It was later suggested in court that the minutes of the meeting were false because Tony Berry was, in fact, in Crystal's car when the meeting opened at 7pm. Berry and Crystal did go to the latter's car (to collect a telephone number) but had returned by that time.

Crystal claims that he had 'no indication' that a board meeting had taken place in that room at Highbury until the following day when he received a fax from the company secretary of the minutes, signed by Sugar. Venables and Crystal are convinced that the board meeting was a 'fabrication', a manoeuvre to remove Venables from office. To back his interpretation, Crystal claims that he spoke to Berry who agreed that no board meeting had taken place at Highbury and that in a letter dated 13 May 'Berry admits the board minute is a sham'.

The agenda for the board meeting on Friday, 14 May was concise:

1. Transfer of nominee share in Tottenham Hotspur Football and Athletic Co Ltd.

2. Termination of chief executive's contract.

3. Approval of new director(s).

4. Any other business.

Sugar and Sandy voted in favour of the resolution to sack Venables. Crystal voted against it. By reason of his personal interest, Venables was disqualified from voting. The fifth director, Tony Berry, who owned some five percent of the share capital, abstained, but he made it clear later, had it been necessary, he also would have voted in favour of the removal resolution.

Venables went to the courts that evening to seek an injunction to be reinstated as chief executive. He also wanted the courts to order Sugar to sell his shares to Venables at a price determined by the courts. His company Edennote launched proceedings at once under section 459 of the Companies Act. The gist of them is that when Sugar and Venables acquired their shares on an equal basis in June 1991, they agreed that Venables would be and would remain chief executive, and Sugar chairman. That agreement, it was argued, continued unchanged, even though Sugar now had vastly more shares.

Venables' court-room argument was that Sugar had breached that agreement between the two of them, because he was determined to take control of the running of Tottenham and so exclude Venables from any substantial part in the management of the club. Venables argued that, in order to achieve his objective of wresting total control for himself, Sugar acted in bad faith in breach of his duties as a director, and therefore demonstrated that he was unfit to be a director of Tottenham.

Venables tried unsuccessfully to force Sugar, through the courts, to sell out to him, gaining a court order restraining Tottenham from acting on the board resolution of 14 May to end Venables' service contract. However, the case never actually went to trial, because the judge refused to grant a continuation of the injunction, especially as there was some doubt whether Venables had the huge funds needed to buy Sugar's shares, something he would only have been able to do had he won his case.

It was impossible to devise any satisfactory management structure for Tottenham while such an acrimonious dispute continued. Venables remained on the board as a director, pending the trial. The enforced cooling-off period brought about by the injunction had done nothing to lower the temperature: Venables and Sugar remained at daggers drawn. The internal row over the negotiations to re-sign Neil Ruddock ensured that that remained the case.

Venables' lawyers had a two-pronged attack: they claimed wrongful dismissal and, at the same time, pursued his more central court battle for control of the club. They sent a letter to Sugar's solicitors demanding to know the reasons behind the sacking of Venables. The reply ran to four pages and detailed 40 reasons, yet Venables still claimed that he did not know why he had been sacked. Sugar commented: 'You know, quite honestly, nine folder outlines all of our allegations. Now, I'm not saying that he has to agree with them, but how can he sit there and say, "I don't know what it's all about." '

Sugar desperately wanted the Spurs supporters to know the truth right from the start, but legal niceties prevented the Spurs chairman from revealing the full story for several months. His first comments on the issue came, a few days after Venables was sacked, in an interview with Sunday Times editor Andrew Neil on LBC. Sugar's anxiety to inform the public was evident, as was his frustration, because his lawyers had advised him to say as little as possible. He knew how the decision would be received by the press and the fans, he explained, and his expectations had proved correct. However, he continued, this showed that the board must have excellent reasons for taking these steps. 'It was a decision which we felt was necessary.'

The offer made to Venables in the letter of 6 May, flung down in the board meeting, was supposed to have been private and confidential. However, it was quickly leaked and dismissed as inadequate, for Venables wanted £6 million out of recognition for his efforts in saving the club and bringing it into profitability. Had Venables settled at this point or at any time prior to the full court hearing, all the accusations and revelations about Venables would most likely not have emerged.

Sugar explained to Neil in the radio interview that he thought the offer was generous, because he was aware of the burden of debt faced by Venables and this would easily clear that problem - much easier than if Venables were to try to sell such a large number of shares on the open market. He also believed that Venables thought he should be compensated for the interest payments he had made as well as for his legal fees.

Sugar barely commented on Venables' involvement with Ashby, saving his most hostile comments for Crystal: 'I blame Jonathan Crystal for everything that has happened to this company in the past two years -1 firmly blame him for everything . . . Terry will reflect in years to come how his dream to run and own part of a football club was destroyed basically by Jonathan Crystal and nobody else.' Sugar made it plain that he detested Crystal because, although a Venables appointee, as a non-executive director, he should have been impartial, a crucial part of his role on behalf of the shareholders. Instead, he was not independent, according to the Spurs chairman, and backed Venables totally.

For example, just before Venables' dismissal, he and Crystal amended chief scout Ted Buxton's contract so that he had the right to unilaterally extend the option agreement by a further two years. It was easily done, as the original 'Expiry of Appointment' clause read: 'The Appointment is for a fixed term of three years expiring on 30 June 1994 whereupon the Appointment will come to an end. Following the expiration of the three-year fixed term, the Company may, as its option, extend the agreement for a further period of two years on the same terms and conditions as hereinbefore described.' However, the two men altered it so it read 'the Company or the chief scout may . . . extend the Agreement . . .'

This meant that if Buxton were dismissed, Spurs could be forced to pay compensation for an additional two years. The additional clause is handwritten, and is initialled by 'JC' and 'TFV' as well as 'EB'. Buxton was indeed sacked as new manager Ossie Ardiles refashioned his backroom staff as most new bosses would do. In effect, the additional clause gave Buxton a five-year contract - and a handsome pay-off - which Spurs contested.

There was another Crystal intervention that angered Sugar, as he was astonished to discover that the club had been landed with a solicitor's bill for nearly £3,750 for helping Neil Ruddock's wife Sarah and David Howells' girlfriend, Debbie Grant, out of a jam. They had been involved in a public fracas and Crystal, in his capacity as Spurs director, instructed a firm of solicitors, Burton Copeland, to sort out the problems which arose from it. Spurs were told that solicitors had to act because Neil Ruddock's performance in the vital FA Cup tie at Manchester City might have been affected while he worried about his wife facing proceedings. Sugar commented on this, saying: 'If you take your wife to a pub and she's involved in a punch-up, you surely wouldn't expect your boss to pay to sort out the trouble.'

However, football is not like any other business and Venables clearly felt he should come to Ruddock's rescue by bailing out his wife. Players, and their families, can receive astonishing support from their clubs, and this can play a large role in keeping them there. Venables and Crystal's speedy actions would have been greatly appreciated by the players, but perhaps it would have helped if they had informed their boardroom colleagues so that the bill did not come as such a surprise.

What had happened was that a number of players had

gone, together with their wives and girlfriends, to a nightclub. While there, the women were abused because of their links to Tottenham. During the argument that followed, one of the adversaries complained that she had been 'cut with a broken glass'. The police had arrested the two women and it was at this stage that Crystal was contacted and Burton Copeland were brought in. The police eventually decided not to press charges against Ruddock or Grant.

Sugar did underestimate the strength of feeling among the fans and made an error in his comment 'that fans are very fickle', explaining that after a few wins it could be that Venables was 'forgotten' and the new manager would be a hero. He also denied that there was much of a protest outside the ground, claiming that most of those present were journalists and photographers.

However, he soon realised the strength of the fans' backing for Venables, and Sugar had a very uncomfortable summer, widely portrayed as the villain of the piece, while Venables remained a hero. During the court case, he was spat at, his home was broken into and his car was wrecked.

Although Sugar played down the role of Ashby as a source of friction while being interviewed by Neil, he was distrusted by Sugar. Within two months of being declared bankrupt, Ashby was taken on by Venables as his personal assistant at a salary of £78,000 (later raised to £90,000), employed in a 'consultancy' capacity. Yet, in at least two letters, he signed himself as 'general manager', a role for which he was disqualified as a bankrupt. Sugar found out about this in September 1991, but was initially understanding, knowing that this can happen in business. However, it was only in April 1992, when Colin Sandy presented Sugar with a six-inch thick dossier on the whole of Ashby's business career, that Sugar decided he had to go.

But Venables refused to sack Ashby. Venables says: 'I was informed that Ashby was a bankrupt in the early part of July/August 1991. I confronted him and told him how annoyed I was that he had not informed me himself.' Venables informed Sugar and accepts that the chairman was very 'decent' about it initially. But Sugar was appalled that Venables continued to support Ashby unashamedly, and his attitude that such a man should be given a chance.

Ashby had a vastly different appraisal of the situation. He was convinced that Sugar's loss of patience with him and other Venables aides was a calculated plan. He argued: 'In my view, both the compilation of the dossier and the subsequent exclusion of me from the board meetings was the beginning of Mr Sugar's plans to weaken Terry.' Venables refused to see why Sugar should not want such a man in such a crucial role. Even if there were good reasons why Ashby was well-qualified to draw such a salary, Sugar did not feel they counted for much. Venables' loyalty to his friend went beyond the call of duty, so when Sugar said: 'Can you not deal with it? Can you not sort him out, deal with him, send him on his way, give him some financial kind of settlement and work it all out?' Venables did nothing.

Despite Sugar's initial comment that he was moving into Tottenham on a strictly business proposition, Venables acted as though football clubs could operate differently. To prove just how strangely Venables ran his business affairs at Spurs, Sugar ordered financial experts to unravel the former chief executive's lifestyle within the company, down to the last penny on his phone bills. It seemed from the files as if Venables' private bills had been paid using company funds for a wide range of items including holidays, a speeding fine of £725 on 21 April 1993, a £30 parking fine, and telephone bills for three numbers. Venables commented that he paid for any private holidays and other personal expenses when asked.

Scribes benefited as Tottenham paid for linen tablecloths, restaurant bills and even a dance floor that was moved to Scribes from Spurs. Scribes menus and artwork were printed and paid for by Spurs, as were some of the pictures on the walls. Spurs celebrations, such as the one for reaching the FA Cup semi-final (at a cost of over £2,500), were often held at Scribes. Ashby used his Spurs account to pay for parties there, such as the one held for Joe Powlawski. It was as a result of this that Ashby's account was stopped, and all expenses had to be signed by Sugar, although Venables signed his own claims. However, Venables denied there was anything untoward in these arrangements.

Many of these items of expenditure have since been repaid, but Colin Sandy commented that 'collection of the money has either been difficult or only successful after some delay'.

In retrospect, given the breadth of issues on which Venables and Sugar disagreed, and where Sugar felt that Venables was not up to the job, even feeling that Venables wasn't devoting enough time to the club or working closely enough with the football management team, perhaps the biggest surprise is not that he was sacked, but that he wasn't sacked sooner. But Sugar hoped that Venables would change and learn what his role did and did not comprise. Furthermore, he knew how popular Venables was, and therefore realised that he had to have some very concrete reasons if he was going to seek his dismissal.

While Sugar might argue about the deal Venables struck over the sale of Gascoigne, there was no doubt that Venables had boosted Tottenham by signing him in the first place. He, too, can point to errors in Sugar's football economics when he recalls the time his chairman turned to him, at the time when the club was wondering how it would fulfil its obligation to rebuild the ground under the Taylor Report, and said: 'There's your stand!' When Venables asked what he meant, Sugar replied: 'We'll knock that Barnaby [sic] out for £6 million to some Italian team, it will pay for the stand.' Venables also cited a conversation with Sugar where the Spurs chairman said he would be happy to finish halfway up the table and reach the second round in both cups that season. Venables viewed this as an 'appalling lack of ambition'. But Sugar is extremely anxious to see the club win major honours.

While Sugar would occasionally show his inexperience in the world of football, his business sense and methods were essentially sound. Venables, for all his football knowledge, had wanted to expand his role and become a football club owner. To do so, he relied for financial advice on the bankrupt Eddie

Ashby and found himself in a series of dealings that were, at best, inept. Somehow, Ashby survived in his job at Tottenham for a few days more than Venables. His performance in the commercial department had been poor, so it was that on 17 May he too was sacked. Had Venables done this himself, he might still be at Tottenham.

CHAPTER FOURTEEN
The Court Case

Part One: The Battle for Hearts and Minds

TERRY VENABLES' popularity was at its peak. Fans bayed for the blood of Alan Sugar, while waving banners in support of the underdog, the man of the people. Surely the bully from the world of high finance and the City could not squash the footballing folkhero. The remarkable scenes as the crowd outside the High Court halted the traffic were manna from heaven for the television cameras.

While Venables was greeted enthusiastically by his supporters, there was an evil atmosphere when Sugar arrived. The Spurs chairman stood up to intolerable levels of intimidation: 'I had some nutters on. They shouted down the phone: "You're dead". I didn't take them seriously, but I did need a bodyguard for a couple of days. There was hate mail, death threats, and supporters' demonstrations.' On the evening Venables was sacked, Sugar returned home to find Sugar Scum Out daubed on the wall surrounding his house. When he attended court, there were 'hostile Tottenham fans in the lobby outside the courtroom itself. When I left I was jostled and verbally abused.' Sugar's family was also threatened. This was not the sort of support Venables wanted.

However, there was no doubt that Venables had widespread and well-organised backing from Tottenham fans and from the media, especially the sporting press. Nick Hewer, Sugar's personal publicity adviser, says: 'I met Sugar and other members of the Spurs board in the boardroom in the morning prior to the board meeting that would decide to sack Terry Venables. There were already crowds at the gates of White Hart Lane. In among those crowds, I spotted Donna Cullen from Good Relations. I knew it from that moment that the support in favour of Venables was being stage-managed. And, it had added spice, because my company had replaced Good Relations as advisers to the Spurs board at the time of the Sugar-Venables takeover.' The excesses of the fans were perhaps inevitable in such a heated atmosphere.

Good Relations' parent company is Low Bell Communications, chaired by Sir Tim Bell, who once plotted an election campaign for Margaret Thatcher while at Saatchi and Saatchi. They had the easier task at the beginning, while Hewer was bombarded and fighting a rearguard action for Sugar. However, he insists that the pressure on Sugar was greater and he reveals how someone broke into Sugar's garage at this time, though he told Hewer not to release the story. They had scrawled across the bonnet of his Range Rover 'Venables In, Sugar Out', the window of his daughter's car had been smashed and the mobile phone ripped out. Despite this intimidation, Sugar kept calm, hired security guards for his home and ensured his family was safe.

Meanwhile, Venables and Good Relations seemed to be having an easy run, although the PR company eventually had to serve a writ on Venables in October for nonpayment of a bill for £11,188.23 for their public relations advice. In five months, reveals deputy chairman Piers Pottinger: 'We had not even received a gesture of a payment, not a single penny . . . There was no dispute over the amount for our services provided. We asked him several times and he assured us that we would be paid. Whenever we approached him he would give no reason why he hadn't paid . . . Then, we were far from pleased when we discovered that he consulted another PR firm and paid them upfront. That was naughty.'

Venables knew he was on his way out once Sugar served a letter offering to buy his shares on 6 May. Venables shrewdly pre-empted his sacking and consulted Good Relations in advance of the fateful board meeting.

Donna Cullen was at the sharp end of the Venables-Sugar publicity battle. She directly advised Venables, became one of his chief aides and confidantes, with close knowledge of his feelings at the time of his sacking and during the court case. Donna, a lifelong Tottenham fan, had also advised Venables when he successfully took over the club in tandem with Alan Sugar. In retrospect, she has mixed feelings about Venables, because 'acting for Terry took over my life for a time'.

Venables' cause was very much helped in the publicity battle by the backing he received from the leadership of TISA, Tottenham's Independent Supporters' Association, who were to become affectionately known as 'Terry's Independent Supporters' Association' on account of their relentless backing of Venables. The catchy motto of their protests: 'T No Sugar'.

TISA had been formed in 1990 'because of the severe financial problems that came to light, and the threat of Robert Maxwell taking over the club'. The aims of TISA were clearly defined: 'It seeks to have a positive influence on the running of the club with the aim of seeing Tottenham prosper.' Steve Davies, a solicitor, was the chief co-ordinator of TISA, which had about a thousand members at the time of Venables' sacking. His allegiance to Venables' cause was unflinching throughout the most hostile times in the battle with Sugar. Had Venables won, his reward might have been a place on the Spurs board. As well as giving Venables vocal backing, TISA collected a reputed £15,000 from Tottenham fans to help Venables with his legal bills.

But it was the performance of Good Relations, and Donna Cullen that got the Venables bandwagon rolling so quickly. After the letter of 6 May, Venables knew what was coming and so arranged a meeting with the agency beforehand. As Cullen recalls: 'We discussed how best to break the story. He knew that Sugar was planning to get rid of him. He knew that the next board meeting was going to be critical. We worked out a clear plan of campaign for our media tactics. I told him to break the story before Sugar, and he did just that giving an interview for News at Ten. If we hadn't done that, we wouldn't have had the press outside the White Hart Lane gates the next morning, even before the board meeting. I suppose it must have seemed organised, but what happened was that Terry was acting on our advice.'

Cullen also pointed out: 'Terry was in touch with Steve Davies a week before his sacking to ascertain [TISA's] position and see what kind of support he could expect. That was down to TISA. Our job was to win the moral high ground in the early days, which we succeeded in doing.' How much of the support for Venables outside the High Court was down to Davies and TISA cannot be ascertained, but the judge believed some unruly fans' behaviour was such that they could be guilty of contempt for their attempts to intimidate Sugar.

Davies and Bernie Kingsley, another TISA organiser, formulated their views after personal discussions with Venables, but they did not initially speak with Sugar. Even when they had the privileged opportunity to study Sugar's affidavit in detail, they still backed Venables' cause until the final moment when Venables sold out his shares, and with it his pledge to fight on for reinstatement as chief executive. Their minds were made up very early on, because they were consulted by Venables four days before the controversial sacking on 14 May. It gave them ample time to plan their campaign of support for Venables.

TISA's summer newsletter revealed just how closely Venables liaised with this group of activist supporters: 'The first indication we had that there were difficulties between Venables and Sugar was in February during a meeting with TV. This was confirmed at the TISA meeting that month which TV attended but at that point there was little indication as to the seriousness of the problem.'

On Monday, 10 May, Davies and Kingsley attended a meeting with Venables who told them 'AMS wants me out'. When the men from TISA asked why, they were told: 'Sugar says that there is no reason.' Venables maintained for months afterwards he was baffled bySugar's decision, despite the fact that his lawyers were eventually presented with a full declaration of why he was ousted.

However, Venables' professed ignorance and Sugar's enforced silence led to much speculation, and increasing the suspicion it was simply a clash of personalities. Venables told Davies and Kingsley about the board meeting and the offer for his shares. He also told them of the meeting on 14 May at which he knew he would lose his job. Therefore TISA were ready with a statement immediately the news broke and they expressed their view that sacking Venables was not in the best interests of Tottenham.

As soon as Sugar saw Davies giving the, TISA view on television, he telephoned him to say that TISA's leadership should not express an opinion until they had heard both sides of the story. However, he had to tell them that he could not explain the reasons for the decision until a later date. Davies pointed out that, from where they stood, it seemed 'that Venables was doing a good job and that until we were persuaded otherwise he must expect us to continue to support him.' Venables was innocent until proven guilty.

TISA members were out in force on the morning of the board meeting of Friday, 14 May, as were many other supporters and hordes of press men. A short statement was read to announce that Venables had been sacked; Venables then emerged 'looking shell-shocked', announcing that he was going to consult his solicitors. Donna Cullen was delighted with how things were going, on the publicity side: 'We certainly gave value for money in those early days, as he had the upperhand without a doubt. Yet, Terry was very nervous about the sort of publicity he would get, and how much the fans would be behind him.'

The early signs were that many of the players backed Venables, notably Neil Ruddock and Teddy Sheringham. TISA also met several other players 'airof^whom expressed their support for Venables and their admiration for his management skills'.

Those fans hostile to what had happened were sure that the timing of Venables' axing was no coincidence: after Tottenham's last league game. Fortuitously for them, there was a testimonial that very evening at Enfield. TISA organised a demonstration there, which was heavily publicised beforehand, and they estimated that 2,500 fans joined in, including Neil Ruddock from among the players. They soon had something to celebrate: Venables had obtained an injunction against his dismissal, albeit for ten days only.

TISA's next step was to call a public meeting for the following Friday, 21 May, at which the popular support for Venables was clear. TISA identified themselves increasingly closely with Venables and, that evening, raised £2,000 and gained 200 new members, with a total of 700 having attended.

Meanwhile, Cullen and Good Relations were working hard behind the scenes. She recalls: 'It was very important to him to have the backing of the fans. For a man who has faced the press so often, it did surprise me that he was always a little nervous before a press conference, and often I had to sit alongside him and prompt him. I rehearsed him before the Sport in Question TV appearance and nagged him to get his act together.' Venables was particularly worried that he would face hostile questioning from Jimmy Greaves, who was pro-Sugar, so she advised Venables: 'If Jimmy Greaves is pro-Sugar, jokingly lean across and suggest he's been offered the PR job at Tottenham.' Venables was a quick learner, and the joke helped win over the audience.

Looking back on the whole controversy, Donna Cullen had this to say of Venables: 'Terry is incredibly well liked -there has to be a reason for that. I feel it is because he is a decent chap. Yet, there is no denying that he would have been far better off forgetting about his aspirations to be a businessman, that has proved to be misplaced. He needed better advice because he was very naive in the business sense ... he was not the Financial Brain of Britain! He allowed most of his financial transactions to be taken out of his hands and they were dealt with by others. He ended up with people who knew his business so well that he was reluctant to break with them. Very early on he was advised to distance himself from Eddie Ashby, but he never listened . . . The nature of the arguments are so damn complex that it is still hard for me to know who is on the side of the angels. But there came a time when I said to myself that I had to put my pen down. I was not getting full disclosure from my client and I backed out much earlier than anyone thinks.

'I felt like the piggy in the middle. To deal properly with a client I need to know all the ins and outs, all the warts, even if they are the biggest warts in history, otherwise how can I give adequate advice about how to handle the situation? I'm not saying there were large warts in Terry's case, but I was not confident that I was in possession of all the information I needed to operate effectively. There was a feeling of uncertainty on my part when I was confronted with questions about Terry's affairs I couldn't answer. I didn't have the answers from the horse's mouth either. I'd ask Terry Venables until I was blue in the face about Eddie Ashby, Landhurst Leasing and Elite Europe.' However, she got no reply and when Panorama accused Venables of fraud, Cullen admitted: 'I was no longer surprised, but the odd thing is that I don't hold it against Terry so much as against his financial advisers.'

Cullen still remains loyal to Venables despite all that has emerged in recent months: 'Maybe he is naive. But I feel he rescued Spurs for the proper reasons, the glory. He revelled in the sheer adulation of the fans. He lived in a false world, but I'm convinced he thought what he was doing was right, and that there was a vendetta against him. Otherwise, why didn't he walk away. He had an offer ... for his shares and he should have taken it; he would have been well off financially.' Talking prophetically, just after Graham Taylor had lost his job, she concluded that he 'should be in the running for the England job. That's where his talents really lie. Perhaps he should have stuck to management.'

Sugar's PR agent, Nick Hewer, knew he would be facing different problems and that he would be fighting a rearguard action. He remembers: 'On the day Venables was sacked, there was a general discussion before the board meeting and I told them that Terry Venables knew every sports journalist in the country, he's travelled with them, drunk with them, he was probably godfather to some of their children over the last 25 years' Hewer understood that the sports pages were always going to back Venables, while the majority of the fans and the players would also side with him. However, Hewer knew that the City journalists were more likely to back Sugar, while Cullen feared that the Sky-Amstrad link would possibly help swing Murdoch and his newspapers towards Sugar.

One of the first actions to be taken at Tottenham after the sacking was for Sugar to hold a staff meeting to explain the events that had taken place. Hewer recalls: 'The mood in the audience was very subdued. Flanked by Tony Berry, Douglas Alexiou, Colin Sandy and Peter Barnes, Sugar quietly outlined the morning's events, confirmed his commitment to Spurs, and, for the first time, suggested that Venables' lieutenants Crystal and Ashby had played a part in the chief executive's downfall. This was an important point, and one that would gain increasing significance in the coming days.'

The crowd outside White Hart Lane was clearly angry, so Sugar suggested they left in Hewer's car, as his would be recognised. Hewer noticed that Alexiou's car was being kicked and he commented: 'I was appalled by the aggressiveness of the crowd and I will need some convincing that it was not all pre-planned.'

A couple of days later, the Sugar side began to gain some support. First, Mihir Bose wrote an authoritative story in the Sunday Times on Ashby's many business failures. That same day, Andrew Neil, editor of the Sunday Times, interviewed Sugar on LBC, and the roles of Ashby and Crystal were again questioned. There was still a long way to go, as was shown when the court case started.

Hewer commented on the 'intimidation' of the crowd: 'I was simply staggered by the viciousness . . . When we left, the atmosphere was white-hot. Two policemen, on either side of Alan, guarded us as we left but, nonetheless, it was terrifying ... To my horror, as I looked across the courtyard, Alan's Rolls Royce was pointing down toward the Strand with a huge crowd outside the main doors waiting for him.' To avoid a potentially dangerous confrontation, they had to sneak out by a back door and into a waiting taxi.

Although Sugar must have been badly shaken by the hostility of the crowd, he insisted that he could say nothing about the real reasons for Venables' dismissal because of the legal actions. Had he done so, Sugar would have been in contempt of court and he was adamant that nothing should jeopardise the strength of his legal position. After the first day's troubles, Sugar's wife, Ann, insisted on accompanying him. But her presence did not stop someone spitting at him, nor did it stop the personal abuse. On another occasion, a group of about ten men, who, unusually, were neither wearing any Spurs shirts and regalia nor were they shouting, had managed to get into the courtyard and were seen swarming round Tony Berry's car, possibly mistaking it for Sugar's. Their quiet demeanour spelled trouble and the police were called to remove them.

Sugar remained perplexed at the feelings he had stirred, his previous involvement with football having been distant. He admitted that he found football a 'Chinese Wall', with the players' department 'a world of its own, very alien to what I had been used to'. He felt out of his depth at first, 'a businessman in the football world'. He went on: 'I decided to stand back and not poke my nose into affairs where 1 was not experienced, like the playing department.' He admitted that it was only once he got into his third year that he felt he was beginning to learn, commenting, perhaps jokingly, 'I might be mouthing off in five years' time.'

Good Relations were just as active after the court case. Donna Cullen notified newspapers of the 'petticoat power' demonstration planned outside Sugar's Chigwell home. She suggested that various wives and girlfriends, and even ex-Spurs players like Paul Allen, would be there. Allen was furious because he had already refused to take part. In the end, only Neil Ruddock's wife turned up with a couple of her friends and children. It was not a spontaneous demonstration, as it appeared on television, because Good Relations had laid on the transportation to get there.

Venables' decision to go to the courts to seek an injunction against his dismissal ultimately proved to be his downfall. It provoked Sugar and his team of accomplished solicitors at Herbert Smith into accumulating the evidence against him, and the closer they looked, the more they found. Sugar, in reality, never wanted a court-room confrontation with Venables, and blames Mrs Justice Arden for granting the injunction on the evening ofVenables' sacking. Sugar disdainfully says: 'The whole thing should have been over there and then on FridayMay. We got a freak decision in the High Court at eight in the evening from what we could see was a lady judge under great pressure. Frankly, we cannot blame her for making the decision she did, knowing that the matter would be passed on to another court for final judgement, and also she was given inaccurate evidence which was disproved at a later date. From the decision to impose an injunction, there erupted months and months of work. We were deluged for the next seven weeks. It was a tale of woe.' He continues: 'Look, there was never any court case. There were just court cases to decide whether there should be a court case!'

TISA's leaders had a privileged insight into the reasons why Venables was sacked. On Sunday 23 May they were given the opportunity to study Sugar's affidavit after a phone call from Sugar in which he simply asked the fans to keep 'an open mind'. Sugar suggested they askedVenables if they could see the evidence the Spurs chairman had filed. Davies, Kingsley and James Loxley attended Venables' solicitors to view Sugar's affidavits. Having seen the evidence they announced themselves to be relieved that there was no suggestion ofVenables taking backhanders, as had been rumoured. They were not unduly worried about the £50,000 paid in cash to McLintock, saying: 'Tottenham may have been in breach of FA regulations by making that payment but that was a long way short of illegality.'

TISA's bland acceptance ofVenables' actions, the surprising use of cash payments and the allegations of 'bungs' being paid was complete. They concluded their report by saying: 'Reading Sugar's affidavit strengthened our view that TV's sacking was not justified.' This was an astonishing conclusion to reach.

Having taken TISA into his trust and found that the minds of their executive were already made up, Sugar protested to Davies on Friday 4 June over the incidents at his home. Their report explains: 'He said that he accepted that TISA were not involved but if it happened again he intended to get an injunction against TISA. It was disappointing for Sugar to take this view - to express and protest a point of view is a democratic right not removed by someone else who holds similar views doing something illegal. In fact, TISA actively discouraged any form of "direct action" and refused an invitation to take part in the protest outside Sugar's house.'

TISA continued to support Venables, even after he lost his battle to remain with the company when the main court hearing got underway on 10 June. The arrival of the popular Ossie Ardiles as the new Tottenham manager was dismissed as 'not really relevant as such, because the real issue was about who controlled the club - Sugar or Venables'. It was also clear to TISA that their stance was a popular one, for they reported a 70 percent growth in membership and announced that they had raised over £10,000.

Sugar clearly felt that TISA were unrepresentative of the views of the ordinary Spurs fan and called for Davies and Kingsley to resign. Ilie Spurs chairman demanded a democratic vote and a new leadership in a letter to Kingsley dated 2 July 1993 and published in TISA's newsletter. Sugar offered to involve the fans, so long as they ceased backing Venables: 'You are entitled to your opinion - I do not have to share it. It is my opinion that you are not a Tottenham Hotspur supporter, you are a Terry Venables supporter and I am afraid that the stance that you havE taken publicly clearly indicates this.'

However, TISA did admit that there was one area in which Venables' actions could be criticised: 'Eric Hall's role is perhaps more questionable, and there is a possible conflict of interest in acting both for Venables and several of the players.' But that was about as far as they went.

However, there were some Tottenham fans who felt that Sugar's decision was the right one. Mark Jacob, writing in the fanzine Spur commented: 'I was concerned about Mr Venables surrounding himself with loyal servants. This has been demonstrated by the appointment of Mr Ashby and Mr Crystal and, indeed, the influence of Eric Hall. On the playing front, this can also be seen by players coming out in support of Mr Venables recently. Surely these players must know who pays their wages. If they have no feelings for Tottenham Hotspur Football Club, I suggest they move on. If the only reason they came to Tottenham was because of Mr Venables, this only goes to prove the theory that Mr Venables has attempted to make himself bigger than the club. If Mr Venables does leave, I wonder how many players will follow him?

'The most important factor at present is for stability at the club. We have a superb crop of young players. They, above all, need a manager they can admire and respect and not one whose string of clubs and pubs have gradually been repossessed and who is constantly looking for get-rich-quick schemes in order to furnish his public image and ego. If Mr Venables just concentrated in one area I feel he would have achieved so much more, but by placing his finger in several pies he has not ween able to focus his efforts in one direction.'

Another letter, highly critical ofVenables, appeared in When Saturday Comes: 'At the outset of their relationship, we were told that Venables would concentrate on the football, while Sugar took care of the finance. It is clear that this did not happen. IfVenables was "the football man", what the hell were Peter Shreeves (1991-92), Doug Livermore and Ray Clemence (1992-93) doing? Venables claims no responsibility for the fiasco of the 1991-92 season, but is happy to claim the credit for the promise of the 1992-93 season. What do you make of that, Doug and Ray? Venables' prolonged campaign has probably cost Clemence his job, as Sugar was forced to bring in Ardiles to calm the storm, whipped up by Venables.'

By the beginning of September, after Venables had sold

his shares in Tottenham, TISA finally decided to try to patch things up with Sugar by saying: 'We have consequently brought our campaign in support of his reinstatement to an end. We consider that it is in the best interests of the club to put its problems behind it, including our differences with you as to the merits of Mr Venables.' And they concluded by explaining in a TISA Newsletter their reason why they had been so consistent in supporting Venables: 'The short answer is because the overwhelming majority of members supported it. TISA's aim is to see Tottenham prosper and, in our view, that is more likely to happen with TV in charge than without him.' But whether that was true became more unlikely as the full implications of his financial dealings inside the club were revealed, threatening the very survival of the club in the Premiership. Being relegated, as had happened to Swindon Town was surely not a way 'to see Tottenham prosper'.

Part Two: The Court-room Debates

Jonathan Costal was Venables' legal guru, but he roused a great hostility in Sugar. Venables came to rely heavily on Crystal's legal advice, but Sugar detested Crystal's involvement with Venables and resented his role as a nonexecutive director in Spurs. The Spurs chairman was suspicious of Crystal, describing his relationship with Venables as an unhealthy hero-worship. Far more contentious was Crystal's attempt to send Sugar to prison on a contempt of court charge. Sugar was convinced it was a diversionary tactic to delay the court hearing from deliberating on the central issue: Venables' dismissal and his bid for reinstatement at Tottenham, forcing Sugar to sell his shares to him through the courts.

Crystal was seen as over-protective of Venables and aggressive towards anyone likely to be critical of the Spurs chief executive. Crystal would enter the White Hart Lane press room, situated in the car park, to warn journalists to be careful of certain stories that might be breaking. He was quick to dispatch warning letters, and was also involved in attempts to try to play down certain newspaper articles in the club match-day programme, even if they later turned out to be true. For example, the club programme once took the unusual step of insisting that it was nonsense that Paul Stewart was coveted by Blackbum Rovers, because he was not being sold - yet not long afterwards he was transferred to Liverpool.

The most potent force in keeping journalists, and their newspapers, quiet was to issue threats of writs and, on occasion, actually serve the writ. Sugar says: 'It's a cottage industry. You know you're not going to court, but a newspaper will pay up £5,000 here, £15,000 there because the cost of defending such actions is so expensive.'

The animosity that existed between Sugar and Crystal surfaced publicly just days after Venables' sacking when the Spurs chairman blamed Venables' associates, and Crystal in particular, for wrecking the harmony within the corridors of power at White Hart Lane during his interview with Andrew Neil. And, Crystal must/have had a significant input in advising Venables to seek injunctive relief from the courts on the evening of his dismissal.

Venables was granted an injunction in the Chancery Division of the High Court before Mrs Justice Arden. It was the first step on the legal merry-go-round that Venables could not stop, or rather would not stop, until it almost broke him financially and he was forced to withdraw.

In his claim to prevent his dismissal, Venables pleaded to the judge that he needed to go with the team to South Africa, although the trip was 'in some doubt'. He also announced that he had an urgent match at Enfield 'tomorrow', and if he did not turn up all the players would walk out on the club. His third claim was that his massive borrowings to finance his purchase of Spurs shares would have to be paid back instantly he was no longer chief executive. However, the Enfield match was taking place that very evening when the case was in court. The South African game had been cancelled the night before and

Venables had already instructed club secretary Peter Barnes to return the match money. The players wouldn't be leaving the club as they were under contract. And, Venables' insistence that his agreements to borrow money were repayable on demand if he no longer held the office of chief executive at Tottenham was incorrect because no such clauses existed in the deal he had done with the Bank of Liechtenstein to refinance his borrowings. On the following Monday, Venables' solicitor was forced to send an affidavit apologising to the court for his inaccurate statement.

Sugar believed that the support of Crystal, a barrister and a leading libel lawyer, was vital in securing the injunction. It was probably that initial success which convinced Venables that it would be worthwhile pursuing Sugar in the courts, but the Spurs chairman insisted that they had persuaded a relatively new judge: 'It was a maverick decision, a freak decision, and from then on all we saw was a succession of delaying tactics designed to put off the day of reckoning.'

Sugar had already made Venables an offer to buy him out on 6 May, but Venables described it as 'derisory'. That offer was for around £3.5 million for Venables' shares and compensation on his contract as chief executive. But he had no intention of walking away with little more than the money to pay off his enormous debts. He believed this was inadequate compensation for winning the battle to buy Spurs. However, he did now need a way out and, through an intermediary, tried to reach a financial solution. Philip Green was the go-between. Sugar says: 'He poked his nose in, but I never made a new offer. Venables wanted £6 million!'

Venables' opening shot in the court-room war was to try to send Sugar to jail. The application for an 'order for committal' was the first item before the judge at 10.30am on Thursday, 10 June. It demanded: 'that Sugar be committed to Her Majesty's Prison for his contempt in seeking to deter, by threatening to discredit his professional reputation, Jonathan Crystal from making an affidavit' in the defence of Venables. Three days before the hearing, the application was made to send Sugar to prison with Crystal's affidavit disclosing an amazing personal clash with Sugar over Venables' case.

What had happened was that a few days previously, on 1 June, Crystal had been working at home on the affidavits for the Venables case when he received a call from Sugar. Crystal insists that Sugar said that he had 'something to show me', although Sugar's version is that he wanted to see him. Sugar rang Crystal on impulse from his car phone early in the morning to warn him that he had information. The court later heard that this information was something which affected his professional career and would have had adverse implications for his family.

Sugar had become increasingly agitated by the importance that Mrs Justice Arden had attached to Crystal's evidence in granting the initial injunction. Sugar became obsessed that Crystal's position as a barrister gave him an unfair advantage: 'I was fighting an unequal battle if Mr Crystal's word was to be accepted more readily than the ordinary man's. I remained fearful that, by reason of the fact that he was a barrister, his evidence would carry a presumption of credibility which my evidence would not enjoy.'

Sugar wanted Crystal to take the train to Brentwood that very day to meet him at Amstrad's headquarters. Crystal was busy for most of the day, but they made an arrangement to meet at White Hart Lane that afternoon as Sugar would be there for a management meeting, although he had to leave at 5.30pm. Crystal arrived at the ground at 4.40pm, bumping into Sugar on the stairs. It was then that Sugar accused Crystal of 'blind loyalty' to Venables. Sugar warned him, as the court was told, that 'if he were to give evidence in a certain form, unacceptable to Mr Sugar, then publication will be made of something which affects his professional career'.

Crystal feared that Sugar was out to discredit him professionally, and thereby harm his family, if he produced an affidavit favourable to Venables. Crystal went to his car and scribbled a note on a piece of paper about what they had said. Once Sugar was told by his solicitors that his actions constituted a contempt, Venables' solicitors in the case, Kanter Jules Grangewood, received a fax from Herbert Smith, representing Sugar, with an unconditional apology. Crystal instructed his own solicitors, Burton Copeland, for the purpose of the contempt charge, accusing Sugar of trying to 'influence the evidence'. Crystal also reported the matter to the Professional Conduct Committee of the Bar Council. Crystal insisted that Sugar's allegations were 'entirely without foundation'.

Sugar was repentant. 'Whatever the difference between our respective accounts of the events of 1 June, I am advised and accept that in the course of my dealings with Mr Crystal I committed a contempt of court. Accordingly, I take this opportunity at the outset of my affidavit to apologise unreservedly to this court for my contempt.'

After Mrs Justice Arden had granted an injunction on the night of Venables' sacking on 14 May and after a one-day hearing proved far too inadequate to hear the full pleadings, the case opened to decide whether to maintain the injunction as Venables proceeded to a trial for reinstatement as chief executive and to force Sugar to sell him l his shares.

Venables' QC, Mr Mann, soon set the scene at the beginning of the first day, 10 June:

> This, My Lord, is a battle of two giants. The first is Mr Sugar and his company Amshold Limited, a giant of the industry. The second is Mr Venables, a giant of the football field, who has made his mark in an outstanding career, both nationally and internationally, and whose reputation is of the highest and undisputed. The battle is over the control of Tottenham Hotspur plc, and through it, its 100 percent owned subsidiary, Tottenham Hotspur Football and Athletic Club.

Among the multitude of accusations and counteraccusations, arguments and legal jargon, Venables' QC put the whole matter very succinctly:

> The position, really, we have to accept is this, Mr Sugar and Mr Venables have fallen out with each other, they do not get on, for whatever reason, and one of them has to go. That is really what it amounts to. Matters have deteriorated to such an extent that it really is unlikely that, in the very long term, they will be able to get on with each other. That implies that we, or Mr Sugar, one or other of them, will have to buy each other out. We ask the court in a petition for an order that we be permitted to buy Mr Sugar out.

Venables' QC then made two contempt charges against Sugar, one relating to the conversation with Crystal on 1 June and the other was that a board meeting was deliberately called at precisely the time the affidavits were due and that these two actions amounted to contempt of court with 'serious consequences'. But Mr Heslop, Sugar's QC, ridiculed the contempt charges. The Vice Chancellor considered 'that Mr Crystal's evidence would be unaffected' by the conversation on 1 June.

The attempts to remove Crystal from the Spurs board were seen as a further effort to isolate Venables and make the interim agreement, worked out on 25 May and stating that both parties would try to work together until a decision had been made whether Sugar could sack Venables, or whether Venables could force Sugar to sell his shares to him, unworkable. But it had already proved unworkable as the problems over contract talks with Neil Ruddock illustrated. It was now impossible for the two men to work together in any sort of harmonious relationship.

As Venables had feared, and Sugar predicted, the case for his reinstatement and the order to buy the chairman's shares was lost. On day three, 14 June 1993, the Vice Chancellor made the judgement that left Venables' professional life in tatters, with him also facing massive legal bills. He announced that, with the club in a state of 'paralysis', the judge could not allow the situation to remain with everyone at the club in a state of confusion. Otherwise, he 'might well have been attracted by a course not urged by either side, which would involve Mr Venables continuing to deal with football matters, but not otherwise. However, there is a further factor which has weighed with me. It concerns the prospects of success of these proceedings.' He went on:

> There is a major difficulty facing Mr Venables. At the time of the rights issue, he appreciated that in future, Mr Sugar would own significantly more shares than he would. This would cease to be a 50/50 company so far as they were concerned. Mr Venables' case is that an oral arrangement was made between them. Mr Sugar said, and I quote: Tn any event, trust me. Even if I pick up all the shares, we still have the shareholders' agreement.' Mr Venables says he understood Mr Sugar to mean that if they ended up with different numbers of shares, they would still share control and, in effect, not seek to oust each other. Mr Sugar denies this. Even if this was said, and Mr Venables' understanding was well-founded, Mr Venables' case for an order under section 459 requiring Mr Sugar to sell his 48 percent shareholdings to Mr Venables is still difficult.

The problem for Venables was, the Vice Chancellor explained, that there was nothing in the written contracts relating to his role which guaranteed the safety of his position, nor was there anything in the mandatory cash offer of July 1991 (when both men asked the shareholders not to sell to them), nor was there anything in the rights issue of December 1991 which related to side agreements about the respective roles of Venables and Sugar. 'There was nothing to suggest that the board of directors did not have the normal right to hire and to fire the company's chief executive or that there was an agreement or understanding that if

Mr Sugar and Mr Venables should fall out, they were nevertheless bound to continue to support each other indefinitely.'

The judge accepted that it was not easy to deliberate on Venables' expectation that he should continue in the running of the public company, pointing out that, at Tottenham, many of the shareholders were fans more interested in success on the field than 'by commercial considerations'. He concluded:

> I do not think it would be right or sensible for me to make an order having the effect of overriding the majority decision of the board and restoring to Mr Venables all or some of his functions as chief executive until the trial. To do this would in all probability merely be postponing the date on which all concerned must face up to the fact that, for better or worse, Mr Venables' appointment has been determined and face up to the consequences of that fact . . . Whether Mr Venables' dismissal was in the best interests of Tottenham is not a matter for the court to decide. That is a matter for the Tottenham board, to whom this decision is entrusted under the company's constitution, although it is a matter on which the shareholders can express their views to the board. I am not therefore making any order regulating the affairs of Tottenham pending the trial.

With that decision, Venables' court-room battle was over, and lost, on day three. Day four, 15 June 1993, was merely the tidying-up procedure in which Venables' lawyers opted against pushing ahead with a contempt charge. Sugar's apology was accepted by Venables' lawyers. The Vice Chancellor still had the option to send Sugar to jail, but as the issue had been dropped, he decided not to. In making this decision he commented on the behaviour of Tottenham fans outside the court, saying: 'Mr Sugar has been subject to physical intimidation and abuse and threats. This behaviour was itself a contempt of court ... It goes without saying that Mr Venables is in no way responsible for this.'

Spurs and Sugar were awarded costs and their solicitors filed a 'bill of costs' against Venables' company Edennote for £400,000. On top of that, Venables' own legal costs are estimated to be around £250,000. Venables sold his 23 percent stake in Spurs for £3 million, but £2 million went to the Bank of Liechtenstein, which had a charge on a large proportion of the shares. Venables also had other loans, as both Landhurst Leasing and Igai Yawetz had lent him money to buy his shares.

Venables' financial security was further threatened by a series of legal actions. Former public relations advisers Good Relations issued a writ for more than £11,000. Scribes was also under pressure from a champagne company, and then General Portfolio went to the courts seeking a winding-up order, claiming £150,000.

It was this financial pressure that had helped persuade Venables to abandon his legal battle and forced him to sell his shares. Tottenham solicitors commented on the costs faced by Venables' company: 'Edennote's ability to pay is in some doubt according to their last set of accounts and the financial information that shows.' Therefore Spurs will have to pay the legal fees in advance and hope that they will be able to get them back. However, Venables still has an outstanding legal action against Spurs and Sugar for unfair dismissal as chief executive.

CHAPTER FIFTEEN
. . . But a Poor Businessman

TERRY VENABLES has always hated the derogatory portrayal of him as the archetypal Cockney barrow-boy 'spiv' made good. But perhaps he will have to be content with the lovable rogue image, for, however he sees himself, his charm, charisma and champagne lifestyle - despite his repeated failures as a businessman - make him seem something of an Arthur Daley-type figure. For, in the final analysis, Venables is a man of modest education, but with great knowledge of football, who found himself in charge of his very own sweet shop in Tottenham Hotspur. Accusations, in court and elsewhere, abound of a £1 million fraud, involvement in a 'bung' to Clough, and breaches of soccer rules on interest-free loans to players and payments to agents. But he is no Al Capone.

The final conclusion on how serious have been his misdemeanours will not be judged by the football authorities alone. The Inland Revenue, the Department of Trade and Industry, Customs and Excise, as well as the Premier League and the Football Association are all currently investigating Venables' activities, with the threat from the Inland Revenue being the most worrying for him, as it has been for other football personalities. Their approach is thorough and unrelenting, taking as long as two years to formulate their case before they make an example of someone in the public eye, such as Lester Piggott.

The Inland Revenue have a special branch of inspectors probing into a whole variety of football-related dodges, with Venables being just one among many who is being investigated. There is a team in Solihull, led by Paul Kendrew, looking into clubs, managers, players and agents. Mike Eveling, press officer for the Inland Revenue, explains: 'Everybody's tax affairs are covered by law, protecting confidentiality, so we can neither confirm nor deny that Terry Venables is involved in an Inland

Revenue investigation. But it is common knowledge that we have a special unit investigating throughout football and we have taken note of any information that we receive from people within the game. We keep our eyes and ears open and note what appears in the press or on television and we follow that up if necessary.'

The Panorama programme, shown in autumn 1993, was viewed with great interest by the Inland Revenue, especially as the programme is yet to receive a writ for its most important allegation, that Venables was involved in a £1 million fraud to help him buy his shares in Spurs in 1991.

The activities of soccer agents Frank McLintock and Eric Hall are under scrutiny after the collapse of Hall's court case against Tottenham, when he submitted an invoice in October 1992 which the club refused to pay because it disguised the true nature of his 'work'. Players have signed affidavits that they paid an agent who was also paid by the club. It was Venables who authorised the payments to the agents from the club, which raises the question: did the agents get a good deal for the player, or for the club? How did the agents manage to resolve this glaring conflict of interest?

Given all the allegations, and the fact that the Premiership set up a three-man enquiry to look into breaches of transfer rules following the references to a 'bung' being paid during Sheringham's transfer from Nottingham Forest to Tottenham, many were surprised that Venables was even considered for the England manager's job, especially as the 79-year-old chairman of the FA, Sir Bert Millichip, has always remained suspicious of Venables and told Sugar that he would appoint him 'over my dead body'. However, speaking in mid-January, not long before Venables finally did get the England job, Millichip commented: 'There are many who would like to see Venables as England manager, but he has a funny reputation.' He continued: 'It is well recognised that I did have my reservations about Terry Venables, but they have been greatly dispelled. There are many, many accusations against him, but when I have asked, no proof has been delivered. There is no proof whatsoever about these allegations. If he was going to jail next week he would not be appointed, but he's not going to jail.' The biggest doubter in the FA had been won over -the way was now clear for Venables.

Rick Parry had advised the committee that no charges against Venables were likely - indeed, he did so even before Sugar gave evidence to the enquiry on 18 January 1994. It is astonishing that the FA has decided to turn a blind eye, because other authorities, such as the Inland Revenue, will not do so if they discover anything untoward. Perhaps the FA fear that once the issue is in the open for one club, many others will be similarly exposed. But, clearly, in their search for a high-profile manager, after so many leading candidates snubbed the opportunity of succeeding Graham Taylor, their hand was forced. Just as Tottenham could not sue their own players for the return of interest-free loans, so the FA could hardly charge their newly appointed England coach.

Sugar, seeing how the situation was going to be resolved, commented the day before he went to give his evidence to the Premier League commission: 'There is no question of me bringing any new information that is going to change any decision the FA may make with respect to the appointment of Terry Venables. There is no way anyone can say that no FA rules were broken - they were. The committee have already been supplied by Tottenham with all the information and there is no secret in the fact that the information includes conclusive proof that FA rules were broken with respect to the way transactions were conducted with agents and that those rules were broken during the period of time that Terry Venables was chief executive since 1991.'

Sugar continued: 'If the FA have decided to choose Terry as England manager, they will have done so based on his footballing ability. And obviously they would have chosen to disregard the fact that he, in his capacity as chief executive, breached certain FA rules. That, of course, is a decision that the FA are entitled to make. I hope, and we all pray at Tottenham, that if they are prepared to waive this in respect to Terry that they will obviously not bring any action against Tottenham and that all the talk of us being severely reprimanded, or even relegated, is also wiped clean.'

Sugar concluded: 'It could be a great day for football and the football industry . . . Terry's back in the game and in work; Tottenham get a completely clean sheet from the FA and no more aggravation with Terry.' Sugar felt Venables' appointment vindicated Spurs. He was wrong. But really he was being capricious.

When FA chief executive Graham Kelly first commented on the Sheringham and Gascoigne transfers, his main concern was for 'the straight managers, the ones who think a bung is found in the bathroom'. He was genuinely shocked over Venables' assertion that payments for agents in transfer deals are 'commonplace' in the Premier League.

The FA would be very disappointed if the problems in English football were compared with the corruption in France and Italy. Kelly was anxious that the reputation of English football should not suffer: 'I don't accept that everybody does it, but anybody who does risks disciplinary action if found guilty of being in breach of the rules. Action is needed in this whole area. But there is a dilemma. Many people in the game don't want agents licensed because it gives certain people a veneer of respectability they would not normally merit.'

It was for this reason that the three-man commission of Parry, Steve Coppell and Robert Reid QC was set up on 4 November 1993, with the aim of looking into previous transfer dealings but also to try to regularise the role of agents. In the current situation, it is clear agents will not go away - there is too much money in the game. Coppell commented that agents had not been too much of a problem while he was manager at Crystal Palace, but he believed that supporters did not like to see 'vast sums of cash disappearing. In future the game needs regulations to ensure that every penny is accounted for.'

Outside of football, Venables is regularly under scrutiny. His company Edennote has been wound up, Scribes West faced similar problems, too. Yet it is this combination of success on the field and failure off it that has encouraged one publisher to pay a hefty six-figure sum (rumoured to be over £200,000) for his autobiography, not to mention the England job, his lifelong ambition that seemed to have become an impossibility after the events of May 1993 and the subsequent allegations. Somehow, Venables keeps on bouncing back, so while 1993 was a bad year, 1994 has already seen a revival in his professional reputation which he hopes can restore his financial situation.

Before May 1993, Venables seemed to have achieved all he could want. He was the football man who could diversify - a very rare breed. He was an author, a television scriptwriter, a board game inventor, the owner of a West End club and the joint owner of one of the biggest football clubs in England - Tottenham Hotspur. He seemed to have it all, yet two successful businessmen who have worked closely with him considered him a flawed genius: Irving Scholar referred to Venables' 'grasshopper mind' - something illustrated by his wide diversification; while Sugar was even more critical, right at the outset of their partnership: 'Venables thinks he's an entrepreneur, I don't.'

Encouraged by Ashby, perhaps, Venables became too ambitious. His previous business failures, such as his tailoring shop, were small-time; Eddie Ashby tried to take him further. It was the presence of men like Ashby and Hall that brought about Venables' downfall at Tottenham. Combined with the way he over-extended himself to buy into the club, Venables found himself out of his league. His expectation that Sugar would finance his dealings and plough money into Spurs, all the time leaving Venables a completely free hand, was unrealistic. So, too, was the belief that they were equal partners. Had he realised where the true power lay within the club, Venables would have survived. Sugar was happy for Venables to have the high public profile at Tottenham - it was one of the chief executive's great strengths that his media relations were excellent - but he was not so pleased if Venables started to believe that it was he who was the key to the survival first, and then revival of the club.

When the power struggle began between the two men, Venables made the fatal mistake of believing that, because Sugar was not 'a football man' like he was, Sugar would throw his hands in the air and shout 'I've had enough'. Sugar did, but not in the way Venables had expected. In the end, in exasperation, Sugar said: 'I've had enough of you.' So it was Venables who left, and not Sugar.

Perhaps Venables also expected too much from Sugar. In buying his Tottenham shares we have seen just how far into debt he had to go - his salary did not even cover his interest payments. It is possible that Venables hoped that Sugar's involvement in Spurs would lift the share price from the 75p offered to Scholar and Bobroff to £2 or more. Had this happened, he could have sold off some of his shares and so brought his finances under control - but it did not. When he eventually sold his shares it did little more than clear his debts and end the crippling interest payments before his creditors seized his assets.

Venables admitted: 'Looking back, perhaps I was a bit reckless or even stupid in taking on this task. Certainly, it has overstretched me financially. I could have been left with nothing. I have lost a lot of money already and the danger remains that I could lose a lot more.'

The second half of 1993 showed just how bad things were for Venables' finances. Laurent Perrier took out a bankruptcy petition against Scribes West in July, backed by other creditors. This was later followed by a writ from landlords the House of Fraser. Meanwhile, an Edennote cheque for £2,500, signed by Venables, to Scribes shareholder Noel Botham bounced; one company in which Venables was a director, Recallcity Ltd, was wound up in London on 15 December on the application of Customs and Excise, who claimed they were owed £41,000; PR firm Good Relations issued a writ for £11,000 against Venables. And so the list went on. Things have improved since then for him, especially as regards Scribes West. Indeed, on 23 January, Venables was quoted as saying: 'The bill to Good Relations has been paid within the last 24 hours, or should have been.' However, five days later, Piers Pottinger from Good Relations stated: 'I can assure you that he has not settled with us . . . The writ remains issued and we shall proceed.'

Given all these problems, it was hardly suprising that Venables' own barrister, John Steinfield QC, was forced to admit that Venables was no great businessman during the court hearing on 29 July 1993, when Edennote was asked to put up £300,000 as security for the costs to pursue his claims for reinstatement and to buy out Sugar. Even this proved beyond him when the details of his affidavit were questioned. It stated: 'As at the 31st of March 1992, £1.473 million was liable to the Petitioner [ie. Edennote, the company used for purchasing his Spurs shares] with a liability to myself and companies which I control, incurred by reason of me and these companies have loaned to the Petitioner a substantial part of the money needed to acquire shares in Tottenham. This position was the same at the 31st March 1993 and continues to be the same today.' In other words, he still claimed to have control over a large proportion of his shares.

Justice Harman disagreed: 'Not a ha'penny is due to any company controlled by Mr Venables, contrary to his oath ... It makes his oath a little difficult!'

Venables' barrister, Steinfield, had little choice but to admit the 'apparent discrepancy' in his client's evidence regarding the £1.473 million. He explained: 'When Mr Venables swore his affidavit he had wrongly assumed that the £1.473 million was a reference to the loans that he had made personally combined with the loans that his companies made.'

'Grossly careless!' replied Harman. 'All you are telling me is that his evidence is not worth the paper that it is written on?'

'I am saying that he made a mistake,' Steinfield insisted.

'It is totally inaccurate on every possible foot ... it does not give me great confidence in Mr Venables' financial abilities.'

'Well, he has never asserted himself to be a person with great financial abilities.' Steinfield was left with no other option but to make this humiliating comment on his client's capabilities.

Venables' decision to try to stand up to Sugar from his position of weakness was misguided. As a result, his reputation has been severely tarnished. Even his supporters now see that he has little to offer beyond his skills as a football coach, which are second to none, and would be enough for most - but not Venables. He wanted to have several options open to him and so increase his personal security, as football management is a risky business. But it was his non-footballing interests that brought him down, even leading to his longest spell out of coaching since he began in that role.

Sugar's assessment of Venables is damning: 'Never mind winning the FA Cup, Terry Venables is such a great actor, notably his TV performances, he deserves a Hollywood Oscar! He might be the Charisma Kid to his fans, but I know him better than that.' He admitted that the decision to sack Venables was a hard one, especially as he knew how the fans would react.

But when Sugar pointed out what he thought was wrong practice, he was disappointed in Venables' response: 'You bring it to his attention, you say to him, "Look, come on, these things shouldn't be done in this way."

' "Right, OK, I know your style. It won't happen anymore." '

But Venables continued to do it his way, so, as Sugar commented: 'In the end you have to say: "I'm sorry, no matter what the fans think, no matter what the outcome is going to be, we've got to do something here." '

Sugar has little sympathy for Venables and his much-publicised problems, which he believes he brought on himself. Besides which, it was Sugar, not Venables, who faced a hostile crowd and had his home broken into. He concludes, regarding his involvement with Tottenham: 'I have gone this far - and I will see it through. More recently I've found the principle of being involved with one of Britain's most famous football clubs incredible, delightful.

The club has been badly scarred by all the unrest of the summer. The healing process will take time - and it will need more than bandages and embrocation. How quickly that healing process is achieved depends a lot on success on the pitch. That is the most important facet of any football club.'

Venables' views on Sugar are similarly critical: 'I think my mistake was I chose the wrong partner for me personally. For someone else, he might be alright. But I don't think he deals easily with partners. He has to be very much a hands-on person who calls the shots. I would think that, to a certain extent, I'm very similar myself as well. But I wouldn't have put all my money in, put it on the line, if I was going to rely on Alan Sugar's wisdom about football. He actually said: "Terry'll look after the eleven on the field and I'll look after the eleven in the bank"... because eleven was the debt we had at the bank at that particular time. That would have been fine if he had kept to that, but he really wants to do the whole thing.

'I just think it's just so unfair and it's misleading to the public, and what concerns me more than anything is that I've always had a rapport with the fans and with the players. I've never shifted from my grass roots and I think to try to discredit me, which I feel he has to do, because all the time I'm not discredited, he will not be accepted. The team will, the manager will, but he will not be accepted.'

More important to Venables was the desire to clear his name - a wish that became essential once the England job became a possibility: 'To have this slur over me is not a very comfortable one. I would say to any newspaper, any television programme, if they can prove it, I'll give a quarter of a million pounds to charity. If they can't, they put a quarter of a million pounds to charity, and if they can't uphold an allegation, don't put it in the first place. They can't prove it, how dare they.'

Sugar has commented that he doesn't think Venables is a 'born villain', and that the allegations against him may have i been brought about by 'the people around him who fix

things for him. So, perhaps only by default he has done something wrong.' He continued: 'He has brought all this on himself. I gave him the best piece of advice months ago, get yourself a top firm of accountants and sort yourself out.'

Venables' defence is based on his belief that he was i sacked because of a personality clash - a battle he now realises he could not win. Venables insists Sugar explained his decision as follows: 'He said that there cannot be more than one governor, one boss, and I said "But you knew that when we started ... Is there anything else?" He says: "No, it's just that there's got to be only one boss and it's the only way it can be."'

Venables has also suggested that Sugar is 'paranoid' that people are always 'stealing from him'. He has complained l that Sugar made financial decisions without proper consultation. Both men did their best to discredit the other, and there was much unsavoury mud-slinging, with each man trying to find as many backers as possible. Even now, many months afterwards, it is hard to remain neutral on the issue.

Both men cultivated their supporters in the propaganda battle. Venables had particularly strong support from the

I back pages of the newspapers, the Tottenham Independent Supporters' Association, as well as friends like Eric Hall, who was the agent for so many Spurs players. He gained professional PR advice from Good Relations. But perhaps

| his most consistent and valued support came from his wife, Yvette.

Yvette recalled that in a year of troubles, the worst moment came when her husband was sacked, and from that i time she helped him plot his campaign. She lived through the torment of the battle with Sugar prior to that decision and the court-room wrangling after it - although she did not

I attend the High Court because she considers herself a I private sort of person.

She remembers: 'There was friction, it started to be unsettled after board meetings. I saw the frustration in him, although he is a man who rarely loses his temper. Then we'd get home and there would be reams of faxes from Alan Sugar. I think he was trying to wear him down. At one stage he criticised Scribes. I wrote him a letter back saying! was appalled that he brought

Scribes into this.' When Venables had the chance of a good offer for his shares, a vital moment in the whole saga, Yvette was a major influence in her husband turning it down and fighting on. 'That was the only time we discussed what he should do. My automatic reaction was "no". If he'd taken the money we don't know what might have happened. It's better to die regretting what you have done rather than what you haven't done.'

She also pointed out: 'Every single football club uses agents for transfers. Are they all doing something illegal? I know deep down that he is a true gentleman. If he had done so much that was wrong why did he go ahead with the court case? Surely, if he were guilty, he would have run as fast as he could in the opposite direction, not leave himself open to scrutiny.'

Another source of support was the libel laws when articles were deemed offensive. One such occasion was when he took offence at articles by one of the present authors in the Daily Mirror on 9 and 10 July in which it was stated that he had entered talks to buy Luton Town Football Club. Venables was still insisting on his ongoing commitment to Tottenham. His solicitors pointed out in a letter of 25 August: 'Our client is totally committed to this litigation [to be reinstated at Spurs and to buy Sugar's shares] and his desire to return to Tottenham and to suggest that he was secretly proposing to acquire a controlling interest in Luton Town portrays him as being both hypocritical and guilty of practising a deception upon the public and those supporting him in his fight to return to Tottenham Hotspur.'

Yet, within a week of the letter being sent, Venables had sold his shares. Indeed, he may already have commenced negotiations to sell them. Nevertheless, the writ was served on 7 September denying any attempt by Venables to buy a controlling interest in Luton Town and complaining that 'the articles dismiss our client's denials of any intention or proposal to purchase Luton Town in terms which portray him as being a liar. As such, the articles represent a serious defamatory attack upon our client.'

Given his financial difficulties, it was not clear how Venables could afford to buy Luton - but he was also trying to buy out

Sugar, too. The articles listed the times, places and people present at the meetings when Venables and Eddie Ashby discussed the purchase of Luton. There can be no doubt that Venables was involved in talks with Luton chairman David Kohler about the purchase of the club. Privately and confidentially, the meetings were confirmed. Kohler and Venables met with two other people also present, one of whom was Ashby. Both he and Venables signed confidentiality agreements. Kohler was convinced that Venables was looking into the feasibility of buying Luton for himself and that he wanted to make an offer when the two men had a meeting in Kohler's Hampstead home.

Kohler gave Venables all the figures, the wage bill and other details. Venables made it clear he wanted to make an offer there and then. But Kohler suggested that Venables went away and read the figures.

Kohler was annoyed that Venables never came back to him with any decision after expressing such keen interest. At least Kohler wanted a courtesy phone call to say that he had pulled out. He contacted Sugar about the potential ramifications of such a deal.

The other key figure in this issue was soccer broker Paul White, who acted as the intermediary between Venables and Kohler. He set up all the meetings and knew first-hand of the interest expressed by Venables in purchasing Luton. The first, informal, chat took place at Scribes West, the second secret conference was at the instigation of Venables. It was for these reasons that the Daily Mirror was not intimidated, as so often happens in such cases, into settling out of court but continued to defend itself. Indeed, it has continued to enquire into Venables' affairs.

More serious were Panorama's allegations regarding the deal with Landhurst Leasing, which it described as a 'fraud'. Venables has insisted the police look into how the programme came by the crucial documents as he believed they had been stolen. The police could find no evidence to support this and, subsequently, Venables' solicitors suggested to the BBC's lawyers that they may have been forged.

Venables seemed to have been given important support in his version of events when Ray Needham, the police officer called in by Venables to prove that the documents used in the Panorama programme had been stolen so as to discredit him, stated, in an article which appeared in the Sunday Mirror on 16 January: 'I am satisfied that Mr Venables has not been up to any mischief. He has been accused of improperly obtaining a £1 million loan. That is simply not true . . . Although I was called in by Mr Venables and asked to investigate the theft of documents, I had to be satisfied that Venables was not simply trying to cover up a £1 million fraud. We could find nothing wrong.'

Venables, delighted by this, commented: 'The loan was perfectly legal. It has just taken a long time for people to start to believe me.' Indeed, Sir Bert Millichip finally publicly endorsed his candidacy.

However, the hext day, Scotland Yard announced that Needham's statement had been misinterpreted, as Needham had been asked merely to investigate the alleged theft of documents and not the fraud allegations.

The Serious Fraud Office stated: 'We are investigating the affairs of Landhurst Leasing plc and we are aware of allegations of misappropriation of funds. We are aware that a company called Edennote, of which Terry Venables is a director, obtained leases from Landhurst Leasing and were among a number of a wide range of clients, but we have never been investigating Terry Venables and we are not doing so.' One reason why this may be the case is that the Serious Fraud Office only deals with frauds amounting to £5 million or more.

Also on 17 January, the Financial Times ran a story quoting Colin Wright, a director of TransAtlantic Inns, as saying: 'We were horrified when we discovered that all the assets of TransAtlantic had been used by Terry Venables to raise a £1 million loan. None of the directors of the company had authorised such a transaction.' The article also pointed out that a further document had emerged which gave more details about the sale and leaseback arrangements for the fixtures and fittings on which the loan was arranged. Venables' solicitors, Burton Copeland, would not comment in detail on the issues involved but did say: 'It is not accepted that Mr Venables signed the lease that you refer to as being dated August 30 1991.'

The article in the Financial Times came at the worst possible time for Venables, reopening the debate about the financing of his purchase of Tottenham shares in 1991. However, he was able to announce that he had managed to sort out his debts involving Trans Atlantic Inns and Landhurst Leasing. He has stated that he has paid a substantial sum to cover his debts to TransAtlantic, now in the hands of receivers. Meanwhile, he has paid £400,000, plus £100,000 a year for the next four years, to Arthur Andersen, the receivers for Landhurst Leasing, in settlement for the controversial £1 million loan to Edennote.

Commenting on these settlements, Venables said: 'I have been working on all these matters for some time. 1 haven't made a big song and dance about it, because I wanted to put the record straight when everything is over. But I have paid out a lot of money.' He also commented on the timing of Bashir and Killick's article, which he believed set out to embarrass him, by saying: 'I don't know how many times I have to keep repeating this: the police have said they are taking no action and I don't know why this persists. Maybe Panorama think if they keep on hammering on about this, people will believe them. If they call it new, people will think it is. I'm getting fed up with it myself.'

Clearly, Venables had to fight the allegations against him with the England job at stake. He commented in a newspaper article: 'There has been nothing solid to substantiate a single allegation against me. I've been the victim of sheer weight of innuendo . . . I'm rescuing my reputation. I shall be around for a long time yet . . . And when I've settled these scores, I will be back working in football . . . yes, in a tracksuit but no, not as manager of Wormwood Scrubs. In a high-profile job.' And they don't come any higher than that of England team boss.

It was back on 21 October that Venables' solicitors

wrote to insist that the BBC broadcast an apology, offer him compensation, pay his legal costs, and never again repeat their accusations against him. If the BBC did this, no writ would follow. *Panorama* will contest any legal action and they are yet to receive a writ. In addition, Venables' lawyers insisted they would seek 'aggravated damages' if the BBC sacked him from his lucrative contract, £150,000 over two years to August 1994, to appear as a soccer expert on Sportsnight and Grandstand, with special brief to comment on the England team. They commented that the programme was a 'character assassination of our client . .. it is difficult to conceive a more wounding attack on his character and reputation.' It had caused 'enormous upset, massive and possibly irreparable damage to his reputation I and standing.'

I There is no doubt that the issues over which Venables I and Sugar fell out included who controlled the company, I who had power over the merchandising wing or the compu-I ter system. Venables comments: 'We fell out over things | like that. There was no mention of any backhanders or anything like that. All that crap has arisen since then.' But Sugar was concerned with more than just who did what, he was also interested in how it was done. It was in the realm of how things were done that Eddie Ashby, whose role in the bust-up Venables downplays, caused so many problems, because his ability was questionable. Venables defends him, saying: 'I've only known him a couple of years, but I've got a lot to thank him for. For one thing, he's kept all my records - every bit of paper ever to come out of I all this, and that will be my defence in the end.'

Unfortunately, pieces of paper serve only to incriminate Venables, rather than to vindicate him. The more he tries to defend himself, the more he is overpowered by the sheer volume of evidence provided by Sugar.

Venables has since commented on the effect the constant barrage of criticism has had on him, and how he is viewed by the general public and Tottenham supporters in particular: 'I feel angry and confused. At first, there were lots of letters from

Spurs fans, saying they were right behind me, how they wouldn't renew season tickets. But after the TV programmes they got fewer. People used to stop me in the street and shake my hand, saying they thought Sugar was . . . something unprintable. But that has stopped now. I feel as though I've been found guilty of something but I haven't done anything. And it is frustrating just trying to tell people that, when all the time they think I'm a crook.' I He even feels that family and friends look at him in a different light: 'I'm beginning to feel like the man in the films who is found with a smoking gun standing over a dead body, knowing that I didn't do it but nobody believes me. It's horrible, like some kind of nightmare.'

Venables has suggested that documents have been tampered with, his offices burgled and his telephones tapped. So worried did he become that he asked the police to look into his suspicions, but they came up with nothing. He concluded in a piece which appeared in the Guardian on 9 November: 'I've been in this business 35 years without a blemish and all of a sudden I'm a crook, I'm naive, I'm a fraud and I'm out of the running for the England job. That's hard to take. I'm totally pissed off.' Yet, within two months, he was the leading candidate for the England post, within three months it was his. Four months later, to the day, his first England team went into action. A new chapter in his life had begun, he could only hope that the old chapters did not come back to haunt him.

CHAPTER SIXTEEN
A Bright New Dawn

TERRY VENABLES' APPOINTMENT as England coach was not only the fulfilment of a lifetime's ambition, it gave him back his credibility. His early success at Wembley, after the disappointments of the Graham Taylor era, captured most of the headlines in his first few months in charge of the England side. But there were other stories that revealed that his off-the-field problems had not entirely disappeared.

The company at the centre of his original purchase of Spurs, Edennote, was wound up in the High Court. Remarkably, Frank McLintock's First Wave Management joined Tottenham Hotspur plc and Alan Sugar in the winding-up petition, claiming they were owed £2,427.80. Given the close relationship between McLintock and Venables, it was astonishing that McLintock's former company should be chasing such a comparatively small sum. The winding-up order also damaged Venables' claim for unfair dismissal against Spurs, because two-thirds of his salary had been paid to Edennote and now the receivers were in control of the company and that claim but Venables has come to an arrangement with the receiver.

Venables also found it difficult to remain within the boundaries set up by his new contract with the FA. When Jimmy Armfield had been discussing the England position with Venables, he had made it plain that the new coach should not be dragged into any courtroom confrontation over the Spurs claim. His two-and-a-half-year contract, which would take him up to the end of the European Championships in 1996, included an agreement that he would sort out his legal wranglings within six months of signature. However, six months on, he had still not dropped his unfair dismissal claim against Spurs.

Of much less importance, though still an irritant to his new bosses, was Venables' involvement in a PFA-backed phone line.

FA chief executive Graham Kelly was forced to reprimand him after complaints from a number of clubs, that these lines were in direct opposition to their own club-call lines and were taking away potential revenue. The clubs were particularly anxious that he should not interview their players. Venables, who had committed to the phone line before the England job was his, subsequently withdrew from it.

There were other embarrassments: NatWest announced that it had demanded payment of £65,000 as a guarantee he had given for a loan to one of his bankrupt companies, Recallcity. Now, with interest, they were claiming £66,493. Venables insisted that the bank owed him money: 'I have no intention of paying this. As far as I am concerned, they owe me money because they wrongfully transferred money from my accounts.'

But one of the longest-running issues in the first part of Venables' reign was his attempt to recoup almost £150,000 from one of his former business associates, Paul Kirby, after he had been faced with demands from creditors of TransAtlantic Inns for £500,000. What made the situation particularly awkward was that Kirby was an FA councillor, the FA representative for New Zealand and Oceania and also the chairman of the FA's publications committee. Kirby had been a director of the ill-fated TransAtlantic Inns, which was central to the Panorama expose of Venables in which it was suggested that wrongdoing involving the company had helped him to buy his shares in Spurs. Panorama claimed that Kirby and fellow director Colin Wright had no knowledge of Venables' activities in their company.

It was a sad end to a friendship that had begun when the two men met during Venables' period at Barcelona. In August 1994, Venables finally issued a writ claiming that Kirby owed him £50,000 in interest on top of the original sum of around £150,000.

Meanwhile, the Premier League continued its enquiry into Spurs, Sugar passed over various documents so that the club could be seen to be making a clean breast of things. One of the most important issues was the relationship between the club, its players and their agents. Because of this, and a series of interest-free loans, the club was fined £600,000, had 12 points deducted from their total at the beginning of the 1994-95 season and was banned from the FA Cup for a season. On appeal, the fine was increased to £1.5 million but only six points were to be deducted.

But all these problems did not alter the FA's support for their man, which must have been a great relief to Venables, who continued to find himself under pressure and his finances under continuing scrutiny. However, in the summer of 1994 it was leaked from the Crown Prosecution Service that there was not enough evidence to prosecute Venables, Clough and McLintock over the Teddy Shering-ham 'bung' allegations made by Sugar in his affidavit to the High Court.

Clough was quick to vindicate Venables: 'I am delighted for him. I have known Terry for a long time and he was a good friend of mine throughout my days in football. I am very pleased that this matter is now out of his hair. It was the only possible outcome, because he knew and I knew there was no case to answer.'

McLintock also commented: 'The worry over this drove me out of the soccer agency business and I still feel the good reputation I had over 30 years in the game has been damaged. If enough mud is thrown, some of it inevitably sticks. I learned that Alan Sugar called in the Fraud Squad to investigate my company and when something like that happens it is bound to be a big worry, even though I knew I had never done anything wrong. I always felt I was just a pawn in a much bigger battle between Alan Sugar and Terry Venables, but I'm glad it is all over now and I'm especially delighted for Terry.'

Venables, too, was very pleased that he had been cleared. 'I'm glad it's all over. Having something like this hanging over your head is not pleasant at any time. I just have to say that I'm relieved the whole case is finished.'

Sugar was less happy with the decision and commented: 'As long as there is air in my lungs and I can breathe, 1 know what

Terry Venables told me, and I stand by every word I had written in my affidavit to the courts. I gave evidence to that effect and nothing will ever change that. My fellow Tottenham director Tony Berry also gave evidence on what he heard Venables say, and he feels the same way as me. It's not just one man's word against another - Tony Berry knows too.'

Berry gave evidence to the police and to the Premier League enquiry relating to a lunchtime conversation with Venables over a meal they had had at Langan's when Venables had received a call on his mobile phone. Sugar says: 'Tony Berry's statements make it clear that Terry Venables told him that a certain manager likes a bung. He got a call from Ted Buxton as he was trying to sign a player. But as far as the law is concerned, you need to have clear-cut evidence in order to bring a prosecution, and the police, after months of enquiries, felt that they had insufficient evidence to bring a criminal charge. It is not up to the individuals to disprove anything, but for the police to prove it.'

Former Tottenham star Gary Lineker has commented on how pleased he is with the way the situation at the club is finally improving after all the recriminations: 'Another reason for the fans to feel ebullient is that, with his signings of Klinsmann and Dumitrescu, Sugar appears finally to be concentrating on the necessities of Tottenham, rather than what seems to the outsider a certain amount of paranoia about Venables. This must be a good thing for Spurs and, for that matter, England.'

However, when Ardiles suggested that Venables should come to White Hart Lane again so that he could see his England squad members, Anderton and Sheringham, in action, Sugar immediately made it clear that Venables would not yet be welcomed back at the club. The publication of Venables' autobiography in September 1994 heightened the feud between the two men. When Venables announced the England squad to meet the United States on 7 September, he read out a prepared statement regarding Sugar following a report in the Sun.

It said: 'I'm aware of the publicity over the weekend that again centred on my relationship with Alan Sugar, the chairman of Tottenham. I've tried over the past six months to keep my thoughts to myself, despite much provocation. But this morning - according to one national newspaper -once more Mr Sugar alleged that I hired a public relations company to organise a near riot outside the High Court. He adds that people spat at him and his wife. He clearly blames me for this, and for a similar incident outside his home. Such allegations he knows to be nonsense. There is no evidence to support them. They are, I understand, libellous. My number one priority remains to produce a successful England football team. But, meanwhile, I shall be considering after the next few days what response is demanded by this latest and most outrageous accusation that has been directed at me.'

Once Sugar studied the contents of Venables' book the writs were quickly served by the Spurs chairman and Tony Berry. Sugar demanded a public apology or would take Venables all the way to the witness box.

However, for most people, the real story was the transformation of the England side, which had begun with the worst-kept secret in football. Since mid-December 1993, it had been apparent that, as much through process of elimination as curriculum vitae, Terry Venables was the man to lead England after the despair of World Cup failure and the ignominious exit of Graham Taylor. Throughout January 1994, in a series of meetings, it became increasingly clear that despite further revelations about his business dealings, the FA had chosen their man.

When the formal announcement was made that Tel Boy was to be the new coach - not manager - there wasn't an interested soul in the country who wasn't aware of his identity. Still, out came the familiar navy blue mohair overcoat for the investiture at the Venue of Legends, Wembley Stadium, and it seemed that just about anyone who mattered was there. The official FA handout before the crown was bestowed made no mention of a name, but the illuminated sign screaming 'Good Luck, Terry' gave it away. There were, surprisingly, few smiles because deep inside Venables had got what he had always wanted - his hands on the reins of English football. It was, he believed, and many in the game shared the view, his destiny to guide England to a new horizon.

In this case the target was the 1996 European Championships which England host and which Venables expects to win. There were no false promises, no messages that he could turn dross to diamonds. Just a commitment to a type of football that he believed was necessary for the demands of the game at the global level. 'I want the England team to play in a manner which brings admiration from the public, which means good football but not fantasy football because there has to be common sense in the approach and the tactics. I am seeking imagination but that does take time.

'It will need to be a bit simplistic and efficient, without alternating systems too much. The quality is undoubtedly there, even if it is not everywhere you'd want it. But I have been excited by emerging players this season. The target is the European Championships, but we do want to win games in the meantime and we must be fully prepared to have the best chance of winning it. I hope in the next two years we will be able to show English football in its true colours. I am bringing to the job myself and my experience and hopefully I can get together with the players and bring the best out of them. The situation is straightforward. It is whether they can pull on the white shirt and say: "I'll show them that I can do it" or whether they shrink a little. I have to find out about them and how successful they want to be.'

As a statement of intent it was encouraging, a man who wanted to put the smile back on the face of English football, to develop a system of play and an alternative to it that players could understand and be familiar with, that was simple yet effective. And, above all, to give English football back its pride.

And so it was that the man who had arrived under a cloud where most other managers depart under one, took charge of the national game with three games of a season to run, matches against Denmark, Greece and Norway, when the focus would be on him. It could not have been easy, for Venables had slipped out of footballing habits, of going to matches to size up players. After all, his last contact with the game had been as a managing director. But he was like a golfer who had left his clubs in the cupboard. Once out on the practice ground, he soon picked up the good habits. And one of his favourite ones was to coax and coach the best out of the enigmatic Paul Gascoigne. After all, he had signed the finest talent in the English game from Newcastle United for a fee of £2 million and then subsequently sold him on to Lazio for £5.5 million.

'Getting the best out of somebody so good appeals to me,' Venables was to say. 'I enjoyed working with him when he was a Tottenham player. And he is patriotic, there is no doubt about that. When he pulls on an England shirt it is important to him. He has a great desire to be a great player but more than anything else he enjoys playing football. He feels comfortable with me. I know him as a player and a person and hopefully this will benefit everyone. The trouble with Paul is that he can't sit still.'

Venables himself was not still for long and one of his first priorities was to take a plane to Rome to see the shape Gascoigne was in, a journey he undertook on Valentine's Day. It was a trip with a two-fold purpose, for he wanted to move on to Genoa to size up David Platt, whom he had never met, with a view to making him his England skipper. The greeting Venables gave Gascoigne in the Hilton Hotel, high above the Eternal City, was paternal and Gascoigne, who had been indulging in a self-imposed silence with the Italian press, was now ready to talk to their English counterparts. 'For me, he is the Number One. I learned so much from him. Where I am in football today is because of Terry. But it is not just me. Everybody who comes into contact with him will learn something.'

And Venables was equally open: 'I am here to talk to Paul about him and his game, what is in my plans as far as systems of play are concerned. One of the problems is the amount of time you have to bring about that change. You have to make it simple because I don't want to confuse players. It is all right having ideas and things I know are correct to do if you have time to implement them successfully. I want to have Paul in my side if he is fit and playing well. The good things he does on a football pitch far outweigh the bad ones he does off it. If he makes mistakes, he should be punished. But you have to look at the other side and the hopes and dreams he has fostered in so many youngsters. There are not enough heroes for our younger generation.'

So Gascoigne, we knew, could be pencilled in the first Venables squad and a fondness for players he has managed at club level would surface again in his early selections; players like Darren Anderton, who was to dazzle for him, and Teddy Sheringham and Neil Ruddock, who he had managed at Spurs and who were involved in his fourth squad against the United States.

But when it came to finding a captain he chose a man he had never met. He and David Platt lunched together in Genoa, talked football and the value of playing abroad and one knew after that meeting that we could forget the other contenders for the captain's armband. It was a case of mutual admiration, for Platt was to say after that meeting: 'When Graham Taylor left the job there was only one man who could have taken it. From a footballing point of view there is nobody better. Though I didn't know him, you hear things on the football grapevine and everybody talks so highly of him.'

There were other, significant, appointments being made by Venables. He shrewdly brought back Don Howe, discarded by Taylor, as one of his coaches, a man of such vast experience it seemed the logical step. And he seconded Bryan Robson, many people's choice for the actual manager's post, because he knew that the then Manchester United skipper was an inspirational figure who would inspire from within the camp. He brought in Dave Sexton, with his long-standing reputation for fostering young talent to run the Under-21 side, and complemented him with Ray Wilkins, another player of vast experience with motivating qualities. It was, by common consent, an almost perfect backroom team.

So everything was knitting into place when his first squad was named for a game against Denmark at Wembley on 9 March. It included Graeme Le Saux of Blackburn, an exciting player converted from winger to full back, Anderton, whom he had signed from Portsmouth for Tottenham, and Matthew Le Tissier, talented but enigmatic, all of them players with a certain flair and panache. And he recalled Peter Beardsley at the age of 33 and long after Graham Taylor had consigned him to the scrapheap of international football: 'I feel his experience will be invaluable,' he said. 'He is a fit lad. He brings the best out of the other players, brings them into the game. This is not really about entertaining as much as having imagination, not to play pretty football but good football and to score goals. It is a starting point for me and I think it is a squad that combines youth and experience. It is designed to be successful within the framework of playing good football.'

And that it did. With Peter Beardsley winning his 50th cap, Darren Anderton and Graeme Le Saux their first, England courted a public that turned up in droves. There were 71,970 of them to see Venables employ a system built on flexibility and movement. There was hype enough on the night, with Venables hailed as some kind of Messiah, and if it was a carnival atmosphere then nobody was complaining, least of all the new coach himself. His new skipper David Platt scored the goal that defeated the European champions, and if Venables had been carrying a sword and shield the reception could not have been more gladiatorial.

The system he employed, and which he would carry through for the next two games, was euphemistically described as a Christmas Tree formation, with Alan Shearer the lone man upfront but supported by players joining him from midfield. 'I could not have asked for much more,' Venables would say afterwards. 'It was terrific and it was just a pity we didn't quite finish them off. But in the time we had to prepare, and bearing in mind this was my first game, I think we did as well as we could have expected. The crowd was a real plus and the performance showed the adaptability I am seeking.'

There was then a six-week break for Venables, a period in which he went to see Germany defeat Italy so as to learn about the Germans, who England were due to play in April. That match was to be frustratingly postponed for reasons way beyond the control of the new coach, a fear that celebrations of Adolf Hitler's birthday would mar the occasion. It was the right decision but served only to take away a yardstick by which Venables was hoping to measure his fledgling side. He tried to maximise on that setback by arranging an England get-together but found, as his predecessors had done, that clubs are reluctant to release their players unless they absolutely have to.

So it was not until May that Venables could get to work again and he used a B international against Northern Ireland to try out players he felt might be in contention for consideration. Notable among them was Steve Bould of Arsenal, getting his opportunity late in his career, at the age of 31, and grasping it in spectacular manner. For his part in a 4-2 England victory at Sheffield Wednesday on 10 May promoted him to a place in the squad Venables named for the end-of-season matches against Greece on 17 May and Norway on 22 May. There was another surprising choice in that squad, too, for Kevin Richardson was summoned to the cause, another player over the age of 30 to win Venables' recognition. 'Some players improve with age,' Venables explained. 'Some are finished at the age of 28 or 29 and others just go on and on. Look at Jan Wouters of Holland as an example, still playing for his country at the age of 37. He plays the central midfield holding role that Richardson fulfils so well. Experience can be more valuable than anything. Just look what Paul McGrath, David O'Leary and Kevin Moran have done for Jack Charlton and the Republic of Ireland.'

And, just to prove he meant it, when his side to play Greece was named, there was Bould at the heart of defence and Richardson in the middle of midfield. 'They are not stop-gaps,' said Venables. 'At this stage, age is not something I am looking at. It is how they cope with international football that matters.'

They both coped magnificently, as England romped to a 5-0 victory on a rain-swept Wembley night. It was galling that here was a side heading for the World Cup completely outclassed, with David Platt scoring twice, Darren Anderton getting his first international goal and Peter Beardsley and Alan Shearer adding to their totals. 'I said that my first job would be to put the pride back in English football,' Venables said. 'And results like that one will help England to become a feared football nation again. That is what I am seeking. I want people to fear us and I have been very impressed about how well we have done in such a short space of time. Most important, we came very close to how 1 want us to play. I don't want to get too excited, but this constituted progress. The result was good and the content of the game very pleasing.'

You could almost have trusted Norway to spoil the party, as they did by squeezing the life out of England with their negative approach which was to make them the most unpopular side of the World Cup. Indeed, had Danish referee Kim Neilson not disallowed a David Platt goal which looked to have been scored quite legitimately, then it would have been a 100 percent record for Venables. It was a disappointing outcome for the 64,327 fans who had come to see England put the record straight against the side that had eliminated us from the World Cup.

But he was not too discouraged. 'From what I have seen in these three games we are capable of competing on level terms with the best in the world,' he said. 'I am not saying we are there yet, but this could be a very good team. I could not be more delighted with the way young players like Le Saux and Anderton have fitted in to a system of play that I like. But I shall also try an alternative way of playing next season, even if that means risking results.'

That promise was fulfilled at the start of the 1994-95 season when the Christmas Tree was put temporarily in the loft to accommodate a more orthodox formation, with Shearer being given Sheringham as his playing partner against the United States. Once again Venables risked the wrath of some sections of the public by recalling John Barnes, who had become a Wembley boo-boy under Taylor, and sending for Newcastle United's Barry Venison when Paul Ince withdrew from the squad. Venison was the latest member of the 30-and-over club, but Venables again dismissed any criticism. 'We talk about being 30,' he said. 'It is like it is a magic number for everyone. I am not saying young players are not important. Of course they are. But when you look at the Brazil side that won the World Cup the average age was 28 with a few 30-and-overs in it.'

Venison rolled back the years as England defeated the United States with two goals from Alan Shearer which had Venables describing him as 'a class act'. But perhaps the real class act for England over the next tantalising months building up to the European Championships in England will be Terry Venables himself.

That is, if he is allowed to.

Because, as he prepared for his second assignment of the new season against a World Cup surprise side, Romania, the high-powered Panorama investigative team were reported to be preparing their second devastating expose into Venables' behind-the-scenes business activities.

EPILOGUE
Terry Venables' Finest Hour

ENGLAND FINALLY STAGED the Euros again, albeit in the most bizarre circumstances, after Covid-19 had forced the postponement of the 2020 show-piece. Inevitably, the 2021 tournament would evoke memories of Euro '96 when football promised to come home and Terry Venables was the England manager who inspired a nation to believe that they had a team to be proud of who nearly won the tournament, the first major trophy since the Boys of '66.

Under Venables England went all the way to the semi-finals; beating Holland 4-1 in the opening phase, a performance widely regarded as one of the greatest of modern times by the national team, and auld enemies Scotland with one of Gazza's all-time great goals. After stumbling past Spain on penalties when they deserved to lose, they then lost to Germany by the same method when they deserved to win! England's football was superb at times and the confidence surging through the team was reflected by Skinner & Baddiel's rallying cry. For a few weeks it really did feel as if *Football's Coming Home.*

Following Euro '96, Venables enjoyed spells at Portsmouth and Crystal Palace as well as a short period in charge of the Australian national team, who were desperately unlucky not to qualify for their first World Cup in 1998 under one of football's great innovative coaches.

It was two years after that agonising defeat at Wembley to the Germans when Terry first tasted life in the FA Carling Premiership, very much at the sharp end, with Middlesbrough. His remit was to save the club from another quick return to Division One, and once more he was ultimately successful. Terry decided his business interests and media work could not allow him the time to take up a permanent role on Teesside, and he continued to work as a pundit on ITV; a high profile role particularly during the 2002 World Cup. Venables was then appointed manager of Leeds United on July 8, 2002. After his spell at Leeds, Terry returned to the international scene with England assisting Steve McClaren.

Venables, though, will be best remembered for his exploits with England, but also best remembered for his failed business exploits with Spurs and his debilitating personal legal duel with Alan Sugar - now Lord Sugar.

Having arrived at White Hart Lane from Barcelona at a difficult time for the club both financially and on the pitch, he galvanised the team to finish third in 1989-90 and signed quality players such as Paul Gascoigne and Gary Lineker. The pair became the most prominent and exciting England players in the 1990 World Cup and would have made a formidable force with Chris Waddle but the Geordie left for Marseille in 1989, the same summer as Lineker arrived. The 1991 FA Cup win was achieved despite the fear the club might fold, although the then chairman Irving Scholar always said that the financial issues were manageable.

Eventually, as detailed in this book, Venables brought in Alan Sugar to devise a rescue plan but their fall out brought further stress to the club with court issues and supporters opinions split. In the dug out Venables was a genius, but he was a flawed businessman.

In a statement from the Department of Trade and Industry, Venables had reached a settlement with its lawyers agreeing to be banned from any directorship, or virtually any other relationship with a commercial operation, for seven years. Accepting 19 charges of serious misconduct, all of which he had strenuously denied for the previous four years, Venables also agreed to pay half a million pounds of the DTI's costs. Three weeks earlier, Venables' friend and business partner, Eddie Ashby, completed a four-month prison sentence for breach of the bankruptcy laws.

Panorama reporter Martin Bashir described him as a "loveable rogue" in the English tradition of Minder. He had charm and charisma but while he was investigated for dubious business practises, Venables was one of the managerial greats, achieving success at both club and international level. Of course Bashir himself is now under investigation for his journalistic methods, and time has been much kinder to Terry. He is not viewed as a crook, but as the loveable rogue Bashir originally described him. At worst he is regarded as a chancer who took the wrong advice from some interesting characters who latched onto him. Terry trod a fine line in his business dealings and sometimes he crossed that line without probably realising the full implications and by taking the wrong advice.

Terry was a crooner, a celebrity act, a charmer, but was he a crook? I don't think so. I enjoyed his company as host at Scribes West in the bowels of the *Daily Mail*'s offices in Kensington High Street but I quickly became *persona non grata* once my investigations into his business dealings kicked in. But when I was there, I could see that while he had one or two genuine friends within the media, he made the rest of the media crop feel like his best mates, and they loved the attention, and sometimes impromptu 'press briefings' over a hearty glass of wine or beer (which their newspapers were picking up the tab for in any case).

Terry, in my view, was no better or worse than MPs entrusted with our votes but guilty of fiddling their expenses. While he loved to hold a mike he also didn't mind a fiddle! Back int he early 1990s, as the battle for Spurs intensified, I suspected there was something more to the story than hitting on the 'big bully' Alan Sugar, and in my journalistic career I never went with the flow.

As Lord Sugar's trusted PR guru, and latterly star of *Apprentice* and *Countdown*, Nick Hewer, wrote in his recent autobiography: "It was ugly, particularly with the footballing press. I was shocked when a well-known tabloid journalist, now writing for a national broadsheet, replied to my question, 'Why can't you take a balanced view?' with, 'Well, you've got to look after your friends.' Looking back, I guess the reason for this is not difficult to determine. Terry Venables, chirpy chappie that he is, was a master at manipulating the back pages of the tabloids and, in fairness, the press in general. He was a man's man, an arm around the shoulder, hugging sort of fellow with a ready wit and with a ready quote always on his lips. He had played at every level of the game, had achieved more as a manger than most and, in contrast to Alan, he was accessible.

"The press went potty, and it looked as though Terry - former England player, renaissance man of English football - had attracted pretty much all the support. But a lone figure, Harry Harris of the *Daily Mirror*, was trying to make friendly overtures to the Sugar camp. I urged Alan to engage knowing that we desperately needed to get a red-top onside, and although The Sun had a greater readership, *The Mirror* was a powerful player."

I am often asked if the then plain Alan Sugar was the man behind all the documents, the smoking gun which shot Venables down in flames on the back pages of *The Mirror*, with arguably the most chilling headlines... 'El Till'. Well, he did not. One of the first and most damaging documents came through my letter box without any identifying marks. I spoke to two or three people I thought might have this incriminating evidence but didn't really think one of them did. Even so, I asked all three to send me this invoice anonymously and left them my address. It duly arrived, and while it might have come from one or two sources, I am pretty sure which one, although I couldn't swear by it.

My investigations might have won awards, arguably more than they did, but Venables' acolytes often sat on the judging panels! I lost my place at the Scribes drinking hole, but also a number of my contemporaries in Fleet Street turned on me. Once I bumped into Venables on the stairs of the Landmark Hotel and he made no bones about warning me off. I was there attending a press conference and no doubt Terry had no idea the media would be there that day. I explained to him that armed with the evidence presented to me I had no choice other than to do my job properly and there was no malice attached, I had no agenda against him, and had always admired him as a genius of a coach. He made veiled threats that it would not be in my interests to pursue my enquiries.

England's Euro '96 performance earned Venables national acclaim, but he walked away at the end of the tournament to fight a legal battle surrounding his business interests and never scaled the same heights again.

★

Yet it is for that Gazza-inspired England performance at Euro '96 that Venables is best remembered. The great irony of course is that the current England boss, Gareth Southgate, missed the crucial penalty in that heartbreaking semi-final loss to Germany. The Euro 2020 England boss was in tears at the end of that match which proved to be the last of Venables' stint in the England hot-seat. Germany beat the Czech Republic 2-0 in the final, and England had to wait 22 years to win another penalty shoot-out with, ironically, Southgate as manager.

Southgate played every single minute of Euro 96 at the heart of Venables' defence in the run to the semi-finals that summer, as he said "The spirit of the team, we are growing that now. That spirit that the public found, the way the tournament grew, the involvement of the fans grew, that is what we want to generate this summer. We had some outstanding leaders in the Euro 96 squad. There were a lot of experienced players, I was a captain of my club but there was also Tony Adams, Stuart Pearce, Paul Ince, Teddy Sheringham, David Platt, all captains at their clubs. We had people who stood up in the big moments and fought together. As with any tournament, you have lads who are not playing in the games and they played their role really well. It's a hard role but they gave themselves to the team."

As Southgate looked ahead to the delayed Euro 2020, he recognised the talents of his former manager, when he said: "One of the most important things I've said to everyone – not just the players, but the support team behind them – is that calm leadership is one of the most important things you can provide in this environment, Terry had a good balance of enjoyment, and knew the moments to have fun and relax, but when we worked he was spot on. He was by no means a disciplinarian, but no one stepped out of line because there was such a respect for him."

Venables sent a special message to the England players ahead of their opening Euro's game urging them to better his Euro '96 exploits and win the tournament. Venables told Southgate's squad, "Gareth knows only too well the excitement and buzz in the country during Euro '96 – and here's hoping they do even better now. Go out there boys, and really enjoy yourselves and we will all be cheering you on." A special film to commemorate Terry's life and focus on Euro '96 was being put together. Those connected to Terry said that he would be watching at home with wife of 40 years, Yvette. A source was quoted in *The Sun* as saying "Terry is looking forward to watching the lads and thinks they have a great chance. Let's hope the boys see his words and they inspire them on to great things. If they do throw off the shackles and go out and enjoy themselves, we could all be in for an exciting summer."

In Euro '96 Gary Neville was aiming to impress at his first major international tournament as a 21-year-old full back, in awe of pep talks from Pearce and Tony Adams in the dressing room. As part of a special Boys of 96 series, Sky Sports News reporter Mark McAdam spoke to every member of the 22-man squad from Euro '96. Sky pundit Gary said: "I wish I could have taken a film with a camera phone of Pearce and Adams before the games, it would make the hairs on the back of your neck stand up to see how proud they were to play for England. Those three lions on their chest, the feeling of pride in their country. Pearce would stand up, Adams would be doing tackles against the concrete wall, it was old school! I get goosebumps thinking about the moments when we scored against Scotland, Gazza's goal, or the night against the Netherlands, it was an out-of-body experience."

Gazza enthused over the management of Terry Venables: "He was the best I worked with. Everybody loved him. Terry

Venables always used to say, 'if you don't concede, you won't get beaten'. In training, Venables would give me the ball and say, 'Take these five guys on'. I'd do it. That was me getting fit. Venables used to record the training sessions so he had this big crane behind the goal. Massive it was and there was a guy up there, about 50ft off the ground, with his camera looking down. So I took the keys and f★★★ed off to the hotel."

Gazza's iconic moment was his goal against Scotland, "Even now people want to stop and tell me about it, they never seem to forget. I have some great memories of that summer." The other infamous moment was replicating the 'Dentist Chair' in his goal celebrations.

Jamie Redknapp recalled: "Nobody really remembers that warm-up win against China, but I do." Venables started Redknapp and Gazza in midfield. Jamie added that Venables told them, 'You two were brilliant'. Redknapp went on: "It was because whenever I got the ball, I gave it to Gazza. That was my game-plan. He never shied away from wanting the ball. We beat China 3-0, then a Hong Kong XI 1-0, and the manager tells us we can do whatever we want to relax."

Gazza said: "It was my 29th birthday so I thought, 'Right, f★★★ this, I'm going out'. So I remember going out to buy some Doc Martens, a big cigar, a bottle of champagne and then walking into the restaurant where all of yous were."

Redknapp takes up the story: "Then we head to the China Jump nightclub and you spot the dentist's chair. All of us had a go, but the person behind the bar decided to take some pictures and sell them."

On flight CX251 to London, two television screens were smashed on the upper deck which the squad had to themselves, as Venables called it 'collective responsibility' as Cathay Pacific, demanded the FA pay them £5,000 for the damage. The high jinks began when Gazza fell asleep, Redknapp and Robbie Fowler shaved off his eyebrows. Dennis Wise was put in the overhead luggage locker. When the media tried to find out who was responsible for the smashed screens, Gazza told them, 'it was the three Scousers'.

Redknapp went to Essex to see Frank Lampard, "we decide to go to Faces nightclub bumping into Teddy Sheringham and Sol Campbell. It was the Saturday night." Venables called Redknapp on the Sunday, 'What are you playing at?' They made the front pages again. Gazza went to see Rod Stewart! Walking up a street. Gazza recalled: "I said, 'Come on, Rod, let's go to the pub, I need a f***ing drink'. He opens up his jacket and pulls out a bottle of vodka. I go, 'Cheers mate!' Then we go to the pub and he goes on the karaoke!"

Jamie broke his ankle against Scotland. He recalled: "Terry said I could head home or stick around. I said, 'Are you joking?' This was the best football tournament/stag do I'd ever been on! There was no way I was leaving."

Before the Euros in 2016 Venables was speaking at the Three Lions pub in London launching Carlsberg's 'Pubstitutions' campaign. Despite the manner of their exit, Venables believed his side lifted the mood of the country for the duration of the event and a bond was formed between a group of players and staff. "The summer was just the summer of a life time," he recalled, "It was the biggest sporting occasion I'd been involved in, where everybody loved it," he said. "Even 20 years on people stop me in the street to talk about it and I still keep in touch with most of the people involved, and we would sometimes, some of the players when we are in town, we get together to relive it, because to us it was magnificent. We did something special, and we could have even won it, but that's life."

The highlight of the tournament? "That would have to be the goal from the 'Magnificent Gascoigne'," he said, reflecting on the iconic moment when the Rangers star flicked the ball over Blackburn's Colin Hendry before slotting beyond Ibrox team-mate Andy Goram for the opening goal of the 2-0 victory over Scotland. "The entire game was special. It was a wonderful team goal and a wonderful individual goal from Gazza," he added.

Gazza might not have seen Southgate as a future England manager but is delighted with what he has achieved in charge of the national team when he said "I am really proud of Gareth, and what he has achieved. In my stage show I always say, 'At Euro 96, I scored my penalty, and I end up in rehab, and he misses, yet gets the England job and a pizza advert – where did I go wrong?'" Gazza spoke to Southgate a few years after he became England manager. Gazza said: "I wish him all the very best. He is so lucky because he has so many great young players. He is a cracking manager. He is a different class, he has them playing really well."

★

In retirement, Terry and his wife Yvette opened a 12-bedroom hotel near Alicante in Spain in 2014, the La Escondia, a one-time hunting lodge dating from 1881, set in 500 acres of olive and almond groves in the centre of the Font Roja National Park. Having first fallen in love with Spain during his reign at the Nou Camp from 1984 to 1987, he stumbled across La Esconida, which Terry describes as being in a "breath-taking" location. "We are always in search of places that are off the beaten track and La Escondia was certainly that, yet such a short distance from the coast," he said when it first opened. The restaurant's menu is centred around vegetables grown in the hotel's garden. "We've eaten some exceptional food in our lives, but the best is always simple cooking beautifully presented using the freshest ingredients," said Terry back then. "Most of the herbs and vegetables are grown on our land by our gardener and the breads and pastries freshly baked in our kitchen. We plan to have a bee hive so guests have fresh honeycomb for breakfast."

The hotel also has indoor and outdoor swimming pools, a spa and a jogging track around the grounds. Bedrooms start from £140 per night and include local taxes and breakfast. The first General manager was Cheila Reais, previously operations director at the Sanderson hotel in London.

The couple spent a year creating their perfect hideaway,

which was being used as a rustic 18-room hostel when they bought it nearly 20 years earlier. "Back then we were looking for a place on the coast and someone suggested we take a look at it as they thought it could make a wonderful house," Terry told *A Place in the Sun*. "When we saw it, we thought it was lovely and in such a fantastic location we decided to go for it. At the time, I was too busy with football to actually do anything with the property, and over the years the ideas changed as to what we would do with it. Then the crisis hit and the big scheme was not an option so we decided to turn it into a boutique hotel." The 'big scheme' refers to Terry's short-lived master-plan for a huge sports resort at the site, which he put forward in 2010, similar to internationally acclaimed La Manga in Murcia, it would have included football pitches, tennis courts, a golf course, hotel and private residences. "We've turned it from 18 small rooms to 10 suites and built two cabins in the woods," continued El Tel, who is a big fan of tapas. "We have also added a large outdoor pool and completely refurbished our indoor pool and spa rooms. The main hotel is finished, but there are a few bits we need to add in the gardens, including a pergola for weddings and a sheltered area next to the pool. If the cabins are a success we hope to add a few more of these. They're a bit special as they are separate from the hotel and have wood burning stoves and their own gardens, so they give the feeling of really being in the country - very romantic!

"Yvette runs it. I am obviously involved to a huge extent too, but she is the one who deals with the managerial side. We used to spend a lot of the year at my mother-in-law's place in Javea, but now we have the hotel we're here most of the time and a few weeks there. We also spend time in London."

I enjoyed a holiday or two at La Manga, it was a venue I knew so well from numerous football trips. One day I spotted Terry strolling along in the sunshine, outside the five star La Manga hotel, oblivious to all around him as he concentrated on the business deal he was hatching on his mobile phone at the time he was still looking for a La Manga style complex resort that specialised in coaching young players. My sources had told me that he wanted to import poor African kids with outstanding footballing promise, and cultivate and develop them into future stars, and then have part-ownership in them to sell onto the elite European clubs. Of course, that was prior to third-party ownership rules coming into effect which would have scuppered that plan had it come to fruition. Naturally, my chances of discussing this grand scheme with him were zero considering our history. Although I knew in advance of Venables' mission in Spain, it was sheer coincidence that I just happened to be spending time in the resort. Suddenly our paths crossed outside the hotel, Venables' jaw dropped, he cut short his mobile phone conversation.

"Don't worry Terry, I'm not stalking you", I quipped.

Terry smiled but was unable to speak. Hours later he had checked out of the hotel and vanished from the resort. Clearly, he could take no chance, and must have feared I was actually following him.

It seemed our paths were fated to cross. Purely by chance we dined at the same Indian restaurant early in 2006, the Bombay Brasserie near Gloucester Road tube station, so yes I can forgive Terry for thinking I was stalking him! But again, as I walked past his table, his jaw dropped open and all he could manage was one of his usual cheeky smiles. "Still, not stalking you, Terry", I said cheerily as I walked on.

In 2016, in an interview in the *Mail*, Terry said, 'Running a hotel is like being in charge of a football team. It's all about getting a group of talented people together who know what their jobs are and what they're supposed to be doing. It's like that with football players. When they know their roles, that makes it easier for the manager. That's what we've done here. We employed keen, enthusiastic and talented chefs, waiters and reception staff with a real desire to succeed at what they do. It's no different, really, from encouraging your players and getting the best from your team. You can't afford to stand still in the centre circle. If you stand still as a football manager, you've lost. It's like that when you're a hotelier, too. You want to be constantly pushing forward.'

Sadly, Terry is not in the best of health as England resumed another crack at the Euros on home soil. Sky TV were in development for a full feature film on Terry Venables' life and times, focusing on the Euros, of course, and asked me to participate, to gain a balanced view. The film was authorised by Terry's family, but he wasn't appearing in it due to his health issues, although there was ample archive material of him.

I was asked by the prosecution team whether Terry had ever sued me, as there was constant speculation at the time the he had. Once I even receive a call from a young lady working for the Press Association asking me to comment about the fact that I had been reported to the Press Complaints Commission. The call was a huge surprise because I hadn't been reported at all. At least, as I discovered later, Venables' lawyers had written to the press Complaints Commission seeking guidance about the procedures they would have to follow if they were going to report me. A couple of Terry's 'pet' journalists were briefed that he had taken legal action, and one of them even taunted me that Terry would see me in court to prove his innocence.

Terry's legal eagles did try a couple of tricks to get me into court. Libel actions can be brought up to three years after the event but no longer, or at least that was the law at the time, a three-year life span. Venables' lawyers waited until the very last possible day inside the time limit to act. His lawyers dispatched a message to deliver the writ, which had to be served personally. The messenger got to *The Mirror* buildings, tricked his way past security, as these guys know how to get these writs personally served, and even reached the third floor and found his way to my desk. Now, all that was left was to see me personally and hand it over - all I had to do was touch it and it was served. So where was I? Well, I was at home on a rare day off. Not doing a 9-5 job, I was often out of the office on assignment at a game, so it was chancy to try to serve this writ on the final day of their three year 'window'.

He also got his lawyers to try to get me into the witness box in a case that was brought by a company against him claiming Terry owed them money, which Venables was contesting. I had no evidence relevant to his case, and his attempt to subpoena me was contested successfully by Mirror lawyers arguing it was simply a side show so that his lawyers could cross examine me under oath where I got my information from. Had I simply refused the subpoena I could have been jailed, but as it turned out the legal argument was strong enough to avoid any of that. However, in this case, the judge branded him 'unreliable' and 'wanton' in his evidence. It made quite a stirring headline on the back page of *The Mirror*: 'You Are Unreliable and Wanton', and there followed a few media articles which were about me as much as Terry, and my reporting on his court cases.

All of this sounds like I had it in for Terry but nothing could be further from the truth. In fact, I actually recommended him to become England coach! Graham Kelly, the FA chief executive at the time, decided it was time the FA came down from its Ivory Tower and consulted some of the constituent parts of the footballing industry about the selection of the new England manger, and as such he asked a small hand-picked group of three respected football writers to give our opinions. We were invited into Graham's room when we were all together covering an England game. Unanimously we agreed that Venables was the right choice.

However I told Graham that, in my opinion, he ought to sort out the Venables 'baggage' in advance of his appointment. If the FA thought he should face charges of disrepute for his financial dealings at Spurs they should be proactive and not use the tired excuse of waiting for legal proceedings to run their course before they could consider any intervention and potential charges.

Of course it can be seen as a legitimate policy as any FA charges might well be seen as prejudicing up and coming court action, but I felt it was imperative in this instance to make an exception; charge Venables, hear a disciplinary case, ban him from the touchline for a month if that was the judgement of the commission, and then he would be clear of these issues and free to concentrate on the England job.

Venables was, indeed, appointed England coach and had a wonderful tournament. However the real story of how his tenure as England boss ended was lost in the excitement of that summer.

The public perception is that his reign ended as a result of dozens of potential legal actions trailing him to the extent that he felt that protecting his reputation was more important than continuing as England coach whereas in reality event the reason he left the England job was that Graham Kelly only offered him a one-year extension prior to Euro '96 and Venables wanted a much longer commitment from the FA, at least until the French World Cup in 1998, which they were not prepared to give him and so even before the tournament began it was known that Glenn Hoddle would be his successor.

APPENDIX

Key Documents

1. The Santin invoice for £200,000 for his work in arranging the transfer of Paul Gascoigne to Lazio (see page 182).

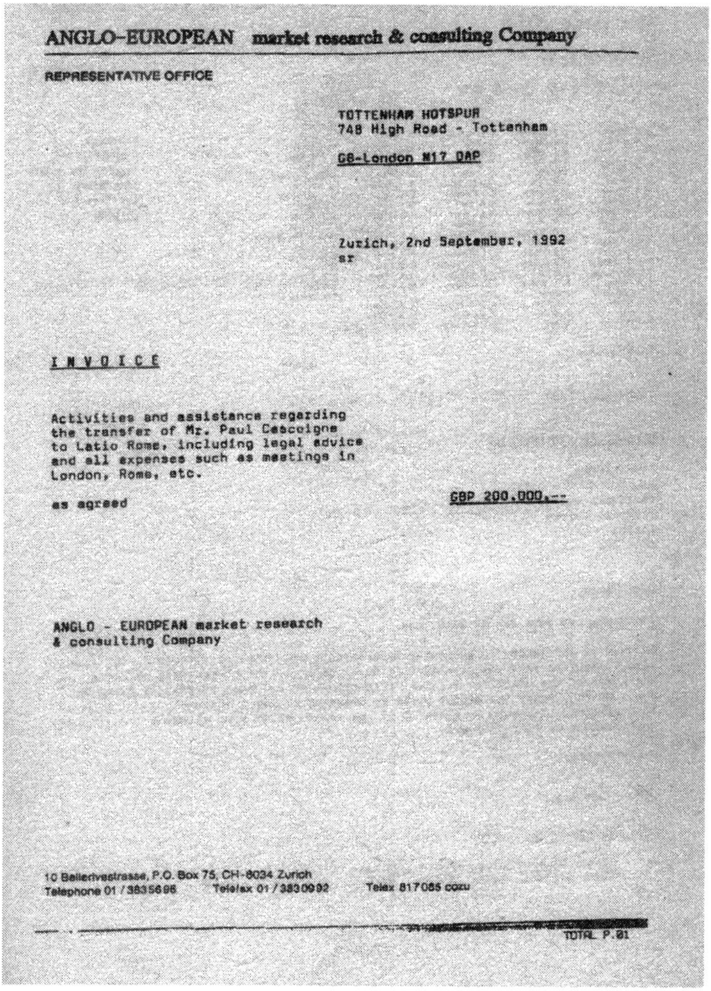

ANGLO-EUROPEAN market research & consulting Company

REPRESENTATIVE OFFICE

TOTTENHAM HOTSPUR
748 High Road - Tottenham

GB-London N17 0AP

Zurich, 2nd September, 1992
sr

INVOICE

Activities and assistance regarding
the transfer of Mr. Paul Gascoigne
to Latio Rome, including legal advice
and all expenses such as meetings in
London, Rome, etc.

as agreed — GBP 200.000,--

ANGLO - EUROPEAN market research
& consulting Company

10 Bellerivestrasse, P.O. Box 75, CH-8034 Zurich
Telephone 01 / 3835696 Telefax 01 / 3830932 Telex 817085 coru

TOTAL P.01

2. The crucial fax from John Campion at Allen & Overy confirming to Tottenham's lawyers, as early as 20 June 1991, that Lazio would pay £5.5 million for Paul Gasoigne (see page 183).

28 JUN '91 12:26

ALLEN & OVERY

J. M. Kennedy
[illegible]
[illegible]
[illegible]
[illegible]
A. J. Herbert
[illegible]
[illegible]
D. St. J. Sutton
K. M. T. Ryan
G. N. Wilson
P. R. J. Holland
W. Tudor John
P. H. T. Mimpriss
[illegible]
P. R. Wood
[illegible]
P. G. Tett
[illegible]
R. H. Sykes
[illegible]
[illegible]
D. L. Mackie
R. G. Davies
[illegible]
[illegible]
M. W. Parker
P. N. Meek
D. H. Weston
R. W. Jones
A. R. Humphrey
R. M. Brown
K. G. Godfrey
M. J. Reynolds
P. A. Owen
[illegible]
J. Cowie
A. C. Keal
D. E. Lewis
[illegible]
[illegible]
P. Crook
[illegible]
N. D. Johnson
[illegible]
Clare M. Maurice
G. J. Kendall
G. M. Pyrre
K. J. L. Jones
C. McKenna
D. C. Hughes
A. D. Paul
C. R. Roberts
[illegible]
[illegible]
J. L. F. Beayne
Julia A. Salt
R. W. C. Turner
[illegible]
S. R. M. Denyer
A. H. Asher
[illegible]
P. M. Watson
M. R. Welling
[illegible] Wells
R. W. Harrison
G. G. Stevens
D. L. Wilkinson
J. A. Stevens
J. M. Goodwin
P. S. Hodgkin
[illegible]
P. M. Moran
D. H. Markey
G. D. Victor
M. A. Segal
S. P. Chater
A. M. Pease
D. M. McGowan
Katherine A. Buckley
[illegible]
[illegible]
C. Henderson
J. D. Thomas
[illegible]
[illegible]
Anne E. Baldock
I. G. Stanley
M. P. Sturgeon
M. W. Friend
Helen M. Hartman-Hall
S. A. Myers
Jayne A. Turner
R. J. Hunter
W. A. Tyser
A. Wilson
C. R. Sheldon

9 Cheapside
London EC2V 6AD
Telephone. 071-248 9898
Telex. 8812801
Fax: 071-236 2192
DX No 73

PB/JCC/ZS

20th June, 1991

URGENT AND CONFIDENTIAL

James Perry
Ashurst Morris Crisp
Broadwalk House
1 Appold Street
London
EC2A 2HA

Dear James,

Thank you for your fax of 18th June.

In view of difficulty in achieving satisfactory insurance arrangements, our client requires that the fitness test to be taken by the player will be along the lines of the draft "performance warranty" which has been previously faxed to you. On this basis the client would be prepared to pay a price of £5.5 million. I should be grateful if you could obtain your client's instructions on this proposal.

Yours sincerely,

John Campion

John Campion

cc Gianni Manca, Manca, Amenta, Biolato, Corrao & C., Edinburgh
Giuvi Biolato, Manca, Amenta, Biolato, Corrao & C., Rome

3. The invoice from First Wave, dated 27 August 1992, the day before Teddy Sheringham signed for Tottenham. McLintock has since admitted it was bogus (see page 196).

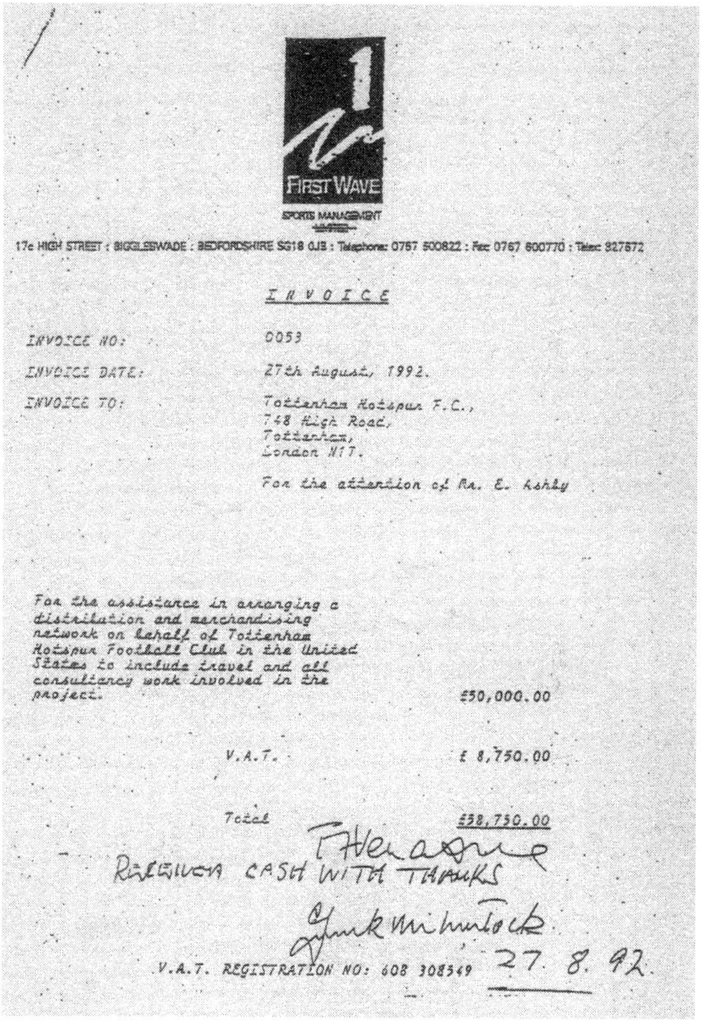

FIRST WAVE
SPORTS MANAGEMENT
LIMITED

17c HIGH STREET : BIGGLESWADE : BEDFORDSHIRE SG18 0JB : Telephone: 0767 600822 : Fax: 0767 600770 : Telex: 827672

INVOICE

INVOICE NO: 0053

INVOICE DATE: 27th August, 1992.

INVOICE TO: Tottenham Hotspur F.C.,
748 High Road,
Tottenham,
London N17.

For the attention of Mr. E. Ashby

For the assistance in arranging a distribution and merchandising network on behalf of Tottenham Hotspur Football Club in the United States to include travel and all consultancy work involved in the project. £50,000.00

V.A.T. £ 8,750.00

Total £58,750.00

RECEIVED CASH WITH THANKS

V.A.T. REGISTRATION NO: 608 308549 27. 8. 92.

4. The receipt, signed by Peter Barnes and Frank McLintock, for the £8,750 which was returned when it was discovered that Tottenham had overpaid (see page 199).

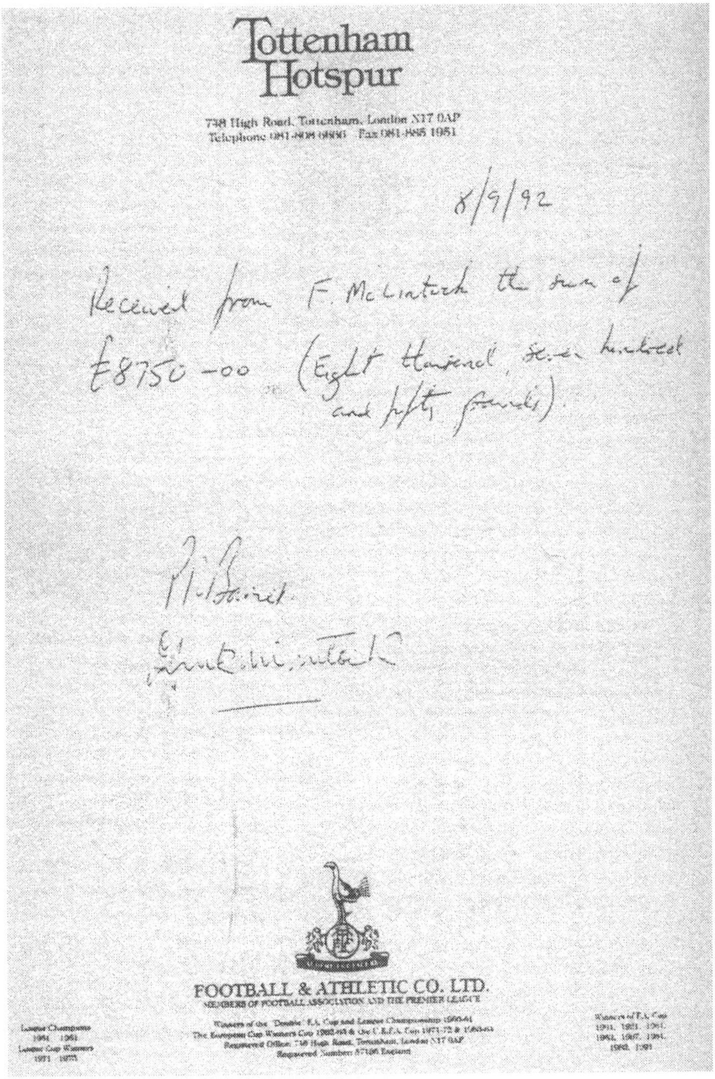

Tottenham Hotspur

748 High Road, Tottenham, London N17 0AP
Telephone 081-808 6666 Fax 081-885 1951

8/9/92

Received from F. McLintock the sum of £8750-00 (Eight thousand, seven hundred and fifty pounds).

FOOTBALL & ATHLETIC CO. LTD.
MEMBERS OF FOOTBALL ASSOCIATION AND THE PREMIER LEAGUE

5. One of Eric Hall's invoices, dated 29 August 1991, that was specifically questioned in the immediate aftermath of Venables' sacking (see page 211).

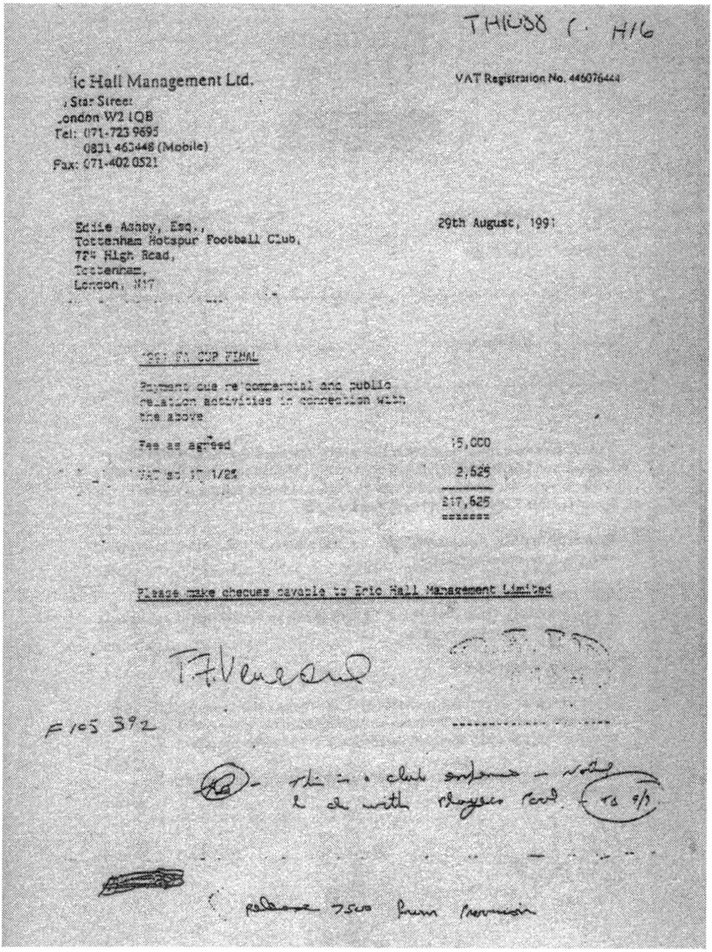

ic Hall Management Ltd.
, Star Street
London W2 1QB
Tel: 071-723 9695
0831 463448 (Mobile)
Fax: 071-402 0521

VAT Registration No. 446076444

Eddie Ashby, Esq.,
Tottenham Hotspur Football Club,
748 High Road,
Tottenham,
London, N17

29th August, 1991

1991 FA CUP FINAL

Payment due re commercial and public relation activities in connection with the above

Fee as agreed	£15,000
VAT at 17 1/2%	2,625
	£17,625

Please make cheques payable to Eric Hall Management Limited

F105 392

release 7500 from provision

6. Sugar's memo to Venables requesting his backing for the view that Tottenham had not reduced their offer to the player (see page 213).

Tottenham Hotspur

4/10

Memorandum

TO: **Terry Venables** **DATE: 23 June 1993**

FROM: **A M Sugar**

subject: ***Neil Ruddock***

You will have seen in the press that we have not yet finalised negotiations with Neil Ruddock over revisions to his terms of employment. Ossie Ardiles is dealing with this and he thought after his discussions with Ruddock on Monday that terms had been agreed but then Ruddock called him to demand more.

Apparently Ruddock claims that the offer we have made is less than one he had agreed with you at the end of last season.

In his memorandum to me of 7 June, Peter Barnes stated that you had discussed doubling his salary (from £75,000 to £150,000) and the previously agreed signing on fee of £50,000 was to stay the same.

Our offer is no less than that.

Could you please confirm that your offer to Ruddock was as I have reported above. It would obviously help Ossie Ardiles in his negotiations if he could say that you have confirmed that and that you believe that Ruddock should accept the offer.

Can you please respond as soon as possible as we obviously want to finalise this matter urgently.

A M Sugar

7. The letter of agreement confirming the loan terms for Nayim, 21 October 1992 - two months into the new Premier League season (see page 241).

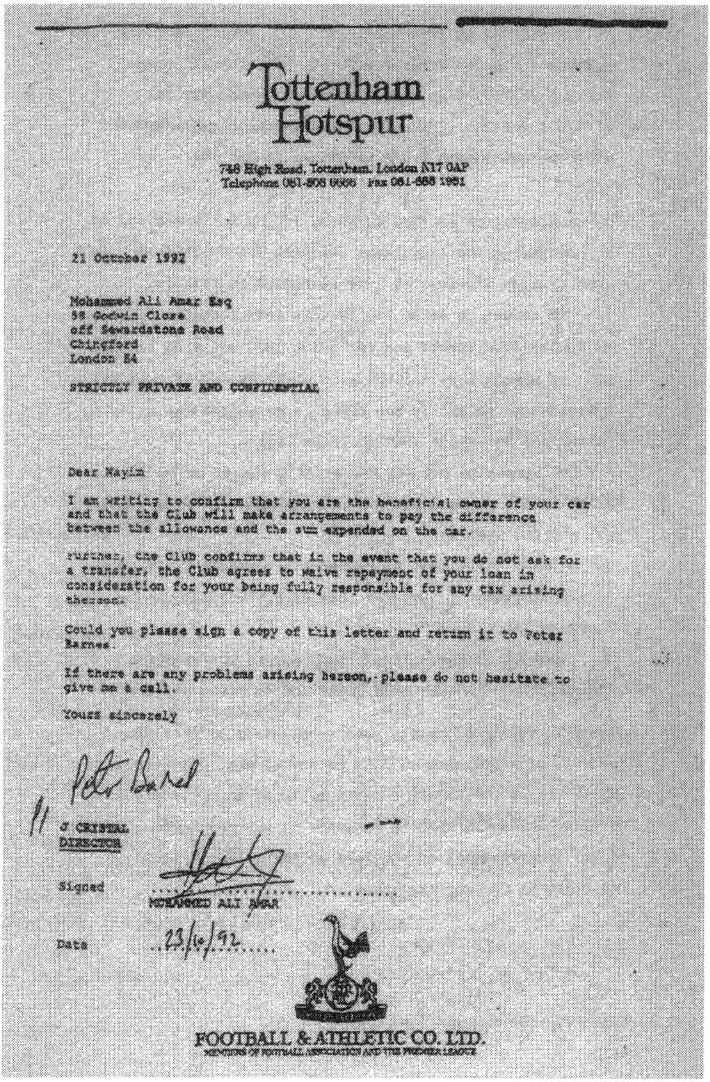

Tottenham Hotspur

748 High Road, Tottenham, London N17 0AP
Telephone 081-808 6666 Fax 081-885 1951

21 October 1992

Mohammed Ali Amar Esq
58 Godwin Close
off Sewardstone Road
Chingford
London E4

STRICTLY PRIVATE AND CONFIDENTIAL

Dear Nayim

I am writing to confirm that you are the beneficial owner of your car and that the Club will make arrangements to pay the difference between the allowance and the sum expended on the car.

Further, the Club confirms that in the event that you do not ask for a transfer, the Club agrees to waive repayment of your loan in consideration for your being fully responsible for any tax arising thereon.

Could you please sign a copy of this letter and return it to Peter Barnes.

If there are any problems arising hereon, please do not hesitate to give me a call.

Yours sincerely

J CRISTAL
DIRECTOR

Signed ....
MOHAMMED ALI AMAR

Date ..23/10/92.....

FOOTBALL & ATHLETIC CO. LTD.
MEMBERS OF FOOTBALL ASSOCIATION AND THE PREMIER LEAGUE

8. The reworded loan agreement between Terry Fenwick and Tottenham which made his repayable loan non-repayable (see page 241).

THIS AGREEMENT is made the day of February 1992 between Tottenham Hotspur Football and Athletic Company Limited of 748, High Road, Tottenham London N17 OAP ("THFC") and Terry Fenwick of [redacted] South Hampstead London NW6 ("TF")

In consideration of THFC agreeing to pay to TF the sum of £3,000 [being two instalment payments due to TF from Hummel (UK) Limited ("Hummel")] it is agreed as follows:

1. TF agrees to waive any further entitlement to payments or monies from Hummel and for which THFC could be liable.

2. TF agrees that such payment shall be in full and final satisfaction of all or any payments or monies due to TF by Hummel and for which THFC could be liable.

3. TF agrees to pay any tax arising out of or by virtue of the above payment and to fully indemnify THFC or Hummel in relation thereto.

4. In the event that TF requests a transfer he shall be liable to repay to THFC the loan of £25,000 made to him by THFC.

5. Save as aforementioned, THFC agrees not to seek repayment of the loan made to TF and to waive all their rights in relation thereto upon termination of TF's present contract of employment by THFC or any extension thereof (whichever is the later) subject to TF agreeing to pay and to fully indemnify THFC in relation to any tax arising out of his non-repayment of the loan or the waiver by THFC of its right to recover the loan.

Signed by and on behalf of THFC

Terry Fenwick

Printed in Great Britain
by Amazon

34603817R00191